WHO IS MY DADDY?

War baby living with a "beast" who was not my father! (Mother's terrible secret)

K. B. Chandler

Grosvenor House
Publishing Limited

This book is published by
Grosvenor House Publishing Ltd
Link House
140 The Broadway, Tolworth, Surrey, KT6 7HT.
www.grosvenorhousepublishing.co.uk

A CIP record for this book
is available from the British Library

Paperback ISBN 978-1-83615-403-7
eBook ISBN 978-1-83615-404-4

This book is dedicated to my angel, my dearest wife, Catherine, who has stood by me through very hard times.

To my four wonderful children, Corinna, Kevin, Victoria and Andrew. I'm a very proud father for all they have achieved in their lives.

Max, Ella, Joshua, and Izabelle, my four beautiful grandchildren.

PREFACE

This is a book about a young man growing up without a father to guide him, or to advise him on the pitfalls of life. From a very early age, I call upon my memory to write this account of my lifetime events.

You, the reader, must make up your own mind about what follows, but everything that I have written is how I and only I remember and believe happened to me during my short stay on this wonderful planet.

It finishes with me leaving training, just prior to joining the fleet as a fully qualified sailor – another story which is in the pipeline.

However, life still goes on, even now in my 77th year, wondering who is, or was not, related to me, who was my father? Over the years, things have got nearer to the truth. I have been given information which I believe could be the truth. BUT MY MOTHER and her FAMILY have kept a deep dark secret, all this time.

I am still, during 2021, trying to find out the full truth of my coming into this world. I am nearly there, details of my father have been confirmed. Still ongoing is the search for my elder sister, Margaret Alma Chandler.

It has taken me approximately 35 years to actually first put pen to paper. I first sat down in front of my computer way back in around 2002, then again in 2009/10, thinking, *Where do I start, how far back should I go?* Why not from the time which had led up to my entering this world? So I sat there, trying to think of the life I had as a youngster, and that is when the memories started to flood in. Memories and life's events came back to me one after the other.

You, the reader, must make up your own mind. Did he really do all this? My apologies if some of the wording causes offence.

CONTENTS

1. LIFE BEGINS WITHOUT A FATHER   1
2. MOTHER – WHO IS MY DADDY?   7
3. MY GRANDPARENTS   16
4. HOLLY ROUGH – BOX HILL   24
5. FIRST SCHOOL/PLIMSOLLS SAGA   29
6. 'OLD MANS' MANY TALENTS   39
7. RED LEYS CHILDREN'S HOME   50
8. FARNBOROUGH AIR SHOW   65
9. START OF MY ILLNESS T.B.   69
10. CHILDREN'S SANATORIUM   74
11. BACK HOME   79
12. SOCIAL SERVICES CALLED   90
13. CHOIR St. JOHN CHURCH   99
14. BOARDING SCHOOL BOYS   102
15. COOK-MEALS/OUTING POINTS   108
16. FINDING CRICKET/FOOTBALL   114
17. ANIMALS/BOWS & ARROWS   121
18. SUNNYDOWN – SCHOOL OUTINGS   125
19. GERMAN MEASLES & VERRUCAS   127
20. SUMMER – TIME TO LEAVE   132
21. TRAINING SHIP ARETHUSA   142
22. ARRIVAL AT UPNOR   145
23. WASHROOM SHOWER TIME   150
24. SCHOOL CLASS ROUTINE   156
25. ASIAN INFLUENZA 1957-58   161

26. COXSWAIN WHALER INCIDENT   167

27. CORNED BEEF SIX BEST   175

28. WHALER INCIDENT DOCKYARD   181

29. T.S. *ARETHUSA* BAND   187

30. CAPTAIN'S SATURDAY ROUNDS   192

31. CHANGE OF SURNAME   198

32. HOW CATHY IN MY LIFE   205

CHAPTER 1

LIFE BEGINS WITHOUT A FATHER

Memories and life's events came back to me one after the other. I am still wondering who is and who is not related to me, who was my father. Things have got a little nearer to the truth as I see it but cannot go into it much further for fear of upsetting others within my family and those who maybe or should be.

I have been given some information which I believe is the truth which I should have kept to myself rather than spoiling a great relationship with my close family members. I have found that life has certainly been far from boring. Very hard at times. Before I start this story, it is going to be very hard to put into writing. However, I am going to give it a try.

Why is it going to be so hard? Well, I have led a life without a father or father figure to look up to, to fall back on for any advice. All I had was beatings, mental and physical abuse. None of my family or classmates' fathers treated them like mine was treating me. So why was he treating me this way? You, the reader, must be made aware that Charles Frederick Francis CUTTS was not my father, but I had to call him 'Daddy'. Being so very young, I knew nothing else but him as 'Daddy'. Every avenue I have gone down so far to find out the identity of my father, my natural father, that is, has led me to a dead end. It is only at the age of 67 years (now 77), I feel I should either be told the truth or find the answers myself. I have tried over the years to ask the question of my mother but to no avail. I am told one thing but when I made enquires it always came to a halt.

At a very early age I learnt how to stand on my own two feet, having been denied any affection or love by both parents. Well,

1

very little indeed from Mother. I did not know what love meant. Love and affection, I had none.

The word 'love' was never heard at all. The only words that were commonly heard around the house were 'your bastard' or 'where is that little brat', and other ripe language. I used the knowledge I had picked up to get from A to B, travelling around the country, by looking after number one – me.

Maybe you might think that is a bit selfish of me but there was only me. My grandparents, on my mother's side, I loved dearly as they spent a lot of their time looking after me. From time to time, they gave me a roof over my head on many occasions from my birth or when I needed it, for which I am extremely grateful. A great debt I owed them but unfortunately could never ever repay. I have asked the question of my grandparents on more than one occasion, but they seemed to skirt around the question. My mother's brothers and sisters, to my amazement, all clammed up very tightly when I asked the question.

I feel deeply sad about that part of this story, which had placed me in a very tight spot. I do not want to open up old wounds for those within my family. Mother should be the one able to tell me the truth, of her own free will. I do not know anything about my father. Even after Mother telling me a story about my father, on my investigation, I'm sorry to say I always came back with nothing. Even at this time of my life I have been told many different stories which I cannot believe or even contemplate to believe. I will cover those points as we arrive at the appropriate junction of my life.

To date, 2021, my inquiries have taken me to question most of my family members, starting with my grandparents, who say nothing as soon as I start asking questions. I have tried nearly all other relatives, with the same results. I tried to question my mother on many occasions but I find this very hard to do.

The old man's details, or 'step-father' or 'common law partner' to mother, are as follows. Charles Frederick Francis Cutts was his name. I was always known as Kenny Cutts to everyone until the age of 15 and hated every minute of being called that – the mickey-taking was endless at school and around other children or my friends who I lived with at the time.

I was placed on the training ship, *Arethusa*, a nautical boarding school, soon after my 13th birthday, in 1957. This is when everything with regards to my name came out into the open at the age of 15-and-a-half, having just passed my examinations to join the Royal Navy in early 1959.

What had transpired was that the Royal Navy and *Arethusa* could not find any record of Kenneth Brian Cutts wishing to join up, so they wrote to my mother to ask the question and to supply my birth certificate. The padre then went on to explain that he had received a letter from Mother (dated 1st June 1959), which he handed to me to read. There, standing out, was the surname of Chandler – my true surname. I cupped the birth certificate in both hands and buried my face into it, the tears flooded out. You cannot imagine the joy that I felt at that very moment.

Mother told the story in her letter. As she put it, during the Second World War she had fallen pregnant with me after meeting this very nice Canadian soldier who was stationed in or around Dorking, in Surrey, on the lead-up to the D-Day landings, which he was involved in. But he never returned as he was missing or killed in action.

Everything the padre was saying to me was just a blur, then I came to my senses. What he was trying to tell me was great news, I just jumped for joy. I told him that from this moment on, I wished to be known as Ken Chandler. It did not take long for it to sink in or for me to get used to being called Chandler, it just came naturally. I did not question it anymore; I was just so happy to know that my name was no longer going to be Cutts. It had been at the back of my mind for a very long time.

Now I could get on with my life but I still had to go home on leave to my so-called parents (the Cutts house on Goodwyns estate in Dorking). The atmosphere was even worse than ever, so much so that I once again moved in with my grandparents in Mid Holmwood.

Fred was always known as my brother, never as a half-brother. News that he was also a Chandler, and not Cutts, came as a very big surprise to me but, having thought about it much later on, my mother's conduct did not really surprise me. During those years, she had at least three children – Margaret (that's another story), Fred, Janet, with Christine some ten years later and me – outside of wedlock. In those days to do it once was bad enough. Her parents had more or less stood by her, letting her stay at home after returning from a young mother's home.

Then, recently, around 2005-6, my sister, Janet (apparently Cutts' daughter), when visiting Mother down in Burnham-on-Sea, Somerset, broached the subject of my father and suggested she tell me who he was as I was trying to get to the bottom of the matter.

During my next visit to Burnham for a visit to Mother one weekend, Cathy and I sat down to tea with her. She suddenly just said to me, "I am sorry that it has not been made clear who your father is or was." Then Mother told me that my father was a Canadian soldier, called Harold Ronstadt. He was such a nice man to her, very handsome, a good-looker, as she put it. "You are just the image of him." It turned out he was serving over here during World War Two and was stationed in or near Dorking. However, he is said to have gone off to the D-Day landings, never to return.

I have, to date, also made enquiries of the Surrey social services office in Epsom as this was the office from which Miss Wright (my social worker) worked from, to gain access to my records held by them. But, lo and behold, I have been informed that all my records have been destroyed through age. The story of my life is in so many records that have allegedly been destroyed. But the main thing was that nobody in authority or administration knew that I had been born until the 1st June 1959, the first date of my registration. So of course there were no records.

I, Kenneth Brian Chandler, said to be born the 12th day of January in the year of our Lord, 1944. Where I was actually born was in the Berrington Hospital, somewhere in the town of Shrewsbury, Shropshire. As shown on my new birth certificate. I believe this momentous event happened whilst Mother, Daisy Ethel Nellie Chandler, had been sent away from Dorking in disgrace to a large house or refuge for unmarried mothers. This was where Mother was sent to complete her pregnancy.

Chaddeslode House, Abbey Foregate, (approximately 150 to 200 yards from the main road). In 1.73 acres of grounds with further gardens and grounds extending down to rear boundaries. Chaddeslode House itself stands away from the town centre. The entrance door is supported by two Doric columns. The house catered for eight unmarried mothers, plus babies, costing seven shillings and sixpence a week (a lot of money during those times).

I was actually born in a former workhouse, Atcham Union (near Shrewsbury), which, during the First World War, was used as a hospital – Berrington Hospital. It was later renamed as Cross House Hospital. Chaddeslode House was a mother and baby home run by the Church of England Diocese of Lichfield.

Most women had their babies and they were adopted soon afterwards. Why not me? I have been in contact with Shropshire County Council, who searched their records for the period of time around that of my birth date. Unfortunately, these enquiries have once again drawn a blank. Everywhere I seem to go, whoever I ask, always draws a blank.

However, they did have a record of Miss Daisy Chandler for about that time who had a child, a boy (possibly me). There were no details of the baby having been adopted. *Why there?* you may ask. All I can say I do not know why. All I know is that there has been a very very dark secret that not one, repeat, not one within the family circle will divulge to me. Every time I mentioned it later in life, when an adult, they went mute! A secret so bad I cannot get to the bottom of.

There is the case of me having an older sister, Margaret Alma. Where and when? Where is she today?

Was it that my mother had been so bad that her parents, Augustine Austin (Gus) Chandler, born 16th January 1887 in Reigate, died 22nd June 1969, aged 82 at Dorking General Hospital, and Ellen Jane Chandler (née Streeter) born 1893, died 27th July 1979, aged 86, did not wish to see my mother or have anything whatsoever to do with her at the time of her pregnancy? Was it not the first time she had transgressed?

Footnote

(Found on the internet in 2021)

HISTORY OF CANADIAN WAR CHILDREN
During WW2 Canadian soldiers serving in Britain fathered well in excess of 22,000 children, many of which were unmarried, single women during and immediately after the period between December 1939 and May 1946 to these women the stigma of being an unmarried mother was too great resulting in the child being given up for adoption soon after birth. Even if the woman kept the child, the law at that time required the parents to be married or the father present at registration of the birth before his name could be included on the birth certificate. Many unwed women finding themselves pregnant who tried to trace their boyfriends, found that the regiment had moved him on and denied all knowledge of his existence. Following the war when the wife followed her husband to Canada, some found that the marriage was bigamous or for some other reason he could not be traced and therefore returned to Britain. Because of these circumstances many Canadian War Children have no knowledge of their paternal father which leaves many questions unanswered.

On the other hand, Canadian soldiers who knew that their girlfriends were pregnant may have been denied the opportunity by circumstance to keep in contact, some may have not even been aware that the child had been conceived. Many reasons may be given but the one overriding fact is that a child however old or father and half sibling has the right to know one another. Due to the passing of time these fathers may no longer exist but there could be half brothers and sisters who would relish the opportunity of knowing their half sibling in Britain. Likewise, the British child would gain the knowledge about their father that was denied them for so long.

The War Children are not looking to move to Canada or apply for Canadian Citizenship. They are aged between 65 and 71 years old (plus) now and most have children of their own and even grandchildren. All they want is to know their roots, not a lot to ask.

Pamela Wilson, Canadianrootuk.org

CHAPTER 2

MOTHER'S EARLY LIFE

I was not the first born to Daisy Chandler. I do know of a possible sister called Margaret Alma, date of birth 14th May 1942 (one-and-a-half years older than me). So, Mother could have been a very young mother of Margaret, just 18 years old, if that. Then to do it again from when I was born must have been very hard for her parents to accept. This sort of conduct was not condoned in those days, it was seen as very bad form to have children out of wedlock, a stain and strain on the family, hence why she was dispatched to Shrewsbury.

From time to time during my grandparents' life, I lived with them at 2 Holmside Cottages. One day, I picked up a photograph situated on the mantelpiece over the fireplace in a prime position for everyone to see. I must have been about ten years old at the time; maybe a little less. The photograph was of my grandmother, Nellie, cuddling and tightly holding onto a lovely little girl, with white (blonde) tight curly hair, looking very pretty.

I asked the question, "Gran, who's that pretty little girl with you in the photo?"

She replied, "Oh! That's Margie, just a little girl who had to go away to Croydon, but she died of an accident in a child's playground, hit by a swing."

Then, a couple of days later, my grandfather also had a tear in his eye or he was crying, which, again, upset me. "Please do not ask any more questions about the photo, it upset your grandmother."

Because of his words I never did ask any more questions. The photograph disappeared only to be seen once much later on in my life. Before contacting any living relatives left of my family, I wish to make this unequivocally clear that I have had a very strong suspicion of who my father was. Those things might prove to be of a local nature and not overseas in Canada. The information that Mother divulged to me after my investigations have proven to be negative and I cannot prove them in any way. MOTHER HAS TAKEN HER SECRETS WITH HER TO HER GRAVE!

During 2007, I addressed a letter to three surviving relatives of my generation to see if any of them had been told by their parents anything of my story. The outcome was a negative answer once again, as far as they were concerned. My Aunt Marge in Somerset, wife of Donald, Mother's younger brother, was also contacted in the same way, however, the answer was a very definite negative, saying she did not want anything to do with the question I had proposed of my birth right. Fortunately, or not, some weeks later, one of my cousins, who I have been very fond of, felt more or less the same as myself. Asking for my permission to follow up on this line of enquiry, she took it upon herself to question on my behalf the other only surviving relative at the time of my mother's generation, Aunt Beryl (wife of Bunny, Mothers' older brother). I gave my blessing; what harm would it cause?

After a lengthy conversation they had together on the telephone, I eventually received a telephone call in return from my cousin. She told me to go ahead and arrange a meeting with Aunt Beryl, to join her for tea at her flat. This was arranged. I do not know how true Aunt Beryl's story is or was, I could only take it at face value at that moment. The only way it could be confirmed was by facing up to my mother, who was still alive at the time, living in Burnham-on-Sea. Unfortunately, she was very ill at time and the question had to be put to her straight, face-to-face, at the right opportunity. Both Cathy and myself arranged to join Beryl for tea at her flat.

My aunt told me that a local fellow, from South Holmwood, was almost certainly or possibly my father, as she had put it. At first, she would not commit herself to say for sure that he was my father (I shall not name him as it may cause too much upset to those close to him. He has since died and his wife, I believe, is still alive and there may be others of this family close to him who are left).

You could have slapped me around the face with a wet kipper; I was so surprised when Beryl did give me his name. It was as if the lost piece of a jigsaw had been found.

As it turns out, I know his son very well indeed. He was a close friend to me when I came home on leave from Arethusa. We first met in a coffee bar in North Street, Dorking which had a jukebox in one corner where the youngsters of the day would crowd around to listen to the 'new' musical phenomenon sweeping the country.

This son of my now-possible father would be in the company of two other lads enjoying their leave period, who were both juniors in the Royal Air Force. I was invited to join them as I too was a junior in uniform.

Most of the girls in the coffee bar at the time came away from the jukebox to crowd around our table instead as the uniforms acted as a crumpet magnet.

There were many good times when on leave from the Royal Navy. We used to go out drinking together in the many public houses that were once on the high street of Dorking. We went with a couple of young men who joined the RAF as boys so we were all in the same boat and enjoyed each other's company. We all became very good friends, 'like brothers do', a small band of brothers, you might say. Three or four of us in uniform and him in civvies, with us proudly showing off our uniforms of course.

I still see him from time to time on the Dorking high street. We exchange news and views, have a chat, but he, I believe, knows nothing of what I have now been told. It now makes these meetings very difficult. I also believe his mother still may be alive today; it would be wrong of me to do any following-up of this story of his father also being my father, making him my half-brother. How odd this would be.

In the case of Margaret Alma, I had been told Aunt Beryl and her husband, my Uncle Bun, wanted to take care of Margaret Alma, to bring her up to treat her as their own. In fact, they had made all the arrangements for this to be done legally – to adopt her. This was not to be, however. As the days were drawing closer, getting nearer and nearer to the handover of the child, Mother took Margaret out one day, saying she was taking her out for the day as a treat – this was fine. The outcome of this was that Mother and Margaret disappeared for two or three days. She did not come home, nobody knew of Mother's thoughts. When she did eventually return to her home, she did not have Margaret with her.

It is said that she went to a large house somewhere in Beare Green or the South Holmwood area, where Mother was in service as a domestic. She gave Margaret to the lady of the house so that she could be brought up properly and have a future; this is what leads me to believe that she may still be alive today.

The story of her being fostered by a family in Croydon and being killed in a swing accident in a child's playground seems very unlikely. No death certificate can be found! My suspicions stem from how certain local persons have behaved towards me, now and in the past. I will try to explain these events as I continue with this part of my life.

A couple of years after this conversation with Aunt Beryl, another cousin and his son dropped in on us for a short visit and stayed for a cup of tea. The conversation got around to discussing the past and he told me that his mother, Hilda, worked with his father in a large house in Capel called Grenehurst Manor. Knowing that my mother once worked in service with Hilda, her sister, I put two and two together and came up with five!

I started to look or find out more about Margaret Alma, yet again to no avail. My Aunt Beryl could not or would not tell me the surname of the people with whom Mother had left Margie – maybe Beryl genuinely did not know their name. Aunt Beryl, bless her, threw another spanner in the works by hitting me with another bombshell. "Did you know that Freddie is not a son of Cutts?" But, true to form, she did not say any more about that subject; maybe she did not know his father.

Cathy and I spent a considerable amount of time talking to Beryl, when, lo and behold, she said, "Christine has the same father as you do," meaning me. My chin hit the floor with a hell of a thud. Cathy and I both had an intake of breath and looked at each other in amazement. Cathy was as shocked as I was.

My next move was to say, "Pardon?" I asked her to repeat what she had said.

"Oh yes, Christine has the same father as you. Didn't you know? she replied matter-of-factly.

It made me feel a little sick. I was so surprised, as was Cathy. It did not occur to me to ask her to give me some sort of proof, which I regret. Aunt Beryl then went into a long statement, informing me of my grandmother's actions in all of this. When I was born, my grandmother was seen visiting the brother (a bachelor, living on his own) who was said to be my father. She would take him homemade cakes and the occasional cooked meals. "Why?" I asked.

The answer I got was to keep him quiet from saying anything to me, to keep him sweet, to make him keep his promise to not say anything. He certainly did keep his word. If this is so, my mother seemed to have been carrying on with this same fellow for a very long time. From when Margaret was born in 1942, right up to when Christine was born in 1960, and beyond, no doubt, until he passed away.

Getting back to our tea with Aunt Beryl; if the things she was divulging to both Cathy and I were true, and the gentleman concerned was my father, whose brother lived opposite my grandparent's cottage and behind Uncle Bun's house, he was also disabled, having very badly formed feet. If the story of my father being a local lad from South Holmwood was true, then when I used to come home from boarding school at Sunnydown, from about the age of ten, and later when on leave from the *Arethusa* and Royal Navy, I used to see him (the brother) watching me. It was mostly from a distance, sitting on his moped or his bicycle, so I made it my business to get to know him a bit better.

I had seen him a lot in the past visiting Mother at our address at Chart Downs. He would visit Mother mostly during Sunday afternoons, when the old man would go to his local for a pint, come with gifts of produce taken from his large garden he had on the Holmwood Common. As I have said, I made it my business to get to know him better. In fact, I got to know him very well. I made it my concern to find out about his disability and to visit him to help where I could. At this point I knew nothing of any connection to him and his brother in South Holmwood. I knew him from his visits to Mother earlier on in my life, so it was not too hard to get to know him.

His Name was Joe, or that's what I called him. I found him to be very knowledgeable and kind-hearted. I got to help him with digging his garden, which was quite large with plenty of fruit trees and bushes of berries, with large plots of vegetables growing. When the visit had come to an end and it was time to leave or say goodbye, he would first of all slip me, as he put it, a little pocket money 'to get by on'. But as I left, he would have tears streaming down his cheeks. The money was always a lot. If I was still on holiday from boarding school or *Arethusa*, he would give me nothing less than a £1 note nearly every time we met. At first, I tried very hard to refuse his generosity (a pound was a lot of money in those days). When holiday or leave was over I had to return, he made sure that he gave me a £10 note which I must say was a hell of a lot of money in those days (more than £100). He told me not to let any of my family know he was giving me pocket money, especially Cutts, as he would take it off me.

So I had to learn how to hide it from others. Upon returning to boarding school or *Arethusa*, I had to declare it, always being asked where I obtained such a large amount of money. I just explained that it was savings from doing extra work while on holiday. Thankfully my explanation was believed so my mother was never contacted about it.

It's now obvious to me that Joe was possibly reporting back to his brother on my progress through life. It makes sense that he was also keeping in contact with Mother, with gifts, when I was much younger when we lived at Chart Down and later at Stubs Hill on Goodwyns.

Since the day Mother took Margie to the family of her employers, Mother and Aunt Beryl have been sworn enemies. So whatever Beryl has said in the past about Mother has caused a rift of bad feeling within the family circles. We all know that in the past Beryl seemed to be a bit of a busy body and said things that other people did not wish to know. Beryl certainly did not get on with Mother, in fact they hated each other. I can see why Beryl was the type of person who called a kettle black, and does not care who knows it, the truth does hurt sometimes.

I have gone over and over what Beryl has disclosed to me. I have laid in bed thinking of what the outcome of all of this might be. How do I come to tell this alleged happening? I have agonised over it in my mind, the more I think of it the more I can begin to believe it, but how do I tell those who are involved in this sad situation? Sadly, I blurted it out at what should have been a celebration of Cathy's and my 50th wedding anniversary garden party to Christine and Janet, who left both being very upset.

I have been in touch with the Salvation Army Family Tracing Service along with two television companies who were tracing long lost relatives, leaving with them a brief account of my history and what I wished to come out of the programme, but so far they have all said they would not undertake my story. Where oh where do I go from here? While there is a chance of finding out what happened to Margaret, I feel something further must be done, but how? If DNA is the answer or is required to get to the bottom of all these questions, then it should be done.

It was soon after being told all this information about my mother's past that I had made up my mind to visit Mother and face up to her with all the information I had been given. As I have mentioned earlier, my first cousin, Peter, dropped in for a chat and a quick cup of tea. We were talking generally about family matters of the past when I mentioned the work that his mother, Hilda, sister of my mother, did during the war years. He informed me that my Aunt Hilda worked as a domestic in Grenehurst Manor House, Grenehurst Park, in Capel, in a village not far south of the Holmwoods. Hilda met her Husband, William (known as Uncle Bill) here; he was one of the gardeners at the big house. Knowing that my mother sometimes worked with Hilda, my next course of action was putting information I had been given together.

I approached the archives of the Capel Parish Council online. No luck there but it gave me a telephone number of the person in charge of the Capel records. On contacting them, yet another blank, they had no records of the staffing of Grenehurst Manor. They did tell me at its height, a large number of staff were employed there. I have not been able to do any other follow-ups. The manor house became the Elim Pentecostal Bible College way after the war years.

Cathy and I had decided that we would visit on this particular weekend, and stay in a bed and breakfast house, if necessary. Unfortunately, during the week before the arranged visit, we received a distressing telephone call from my sister, Christine, telling us that Mother had been found lying in the hallway at the bottom of her stairs by the local postman, who noticed that her curtains had not been opened. After looking through the letterbox to see my mother, he immediately called the emergency services and Mother had been taken to Weston-super-Mare hospital and was in a bad way. We travelled down to see her in the hospital. Whoops! There goes my face-to-face encounter with my mother as she was in no fit state to answer or deny anything I put to her. Unfortunately, it turned out that her health had got progressively worse and worse, and she fell into a sharp downward slope of ill health until she eventually died on 10th December 2010.

Now I am in a position of trying to prove the information obtained from Aunt Beryl. I surely have to tell Christine and the others of what I have been told. Do I go straight to this 'friend' (his son) of mine and upset his apple cart? Maybe he already knows something. Oh, what do I do? I have tried to investigate it on my own, I have tried to get hold of the 1942-1943 census to ascertain the work that Mother was involved with at the time, but unfortunately that census was put on hold due to the War and there is a 75-year exclusion of access to the files. I do have further suspicion that his son may know of the situation. I have seen him lately in the town and he has crossed the road to avoid me, or am I getting too paranoid?

There is another reason why I think he may know. In the late 1990s I joined the organisation and became a member of Masonic order by joining Lingfield Lodge 7802, who met at Nutfield in Surrey. Within Masonry circles, it is suggested that you should try to visit as many of the other lodges as you can as they are nearly always slightly different from that of your mother lodge (Lingfield). So living in Dorking at the time, I decided that I should visit Dorking 1149 to see how they do it. I arrived at Dorking Lodge, and who was the first person I met? No other than the son of my alleged father, my friend of many years. The surprise shown on his face was to behold, it was the same as you might see in a face of one who had seen a ghost. However, in Masonic circles, it states that 'if one were to visit a lodge in which there is a brother with whom you are at variance, or against whom you entertain animosity, it is expected that you will invite him to withdraw in order to amicably to settle your differences, which being happily affected, you can enter the lodge and work with that love and harmony which should at all times characterise Freemasons'.

Since that first visit to Dorking Lodge 1149, I have joined the Dorking Lodge as a member. My friend has not put in an appearance now for over 17 years. Is he at variance with me? I do not know. He pays his subscription every year, members are in contact with him, but yet he still has not attended a meeting since that first meeting so many years ago. It does make me feel that there is something to the story of him maybe being my half-brother. I have been toying with the idea of hiring someone to trace what my mother's life was like.

CHAPTER 3

MY GRANDPARENTS.
GRATEFUL THANKS FOR ALL
YOU DID FOR ME

Now, getting back to my grandfather (Gus) from the Pointz Castle steam trawler. Grandfather (known in the Royal Navy as 'Taffy' as he came from Swansea) joined the Royal Navy at the outbreak of World War I. He did his training as a steam turbine engineer at HMS *Vivid* (now a naval reserve base in Plymouth) but he was soon to join the Home Fleet under Admiral Beatty at Invergordon in Scotland where he joined the battleship HMS *Benbow*. He took part in the great battle of Jutland, when on *Benbow*. He told me of long hours at 'action stations' in a hot engine room, as a stoker shovelling coal into the great big furnaces to keep up steam to the turbines. During the First World War, he also took part in the battle of Dogger Bank in the North Sea. I am not sure what ship he was on at the time but he did tell me he also saw time on HMS *Valiant* and HMS *Iron Duke* (both battleships) where he spent a lot of time at Scapa Flow in Scotland, which was being used as a base for the Home Fleet. Granddad also went to the Falkland Islands to do battle during World War I, but on which ship I am not too sure; I think it was the *Valiant*. So, he had many battles to fight and made it home afterwards. He must have won the medals of the day but I do not know who has them now; I would love to have even seen them.

Returning to civilian life, Grandfather first returned back to the Swansea area to find work, which after the First World War was very short in South Wales, leaving him to find work elsewhere. So off he set, walking from Swansea to Reigate, the actual place of his birth. Yes, I am told he walked all the way, during one of the worst winters on record, with just a few belongings. How long it took him I can only imagine. Apparently the boots he was wearing when he arrived at Reigate had been totally worn out, he had used cardboard inside them as soles in the boots. Imagine it walking all that way just to find work.

He did eventually find work; I am informed he joined up with his brother William (Great-uncle Bill) who lived in North Holmwood, father of Brian Chandler of Chart Downs, who managed to get him to work in making bricks in the North Holmwood brickyard (now Holmwood Park estate). He lived in accommodation supplied by the brick company, in what is now Watham Road, North Holmwood. The building consisted of a long wooden bungalow (not unlike an Indonesian longhouse I saw in Borneo) which seemed to be raised off the ground on stilts with a high stairway to enter it. I do remember seeing these wooden bungalows during the early '50s and '60s. During his work there he had an accident, where a clay hopper (something like a small dumper truck which carried the clay to the factory) came away from its rail and fell onto him, trapping and leaving him with head injuries. As a result he was left out of work for a time.

When I was young and living with my grandparents, he worked as a linesman for the AJS (not sure what the initials stood for) but I do know that he worked for the Electricity Board, based at what is now known as Rough Rew, which was situated behind where we used to live in Flint Hill Close. His job was to keep all the overhead electricity wires clear of any obstructions, like trees and other plants. He also helped with clearing and putting up telegraph poles which supported the overhead wire cables.

Granddad always would carry his tools with him, everywhere he went. These were very sharp and I mean *sharp*. Axes which could cut a bough of a tree in half with one blow. He also had this large scythe which was a tool used for cutting long grass and bramble bushes, with a long curved cutting blade, very sharp, set at right angles to the handle, on the end of this long handle which in turn had two smaller handles attached so that the tool could be held in each hand. It was swung from side to side in a cutting motion to cut the grass, etc. Other tools he carried were sickles or 'fagging hooks', smaller grass cutting tools. Granddad used to wear heavy boots, with leather gaiters halfway up his legs, for protection against being cut by his tools. I used to help him take off his gaiters and boots when he came home from work. He had a particular way of securing his boots, by a single long leather boot lace, which he would tie a knot at the bottom hole in the boot, then thread this single lace though all of the holes to the second from top hole, then rap the lace twice around the ankle, tucking in the loose end under the lace which went around his ankle, it never came undone. Then I used to have his slippers ready. When he would sit in his chair next to the open fire grate, I used to sit on the carpet beneath his feet. He would turn on the radio (they did not have a television in those days – could not afford it) for the six o'clock news. Afterwards he would tell me where he had been working that day.

The family, my grandmother and cousins and I, used to sit on the common watching for the dark green AJS lorry to pull up on the main road, opposite to what used to be the Norfolk Arms public house. We watched Grandfather jump down from the back of the lorry, and we would all run down the common to meet him. I say 'we' – that was Peter, Valerie, my cousins and myself. He would never let us handle or hold any of his cutting tools, they were always very sharp. When the AJS depot started to run down its staff, Grandfather was one of the first to go, as more modern cutting equipment came into being. So he took up gardening for some of the large houses around Dorking. He was a fantastic gardener, knew everything about it down to the Latin names of plants.

Now, my grandmother, Ethel Nellie (née Streeter) – most people called her Nellie – was a well-built woman of about five-foot-one-or-two, very thick set, not fat, just broad, you did not mess with her, a no-nonsense woman. My memory of her was of a very hard worker, always having her brick copper boiling away in the corner of the kitchen. Now this copper was where she would wash all of the clothing. (no washing machines in those days). It was made of a copper basin of about three or four feet across, about three to four feet deep, which had to be filled with buckets of cold water from a single cold water tap in a large earthenware white sink in the kitchen. No running hot water taps in those days. To light this large copper, built underneath was a large fire grate, which had to be lit using kindling wood and paper, often we would start it by taking a small shovel and take the burning ember from a large cooking stove in the dining room, or from the front room fire if alight, place the embers under the copper, then put on the kindling wood, if they had coke place some onto it and off it would go. Once boiling it cleans the clothes and the smell of washing powder and steam from the copper fills the house. I cannot remember that house ever being too cold, mostly it was very warm indeed.

The toilet was built onto the side of the house, but to use it you had to go outside the back door and into the toilet. They did not use toilet paper as we know it today, nice and comfortable and soft, but hanging on a hook would be pages of the *Radio Times* or newspaper pages cut into strips of three and hung on a piece of string on a nail made into a hook. You had to rub the paper between your hands to make it feel a little softer. It got very cold out there in the winter, so you did not spend too long sitting out there. (The print on the paper would come off in your hands, Lord knows what your bottom looked like after being rubbed with a newsprint).

All the cooking was done on this great big black fire or grate, situated in the dining room, which had several hobs on it, again a solid fuel was used like coal, coke or mainly logs of wood. There would always be a very large black kettle boiling on the stove, which had a black bottom, the blackness cause by the heat of the hob. Later on, the landlords put in a small gas cooker with a couple rings on the top with a small grill, with an equally small oven, but Gran seemed to manage on it. She was a fantastic cook.

Bath time – that was another ordeal. There was no bathroom, just a scullery or the little kitchen sink; the scullery or small kitchen was not big enough for using the bath. First you had to go outside in whatever weather, snow or shine, take the large galvanized tin bath, which was hanging on a hook on the back outside wall in the garden, next to a large apple tree. We had to carry it or drag it, as it was too heavy for us children, into the dining room area, moving a large wooden table to one side. This routine happens at least once or twice a week. Mainly on a Saturday, the tin tub would be brought indoors and filled with boiled water from a variety of pots and pans, or taking water out of the copper in the kitchen, as each of us took our weekly bath. In the meantime, the copper had to be lit and filled with water, which, when hot enough, had to be transferred into the tin bath on the floor of the dining room. In those days, it used to be the man of the house who got the first bath, followed by the rest of the household all the way down to the youngest member of the family, me. By then, the water was so dirty you might not be able to see such a little one in there, hence the expression about 'not throwing the baby out with the bathwater'. The house had no central heating but it was always warm in the winter.

As I remember, it was rather a crowded house, although I could have been perfectly happy there if I had been born into another family, but being out of wedlock, it was a different story. My family was against me from the start. My crime was that I was not really wanted or welcomed. I did not understand why all this was happening, very sad to say but that was the attitude of people back just after the Second World War.

Later, when Cathy and I were living in Singapore, my grandparents had to move out of the cottage at 2 Holmside Cottages because the landlord wanted to modernise the house and live in it himself, so the local council had to find the grandparents somewhere else to live. They placed them in Wenlock Edge, the high-rise block of flats on Goodwyns Estate. Granddad was very upset about all of this, firstly, being told he had to get out of what he knew as his home and precious garden. All the long hours he had put into making it his own pride and place, where he could wile away his days doing what he loved best, his gardening. He said if he would have to live there in Wenlock Edge, he would die there. It was not long before he became very unwell, eventually being placed in the Dorking Cottage Hospital in South Terrace, Dorking, where he just gave up living and passed away. A very sad day for me.

Grandmother could not manage living in the high-rise flat so she was moved once again into the old people's accommodation on Rough Rew. This is where the photo of Margaret appeared on her mantelpiece once again. On one of my visits, she saw me looking at it. She just stood up, went to the mantelpiece, and lay the photograph upside down. She did not say a word. It made me feel so sad I just left without even saying goodbye. From that day, I did not like going around to visit Grandmother, but I made it my duty, not a chore, just to make sure she was all right.

At the time of my birth, I know my mother was working in service, as a domestic, for a large house somewhere nearby, but where, I still do not know. Maybe when she was sent away because the disgrace of being pregnant was too much for her parents and employers. Well, sometime soon after being born, my mother must have returned to 2 Holmside Cottages, to live with her family. My memory of this time is really very vague; well, I was only a baby or very young.

World War II was still at its height, I do know, because of the stories told to me about being blown out of my pram by a doodlebug flying bomb which had landed and blown up in a field near to the house on Holmwood Common. Stories of how my mother, after returning to Holmwood, had to find further employment. I believe she worked for Lyon's Tea Shop on Pump Corner in Dorking. There were several stories of her bringing home iced cakes for tea, to have them taken from her by my grandmother, to be broken up and given to the other children first, like my cousin Peter who was a little older than myself. I am told I hardly got any. Whether that is true or not I do not know.

I am also told that, for some reason or another, at this early stage of my life, I lived with my Uncle Bill and Auntie Hilda, mother and father to Peter, my cousin on the Holmwood Common, in a little cottage called Vine Cottage, still there today. Later, Auntie Hilda and Uncle Bill had more children – Valerie, Iris, Michael, Leslie, Nigel and Margaret. All first cousins. My first memory of this stage of life was again very vague, of playing out on the common with Pete, building our camps in the bracken. Uncle Don, my mother's younger brother, would take us out onto the common, or up into the Redland woods with his air gun. He had a lovely pet dog called Spiv, a black mongrel with a bit of Labrador in him, gentle demeanour. When it snowed, we would all build snowmen either on the common or up in the Redland.

I can remember watching and waiting for the men (Uncle Bill, Uncle George) to come home from the pub, The Plough at Blackbrook, or the Norfolk Arms. Uncle Bill was still in the RAF at the time and Uncle George was in the Royal Navy as a seaman in the gunnery branch. He was a Geordie through and through, who was mainly doing convoy work during the war in the North Atlantic, later to be on boom defense ships. He married Auntie Doris (Alma), born 21/10/1921, died 8/11/2007, who was also serving in the WRNS (Wrens) as a leading cook. They met in Plymouth, where George proposed to Alma while standing in line at a cinema. They never did get to see the movie because a bomb fell on the building. Both survived the war, Auntie Doris (or Alma, no matter how she was known to me) was unfortunately struck down with scarlet fever during 1942 and was discharged as a leading cook from the Women's Royal Naval Service due to bad health. I am sure this contributed to her being struck down with Multiple Sclerosis in later life, which gradually got to be more disabling. She was finally placed in a care home in Frimley to see out her last days.

Following World War Two, George and Alma tried to settle in Newcastle area but Alma became so homesick that they both move back down south to Chart Downs in Dorking, where they settled for a short while before moving to Appladell Road in Leatherhead, having had a family of William, Maureen, Linda, and Peter. More cousins.

I am also told Uncles Bill and George used to get me drunk on cider or 'scrumpy' just for a laugh, so they could watch me banging my head against the wall. I remember that Uncle Bill kept this very vicious dog which was always barking, locked in a shed in the back garden, at Vine Cottage.

My mother had by now moved back to live with her parents. Not for long as it was about the time she had met up with this bloke who, in the early days of my life, I thought to be my real dad! He and my mother lived together as man and wife (common law) along with me, my brother Fred, newly born, and a brown and white mongrel dog called Toby, and a pet jackdaw called Jackie.

CHAPTER 4

LIFE AT HOLLY ROUGH, BOX HILL

My next memory is around the age of four years, living in an old type of hut, something like a really old railway carriage, up on top of Box Hill. Ashurst Drive, to be more accurate. It was situated on land, which must have been owned by a family called Clarke, in an area known as Holly Rough. It seemed to be balancing on the side of this hill in the woods. To get to it, we had to walk down a dirt track, past Clarke's large house, down this steep hill, where perched on the side of the hill was what the 'old man' called our bungalow. It did not have any gas or electricity, running water was from a single cold water tap outside the back door. The toilet was an Elsan type of thing, in a small hut outside.

The 'old man' – I could call him many different names but due to my age I knew him as 'Daddy' – was a Mr Charles Francis Frederick Cutts (more of what I thought of him later as we go along with this account of my life). Born 1899 or 1900, a bigamist. At the time he met up with mother to have this relationship, he was already married to a lady called Jessie. He died in 1978. At the time he met up with Mother, he was living in Bexhill-on-Sea, East Sussex. He was a bricklayer/labourer. What connection my mother had with Bexhill-on-Sea I do not know, or how she got to know the 'old man'. He had five sons with Jessie. Frederick, born 1921, died 1979, at just 58 years old. David, born 1922, died 1956 – he was only 34 years old. Francis, born 1923, died 1993; he was 70 years old when he died. Ronald, born 1935, married to Irene. They have two children, Ricky and Sue, both married. The 'old man' could not have long been out of the army – Queen's Own East Surrey Regiment. He managed to survive World War

Two – worse luck. Found out later he originated from Camberwell, London. At no time did I ever, as far as I know, meet any of his family. Have not done so to this day. I have had no contact at all with them, although Christine (my sister) has been in contact with them. As for Fred and Janet, they do not want anything to do with them either. For all intents and purposes, he was my dad, I called him Daddy (which still hurts me today). I knew nothing else, until later in my life.

It was around this time that I remember the snow, the great freeze, we had in 1948. There was the 'old man' digging his way out of the bungalow, digging a tunnel so that we could get out as we were snowed in to clear a pathway, with the snow piled high on either side of the path. This was very exciting for a four-year-old. It was like living in an igloo for a time. It seemed to become nice and warm inside as I remember. The weather during this period was very, very cold outside; it went on for months, becoming extremely cold. We had to sleep under extra-heavy overcoats to keep warm at night.

We lived our mundane life there on the 'Roof of the World', well, it seemed that way to me at that age (no, not the caravan site of the same name). I can remember that my 'brother' Freddie was only newly born so I must have been four-and-three-months-old. I remember the old pram that was Fred's carriage. A big black thing with large wheels on the back, a smaller set of wheels on the front, a large black hood, which could be raised or lowered. Mother, at the time, worked as a cleaner at the Hand in Hand public house, and for various other large houses in the area. I spent a lot of time in the bar at the Hand in Hand public house, with Fred in his pram, watching mother on her hands and knees scrubbing the floors as she cleaned up.

My first memory of this period (people say memory is a good thing) is at breakfast times, mainly because, even at this early age, I had to clean out the fire grate, take the ashes outside in all weathers and throw them onto the path leading to the bungalow all from the previous day's fire. Then I lay the new fire, screwing up old newspapers, laying it in the grate of a small, square enclosed fireplace (possibly a wood burner) which had a double door on the front. A couple of pots or a kettle could be stood on the hob on the top to keep hot. I placed chopped kindling wood on top of the screwed-up paper, then carefully lay small lumps of coal on top of that, but I cannot remember ever being allowed to actually light it. Once that was done, I had to collect fresh water from an outside tap for the 'old man' to wash, shave and for his mug of tea (a very large white enamel mug with a blue rim – army issue, I think).

When that little chore was finished, I had to fill the Primus stoves with blue paraffin; they were little pressurised brass cooking stoves, with a single burning ring on top, with a round tank for the paraffin at the bottom. On the side of the Primus tank was a small handle, which had to be pumped to build up pressure in the tank, which in turn fed the heating ring through a small jet. The primus stood on three short legs. To light the Primus, you had to pour a very small quantity of blue methylated spirits into a little canal or small reservoir, situated just under the burning ring. To get the burner to light, one had to set light to the methylated spirits, let it get hot, with a nice blue flame, then release the pressure from the tank, which would then burst into flames as the modern gas ring burners do today What I had to do was then pump up the pressure, without knocking it over, or spilling the methylated spirits, then strike a match, light the methylated spirits in the reservoir, quickly turn another knob to release the gas pressure I had already put into the tank. A very dangerous operation even for an adult, let alone a little boy of five years old. Standing back; hoping it would not backfire on me. I turned the pressure knob so that I got a nice blue flame going. I had to make sure that at least two of the three Primus' were working properly. To see that you had the required flame, you had to keep the pressure jet clear with a little tool, which had a small, vertical needle in the end that you had to move up and down in the jet to keep it clear and clean. A very dangerous practice; I would think in today's environment it would not be allowed.

Well now we had a little heat going. Breakfast could be cooked for the old man. Then after he had his, possibly bacon with maybe an egg or two, I got mine – porridge, if I was lucky, or if available, but hot bread and milk was the breakfast of the day, I was lucky if it was hot. Sometimes I remember getting a little sugar on it; sugar was still rationed at that time, so were sweets and chocolate, which Mother had to get from the shop after handing in whatever ration book she had to use. Sometimes, as a treat, I got sugar on my porridge, most of the time it was eaten with a sprinkling of salt (as they do in Scotland). On occasions, I actually got a bread and sugar sandwich – no margarine or butter – which was indeed a very great luxury.

Another task for me to do was fill the oil lighting lamps with blue paraffin (no electricity). The lamps consisted of a high, fluted stand which had a fuel tank on top, something similar to those of the Primus stoves but a little smaller, with a long, fluted glass tube. Under the glass tube was a wick which could be moved up or down to gain the best flame for the brightest light. I remember scraping off the old burnt part of the wick with a sharp knife and trying to cut it straight with scissors for the next time it was lit. Yet another very dangerous feat to undertake.

At this early age, another of my jobs was to run errands for my mother, namely go up to the shops on the main road for a loaf of bread, eggs, or for some milk. It was a walk of about a mile, up the dirt track, past the Clarke's house and their very large motorboat in the corner of the car park for the house. Out onto Ashurst Drive, well, you see, there was a large house on the left towards the top of Ashurst Drive, which had a large four-bar gate. Behind this gate were these two dirty Great Dane dogs, and a couple of Alsatians, owned by the people living there. One day, one of the Alsatians had got out and stood in front of Mother who was pushing a pram with Fred in it and me holding onto the pram handle. This dog was barking at us and baring its teeth, growling so very loud. It would not go away, frightened the wits out of me. I do not know how Mother felt; she must have been very scared too. We stayed there ridged, frozen to the spot with fear. This snarling dog, bare white teeth showing. It seemed like ages before a man stopped his car, or was it just a truck? Cars were very scarce in those days. He got out and shooed the dog back into the house's garden and shut the gate. So, we could get on our way walking up to the Council's clinic, which was being held in the Box Hill village hall, to get our free orange juice and cod liver oil. I had nightmares about that dog for many years, a long time.

On many a day, I would be sent up to the shops for this or that. I had to run the gauntlet of large barking dogs, snarling at their gates. They were enormous. I was petrified of them, and if they were out in their garden, I would just freeze until an adult came along and rescued me, by walking me past these dogs. It normally took me about two hours to walk to the shops, get a long loaf of bread, then return back home, past these dogs. By the time I had arrived back home with the loaf, normally a bloomer, which at one end had what I now call the 'knobby', the other end was open, where it had stuck to the other loaf alongside it in the baking tray. This open end was easy to get into. Nicely fresh, soft baked warm bread, still one of my favourites. I would get, well, a little hungry walking up to the shop and back. So I would pick out a little pinch at a time and eat it. The hole got a little larger the longer I was out shopping for Mother, and in the end I had eaten what could be described as a large handful, which meant I got a large handful alongside my ear from the 'old man', when I eventually arrived home, for eating the bread, and another for taking so long to get it.

CHAPTER 5

STARTING FIRST SCHOOL

ST. MICHAEL'S IN MICKLEHAM AND THE PLIMSOLL SAGA

Soon after I started going to school at St. Michael's in Mickleham. Oh boy, that got me into a hell of a lot of trouble. As far as my 'old man' was concerned, everything I did could never ever be right, it was always wrong. My first recollection of school life was that I had to walk up to the Hand in Hand public house to meet the school bus. It was situated a little further on from the shops, so it was quite a walk for a youngster's little legs. The bus or coach service was managed by the local council, who hired a local coach firm in Dorking to run this bus service. This one was run by the husband-and-wife team and called Lipscomb Coaches of Junction Road (where Waitrose supermarket is now situated). The driver was called Jack and his wife was called Nina. She was his assistant and looked after the children on his coach. We children called her 'Auntie Nina'. The school pick-up was the car park of the Hand in Hand public house near to the shops, first thing in the morning, in all kinds of weather. Mother would take me to the school bus when I first started going to school, but after a while I would have to make my own way by walking up to the Hand in Hand to catch the school bus.

I had this slight problem with walking up to the shops or to the school bus on my own. Whenever I had to go to the shops or to catch the school bus all by myself, those dogs would come barking up to the gate, I just froze, until they got called in by their owner or when they got tired of barking and just went away by themselves.

One day I had to wear this 'new' fawn-coloured raincoat or mackintosh to school, which Mother had got at the latest jumble

29

sale in the village hall. Off I went one morning in my 'new' coat, I felt like the bee's knees with it buttoned up on the left. I got to school, got off the bus, on the Mickleham bypass, where the Italian restaurant is situated today at the Bittoms Hill, bottom of the hill. You then had to walk up to the school. Anyway, when I arrived in the school playground, one or two of the bigger, older boys started to call me names, girls' names or 'sissy'. I did not know what was going on. It turned out my 'new' coat was a girl's coat, with buttons on the wrong side. Pretty smart, those older boys, knowing it was a girl's coat. So did I from then on.

I refused to wear it again that day, even when it rained at playtime, until it was time to go home. Well, this little lad of five years of age, me, I had enough of being pushed around in the school playground, being called girls names by these bigger boys, the bullies of the school. So I found a sharp piece of metal, got the coat, placed it on the metal and tore a nice big L-shaped tear in the back. *That's fixed that, shan't be wearing that again.* Wrong. BIG mistake. Not just a big mistake but a very bad mistake. When I got home, I tried to hide the coat. I did not get away with it. It did not take long before Mother found it stuffed under my mattress; boy, did I get a hiding. Her favourite tool for this was a feather duster fixed to a bamboo stick. Boy, did that bamboo stick hurt around the back of your thighs. and then I would be sent to bed without any tea, starving hungry.

Mother would follow that up by saying, "Wait until your father gets home."

This is when I remember I really got to know the 'old man's' army belt very well. Every time he looked at me in a certain way, I knew I was going to get a good thrashing or belting with it. I knew I was going to get that leather. Sometimes I may have deserved it, getting a whack or two, but he seemed to get great pleasure out of it. I really got to hate that man. *How could your dad treat you like that?* were my thoughts at the time. I can also remember him coming home from work a little bit under the weather sometimes, from his visits to his favourite hostelry, having stopped off for a drink in the pub, which meant I was more than likely to get a good hiding for doing nothing, just for being me! He was not always under the influence through drink, so that was not an excuse for him to hit me for no reason. I remember he was sober most of the time, so that didn't really affect what type of hiding I would get.

Off I went up to the Hand in Hand the next day, now dressed in my repaired fawn Mackintosh, with this big 'L' on the back, to meet the school bus. As soon as the bus was out of sight of my mother, off came the coat, which got stuffed down under one of the seats on the bus. So I arrived at school minus the repaired Mackintosh. Fantastic; the boys would not now be able to call me names.

It was several days before my fawn Mackintosh was found to be missing. At first, I told Mother that a boy had taken it from me and thrown it away. I think she had reservations about believing my story, until one day she met the school bus. Auntie Nina said to Mother, "I think Kenny has forgotten his coat, he dropped it under the seat." She handed Mother this creased and screwed up coat, which had been pulled from my hiding place. Another sore backside for telling fibs, and a 'wait until your father gets home'. That's a phrase I got to hate over time.

The school bus was owned by Lipcombs Coaches of Junction Road, Dorking. The driver was a very large, jovial man with a big round cheerful face and a big red nose. His name was 'Uncle Jack'. He was helped by 'Auntie Nina'. They were Mr and Mrs Peters of Junction Road, Dorking. These two lovely people would look after us on the school bus. The school coach would always take the same route every day, by leaving the Hand in Hand, drive down towards Headley, at the junction turn left along Headley Common Road, opposite the cricket pitch turn left down Tots Hill towards Tyrell Wood, going through a 'tunnel of beach trees' past the golf course at the end, down to Givons Grove roundabout, past the petrol station with its thatched roof, turning left along Mickleham bypass, past the Old Forge Transport Café, then to the school. On the return trip, they would drive off from school, turning left, through the village of Mickleham, passing Juniper Hall, turn left, going up the zig zag, along the top of Box Hill, back to the Hand in Hand.

We, the children, would be met by our parents. Sometimes Mother could not be there to meet me, either still at home suffering one of her headaches or some other sickness. So I often would make my own way home. To avoid the dogs in Ashurst Drive, I found a shortcut (or what I thought was a shortcut) down through a copse, across a small piece of common land, which came out at the back of our bungalow. Today you would not be allowed to let your children walk such a distance in woods, over a common on their own, for fear of an approach from some strange person or other.

This became my downfall on many occasions. I would get off the bus, walk home on my own, but sometimes, halfway into my journey, I would want to go to the toilet to do a 'number one'. But after once being told it was dirty and very rude to take down your trousers to do your toilet where other people might see you, I tried my very best to hold onto it until I got home. Oh no. Many times I could not make it, always within sight of home. I could not hold on any longer, yes, I messed in my pants. At first, I would try to clean myself up, with leaves or damp grass, which made things much worse. Instead of being comforted, or told it did not matter and being cleaned up by Mother, all I got was another clip round the ear, or rather a good smacking around the legs again! Then those words 'when the old man gets home from work'. Off with his belt. I really got to hate that man – no, not a man – an animal.

Often, Mother would give me a letter for my teacher. I, in my tiny little mind at the time, thought they were saying bad things about me, even to this day I could not say what these letters were for or about. However, I was scared out of my wits, whatever the contents of the letters were. So I used to tear them up, or hide them in my special hiding place. There, no one could ever find them, or so I thought. My hiding place is a nice place in the hedge, brambles and all. *No one will ever find them there.* Nobody could even see them, let alone reach them from the pathway. Wrong again! Well, people could not see them, but not until the winter months set in at least. When the leaves on the bushes fell off, the brambles lost their leaves as well. On walking up to the school bus one day with Mother and Freddie – oh no! Even I saw them. There in a nice, neat (I was neat for my age, I had to be) pile were the torn up letters, there to be seen by all who passed my hiding place – that meant Mother. Oh dear, another good hiding. Out came that bloody duster. Another hiding from the bamboo stick, her favourite weapon, on the back of my legs or upper thigh.

PLIMSOLL INCIDENT

Another incident. Mother had been to the jumble sale once again; it was one of her pastimes, or the only place that she could afford to buy clothes to keep us dressed. She bought me a nice 'new' pair of white plimsolls, you know the type, white canvas uppers, rubber soles. This was during the summer, so the school had a sports day. One day, I had to take my plimsoles to school for a practice day and to get ready for the actual sports day. Sack, egg, and spoon races. We all had to have our plimsolls – nothing unusual about that, you might say, but it was for me. I forgot to take them home with me one afternoon after school.

Here we go again, I got a big telling off from Mother, with the phrase I had heard on many occasions: 'you wait until your father gets home'. I tried everything to hide when I heard his motorbike coming in the distance. I even went to my bed, got right down under the bedclothes, pretending to be asleep. Having parked his motorbike and walked a short distance down to the bungalow, taken off his coat and boots, stood in front of the fire hearth, warming his backside, demanding his mug of tea, he noticed I was not around, Fred was playing on the floor, but there was no sign of me, this prompted him to ask Mother where I was. She told him I was hiding from him as I had not brought home the plimsoles from school. This did not do me any favours whatsoever. I could hear him moving towards my bed. I had the top bunk, Fred slept in the bottom one. The old man came at me, pulled me out of the top bunk by my hair, I can feel it today, and introduced me once again to his blasted army belt, and I really started to hate this man who was supposed to be my dad. Freddie was running around and started screaming, then hid in the bottom bunk. He was only a little baby at the time, maybe two years old.

The old man's next move was to frighten me senseless. He grabbed me by the throat, his whole hand went around my throat, and the collar of my shirt, then in one motion he threw me out of the bungalow in a rage, yes, right out of the bungalow, not just the room. He told me he would have me put away in a home if I could not do as I was told, that he would bloody well kill me if I did not bring those plimsolls home with me the next day. After what seemed like hours, out in the cold evening air, I crept back in and passed him sitting in the corner, mending one of his so-called antique clocks which he also collected (or stole). I was very scared he would kill me. Off I went to bed; Fred was still bawling his head off, so it took me some time to get off to sleep.

The next day arrived, a nice bright crisp summer's day. It should have been a nice quiet walk up to the Hand in Hand to meet the school bus and off to school. Unfortunately, things did not go according to my plan. You see, having got up just a little later than we should have done, Mother was not feeling too well again, must have been that time of month? The 'old man', bear with a sore head, had gone off to work as a builder's labourer. Little Freddie was doing his usual act of bawling the house down, me having to go through my daily tasks or chores.

All this made me a little late. As I said, it was a nice sunny summer's morning, Mother let me walk to the school bus on my own (I must have been about five or six years old by now). I took a leisurely walk at about eight in the morning, up the hill toward where the school bus was waiting. I had no concept of time, taking a nice leisurely stroll in my own time.

Oh no. As I came within view, I could see the school bus already at the stop; oh no! I started to walk a little quicker; oh no! I could see the school bus start up by the smoke coming from its exhaust, then it was seen to move off, disappearing down the road. I then broke into a run, running as fast as I could, yelling for the bus to stop. I felt so sick after trying to stop the bus that I collapsed by the side of the road, out of breath, legs aching, crying my eyes out. This was one of the days that I really, really wanted to go to school. If I didn't I really thought that I would be killed by my dad! I was just about to turn around and go back home, when this thought struck me with fear. *I'll have you put away in a home, I'll bloody well kill you if you do not bring those plimsolls home from school.*

Petrified, I thought, *I cannot go back home, I must get to school, and I must collect and bring my plimsolls home.* There was only one thing for it – to get to school. So I turned around and off I went. I first started by running, but soon got tired of that. Before I got to the end of Boxhill Road, passing some of the farms, I had to have a rest. I could not run much further – should I go back home, or should I get to school, what should I do? It did not take me long to make up my mind, I had to get to school so that I could bring home my precious white plimsolls or I would be killed. I could not let that happen. Up I got, determined now that I should get to school before assembly. At the end of Boxhill Road, I turned left onto Headley Common Road. I did not have a clue how long I had been, or even what the time it was. I had no fear of the cars that passed me; remember I was only about five, maybe six years old, and only very small for my age. Yet not one person stopped to see what I was up too.

I reached the Headley cricket pitch and had to rest for a while. By this time I was getting rather hungry, I had no sweets, they were very rare anyway, and I do believe they were still being rationed following World War Two. I had not got any money, not even for school meals, as I got those free due to Mother's circumstances. So, I started to eat the grass at the side of the road, and then I came across a crab apple tree, I started to eat some of them, but they were very bitter.

Off I started again, trying to remember which way the coach took us. Turning left after the cricket pitch, I walked down along Leech Lane, or as it was known locally 'Tot Hill', a winding narrow road. Carrying on, into Mill Way, which was still so narrow, but first went down a steep hill and up a steep hill on the other side. I passed Nower Wood, down through Tyrrells Wood golf course. It was here that I really started to hurt as I was getting tired and very hungry, but there were plenty of beechnuts and blackberries, which I collected as I walked. I had also picked a few damsons. I also started to eat hawthorn leaves, these I was told about by Mother so I knew by the name of bread and cheese. After a rest and watching some of the grownups playing golf, I carried on walking, onto Reigate Road, which came out onto the Beaverbrook roundabout. Then it was downhill all the way on the Leatherhead bypass road to the bottom at Givons Grove, the petrol station at the bottom of the hill, which had a thatched roof in those days. I turned left at the Givons Grove roundabout and walked along the dual carriageway. At that time, there were no hatched areas on the road, and vehicles used both lanes in those days. Large lorries would be thundering past; sometimes I had to climb up the bank to get out of their way, but still not one person stopped to see what this young boy was doing on such a dangerous road. On one of the now dangerous Mickleham bends, was situated The Old Forge, a transport café. I even walked past that without anyone paying me any attention; by this time it must have been around three in the afternoon. Still, I had to get to school, I knew by now that I was going to be very late for assembly; I felt I was in for another telling off from the teachers.

Anyway, I pressed on; I knew that I was almost there as the small corner shop came into view, which was situated where the Italian restaurant is now, at Byttoms Hill/School Lane. This is where the school coach would stop. It is 5.8 miles from the Hand in Hand (measured later on in my life, because I cannot even believe that I walked that far as a six-year-old, and nobody ever challenged me or asked what I was doing or where I was going).

As I came around the corner, I could see the school bus was waiting, collecting the children to take them home again. I could see the other children getting onto the coach, However, as I got closer, I could see that it was starting to pull away, it was leaving without me again, and I started to run after it, shouting and sobbing but was so exhausted.

As luck would have it, Auntie Nina was checking the children already on the bus by counting them. When she looked up and caught sight of me through the rear window of the bus, I was still running down the road. Suddenly the bus stopped. Auntie Nina came running towards me. I collapsed into her arms sobbing my eyes and heart out. Then the questions started. Why was I there, where had I been, etc., etc. I then told her the story about my plimsolls; Auntie Nina then took me up to the school where I had to repeat my story of how I got there. Nothing more than a miraculous feat, walking all that way just to get to school. Must have taken me seven hours. How lucky to even get there, as the bus was leaving to go home, what luck. Then to be spotted by Auntie Nina. After getting another telling off from the headmaster, then given something to eat and drink, I was taken to the cloak room to my peg. Hanging there was my blue bag, inside, those darn white plimsolls. I was then taken back to the coach. All the other children thought it great fun, cheering me, and asking questions of what had happened to me, where I had been. The coach was now late leaving to get them and me home and everyone home. We arrived back at Box Hill, a little later than normal. However, Auntie Nina had to tell my mother and the other parents why they had been held up and what I had been getting up to, how I had missed the coach in the morning, how I had walked to school.

I bet you can guess what happened when I got home. Yes, another thick ear, and 'wait until your father gets home' but why? I had carried out the old man's wishes, got to school and did exactly as I was told and brought home those plimsolls. No matter, I still felt that bloody belt of his and was sent to bed with no tea, after going all day without any proper food. As you read this you may think to yourself, he's making up this story, but believe me this is truly what happened as I remember it.

It was around the same time that I had another 'little' – well, a bit more than a little – incident. I have already told you that we lived on Clarke's land. They had a son called Peter, about the same age, maybe a little older than myself, and he was a great playmate. One afternoon we were mucking about, around where they had their large motorboat. I think we were actually playing pirates on it; we were sword-fighting with sticks. As young boys did in those days, we played with anything you could get hold of. Peter got me in one of my eyes with this stick, which broke off. I cannot remember if it actually entered my eye, I cannot remember much of what happened then, but I woke up in the children's ward of

Dorking General Hospital. I think I was very lucky that the stick had gone into the side of the eye socket and broke off. How long I was there for I have no idea, memory a bit dickey, or what damage was done, but wearing an eye patch for some days after, I really did feel like a pirate. Peter Clarke came and visited me in floods of tears as he thought that he had blinded me, with me sitting up in bed with this pirate patch over one eye. It could not have been very serious, as I had very good eye sight in both eyes until way after my 50th birthday. I can remember, however, my mother bringing me hard boiled eggs for my tea while I was in hospital. I hated eggs, especially boiled ones; they always made me feel sick, always repeated on me, this horrible gassy smell when I burped.

CHAPTER 6

THE 'OLD MAN'S' MANY TALENTS

The old man had many 'talents'; thieving was one, I am sure. He had a number of motorcycles during this time. He could and often did strip those bikes down to their very last nut and bolt. Then rebuild them. One bike he had was a BSA (Gold Star, I believe) with a sidecar, which he used for taking us to various places. A very frightening experience, sitting in this side car, so close to the ground, nothing much in front to protect you. He had this BSA for a long time; it was his pride and joy. I could always tell when he was coming home; I could hear his bike from miles away, I got to know the tone of the engine. He would often take us to Leatherhead in the sidecar, so that Mother could do some shopping, or drop us off in Dorking, which meant a bus ride out to Mid Holmwood to see our grandparents. We would stay for tea. Then when it was time to go home, we would catch the 414 London Country bus, which would take us through Dorking and out to Brockham Lane, where we would get off. From there we had to walk up the 'goat track', a very long high sloping footpath to the top of Box Hill which came out by the Roof of the World caravan site. A long and hard climb for anyone, let alone Mother with her shopping and two young children in tow, pushing or pulling a pushchair. We often took this route home when the old man was not around, which was not very often.

Mother often took us for a walk along the main road at the top of Box Hill to the 'lookout', where we would play for a while. On the way back we would stop off at the Upper Farm caravan site where they had a swimming pool. Both Fred and I used to go into the water to have a little fun. Often, I would come home and find a motorbike in pieces on the front room floor, being told off and told not to touch anything. Often different makes of old bikes. Another passion he had was for old clocks, antiques, as he would call them. He could take them apart and clean them, put them back together and they worked perfectly. I think he used to repair these clocks as a sideline for other people, maybe the bikes too.

The old man, also used to do odd jobs for people in the area, labouring jobs such as digging footings for houses, trenches and the odd cesspool, or pit, a large, covered hole for collecting or storing sewage or wastewater. On the odd occasion he would take me along; it was not to help him. I think it was to get me out from under Mother's feet. More than not, I would often get told off for doing something wrong, like one time he had dug this really large hole that he needed a ladder to get in and out of. Even at that early age, I would have thoughts about how I could 'do him in' So there was the old man, standing admiring his handy work. Standing on the edge of this very large deep cesspit, which he had spent a number of days to get to this stage, brushing the sweat from his brow, he had already pulled the ladder out. I was nearby, saw my chance, even at only six or seven. I took a run at him, hit the back of his legs with my shoulder (rugby tackle style). The last thing I saw was him lose his balance and topple face first into the hole with a horrible scream. I did not turn around or stop running for some half a mile or more, until I got home.

Met by my mother, who tried to get out of me what was wrong, I eventually stammered out that I had killed my dad, that I was so sorry, it was an accident, I bumped into him and he fell into a large hole. Mother immediately bundled Fred into his pram, grabbed my arm, half-running me, half-dragging me around to the property where my old man had been digging this cesspool. By the time we had got back there, he had managed to get out by climbing up the side. I was greeted with "What the bloody hell do you think you are playing at; are you trying to kill me?" He thought that I had done the right thing by running home to get help, so on this occasion I did not get the good hiding I thought I was going to get.

Then there was one bonfire fire night, November 5th, the old man had brought home a few fireworks. He made a bonfire in a clearing, on the slope, near to our bungalow. It got nice and red-hot so mother supplied a few potatoes, placing them into the hot coals, along with the chestnuts (we were surrounded by chestnut trees) to roast. There were chestnuts everywhere you looked, when they cooked, we had these nice hot spuds to eat. The old man let off what fireworks we had. Mother, Fred and I had a packet of sparklers, and both Fred and I were having a bit of fun, enjoying what he had brought home for us. Then the old man said he had got some bigger and better bangers indoors; we were told to hang on and wait where we were for a while. "I'll go and get them," he said. Some minutes later he appeared from behind this large tree, telling us to stay where we were, as we were in a safe place. The old man said he was lighting one of his fireworks, which had a big bang. What the silly sod had done was to get his Belgian .410 shotgun out, a single-barrelled gun, put a cartridge up the barrel and fired it up in the air. You could hear the lead pellets going through the branches of the trees. Yes it was a big bang, then another, and another, he let off about six of these cartridges. He was trying to hide behind a large tree so that we could not see the shotgun. We two boys were thrilled they were large bangs. Off we went to bed having had a great time, with our roast jacket potatoes and chestnuts, straight out of the fire and all.

We got up the next morning and on our way up to the shops with Mother and Freddie, we passed our burnt-out bonfire, from the night before. Like young boys do, we went to see if it was still a light and I started to kick a few burnt embers around and poking it with a stick, but they were all out. While I was doing this, Mother was walking past the next bungalow to ours, which was owned by a Jock Hess Law, lived in Redruth, Cornwall, who used the bungalow as a type of summer holiday home. Well, as Mother was passing Jock's place, she froze as though she was going to have a fit. She really looked very ill. "Oh my God!" she screamed. I thought I had once again done something wrong in scattering the ashes from the bonfire. Mother just turned and ran back to our house, shouting for the old man to get up and come and see what he had done. You see, Jock Hess Law had made this bungalow himself, the main materials used on the walls were asbestos sheets. The old man's bangers from the night before must have been pointing at point blank range towards Jock's place. The silly sod had peppered the bungalow with thousands of little holes, but not only had they gone through the outside walls but some had travelled all the way through the inside walls as well, some even came out the other side. Cracking a couple of windows too.

You should have seen my 'old man's' face, what a picture. I remember the panic which set in, both him and Mother shouting at each other, she saying he was a stupid old fool, in very bad language, amongst other things little ones should not hear, or words to that effect. Him shouting and swearing. Loud discussions on what to do next. Luckily, Mother was entrusted with the keys to the place. She used to look after it while Jock was away, kept it clean and so on, generally keeping an eye on it. The old man at the time was in the building trade. Amongst other things, he had access to building materials. For days after, there was my old man trying to fill in all of these holes. In the end he had to redecorate the inside as well as the outside.

This brings me onto another episode in the life of one Kenneth Brian Cutts; a very young life up until now. Being very inquisitive at an early age, I needed to know how my 'old man's' bullets had made such a loud bang and how the holes in the next door's bungalow had worked, so I tried to find out where they were kept. Sure enough, I found a locked metal cabinet. Next course of action, I had to find the key. I had a fair idea where to look because I used to watch his every move, he was always hiding things from us, Mother as well. Even at an early age, I could see what he was up to. Finding the key in one of his brass cigarette boxes, one of his so-called antiques, I found where the old man had hidden his shotgun cartridges. I decided that I wanted to know how they went bang. I took a few out of the box, went into the woods, not a few paces from our pathway to our bungalow. There I sat trying to make these things go bang, I was holding them in my hand, hitting them with stones, throwing them onto a stone, still they would not go off. *I know*, I thought, *I'll get some matches*. I found a box of matches, tried to set them alight, no joy there either. I had run out of matches. *I know, I'll go and get some more*. I knew quite well that Mother had put them out of my reach or so she thought. So, another box was called for. I was still unable to light these cartridges. Next course of action. *I know, I'll get a hammer*. Luckily, I could not find one, but did find a small hacksaw. *I know, I'll cut them in half*. So I set to sawing this cartridge in two, and out burst all these little round pieces of lead shot, and inside was this wading. *Now what do I do to make them go bang?* Pulling out all the wading from three of these cartridges, I struck a match and touched it to the wading. Whoosh! The wading went off, dirty great bright blue flame, large white cloud of smoke, the flame took my eyebrows, my curly blonde fringe, burning my face slightly. I quickly tried to hide what I had done, but how do you hide thousands of little pellets of shot, burnt matches and cartridges that had been cut in half? Well, I covered them in dirt and leaves. *Nobody will find them now!*

There was no bathroom as such in our house; just a bowl of water, or even a bucket, water came from a small standpipe outside the back door. Anyway, I calmly went to my bedroom thinking, *if I washed my face, no one would notice, I'll get away with it*. WRONG AGAIN. So, moments later, Mother came in from doing something outside. Oh no! Mother had another screaming fit. "What have you done to yourself?"

I replied, "Nothing, Mummy," as if nothing had happened.

It went on. "What have you been up to?"

"Nothing, Mummy." I answered every question with a 'nothing'.

She then went into the kitchen, straight to where she stored the matches. Lo and behold, there were a couple of boxes of matches missing. "You've been playing with matches, haven't you?"

"No, Mummy."

"Oh yes you have, look at your face, your hair is all burnt." This time I got her favourite weapon, the feather duster, feathers on the end of a bamboo stick or handle. I received the handle right across the back of my legs. "I'll teach you to play with matches!" she shouted. Alas, she never did give me any lessons on how to play with matches!

Obviously that was not the last of the affair; I got the usual treatment from the 'old man' for playing with matches. Well then, a few days later, came the time when the 'old man' would take out our dog, Toby. He was a lovely terrier type, a bit of this and a bit of that; he was brown and white, rather hairy, a bit of a rat catcher you might find on a farmyard. Both would go out onto Headley Common, to shoot some rabbits or whatever game there was to shoot for our Sunday lunch.

When the old man went to his gun case to get his gun out, oh no. I had, in my childish panic after trying to blow up myself, forgotten to lock the doors on his cabinet. Also, the old man went to where he kept his ammunition. Then the whole wide world erupted. There for all to see, were a few cartridges missing. He hit the roof, grabbing me by my shirt and shaking me hard. "Where are they?" he asked me.

"Don't know," I said.

I thought the end of the world had come early. I got the biggest hiding so far; I was thrown from wall to wall and then back again. I denied everything. I could not sit down for days after; my backside hurt so much, my head hurt from crashing against the walls. He shouted, "I'll find out, you know!" Find out, he did. Well, it took a couple of days for the wind to blow away the leaves that had hidden my little 'pyrotechnic bonfire'.

There for all to see, just off the pathway, was a little pile of the damaged cartridges, sitting in this burnt patch of ground. I tried to blame Freddie, seeing how he was far too young to know what was going on, barely able to walk himself; I had little idea anyway myself. This time I think the old man did nearly kill me. Apart from me trying to kill myself, Lord knows how I did not kill Freddie as well. I tried hitting the cartridges with stones, tried to set fire to them, how did I just get away with burning my face a little bit, singeing my hair? It took a long time for everyone to get over that little episode of my life; it taught me that I should not play with fire, matches, or any other volatile substances.

I attended St. Michael's School in the village of Mickleham up until I was about six or seven. I remember it was a nice friendly place, with plenty of friends to play with. The teachers were very nice to us. One Christmas, in the school nativity play, I became a shepherd, wearing one of Mother's tea towels wrapped around my head. In the school, during the summer, we had to dig a garden and had to plant seeds. We had great fun watching these plants grow, being taught how to make flowers and vegetables grow.

Halfway through the morning, after our first play, we had to return to our classes when the milk monitors had to place a quarter pint of milk, which came in a small bottle with a cardboard top, which you had to pull to release the milk. A good pastime was to stick your thumb on the cardboard top and to press hard so that it would squirt up in the air and onto your desk, the milk was normally accompanied by a small current bun. At lunchtime, the whole school had to make our way to the playground, forming lines in classes, and then we had to hold the hand of the person next to you, normally your best friend, which meant a little jostling to get next to your chum. Then, with a teacher leading, we had to walk along this footpath, across a field or recreation ground to the Mickleham village hall in Dell Close. There we would have our school dinner. Sat at long lines of tables with long benches to sit on. After having had our lunches, all the classes had to lay on small mattresses for up to maybe 15 minutes to rest. Then it was back to school, the reverse as when going to dinner or lunch.

On hot summer days, the class sometimes were to miss our rest in the hall, we would sometimes be allowed to sit quietly on the grass of the recreation ground. Halfway along one of the footpaths was this very large walnut tree. On the way back after dinner we were allowed to play for a while. One day we thought we would collect some of these walnuts, much the same way as one would collect conkers, by throwing things up into the tree to knock them down to the ground, then we would crack them open and eat these nice fresh kernels. On one of these days, a number of us had eaten far too many of these ripening nuts. Midway through the afternoon in the classroom we became violently sick; the doctor was summoned to the school. I think the teacher thought it was something we had eaten for dinner. There was such a panic, until one of the boys was sick in front of the ensuing entourage of doctors, nurses and teachers. There for all to see was a pile of regurgitated walnuts. I have hated walnuts ever since, but could not stand the taste after that. Still cannot eat them, finding the taste rather off.

During the years up until this time – it must have been approaching 1950 – we used to watch all the old aircraft flying over in squadrons, many a Spitfire, Typhoons and I remember most of all the Mosquitos but more exciting were the new jets, the Meteors and Vampires, they made a lot more noise.

Oh yes, I have not told you about the two pets we had while living on Box Hill, well I have only mentioned them in passing. However, we had this lovely bits and pieces dog, he was brown, and white, longish shaggy hair, one black patch over one eye. His name was Toby, a good guard dog, which was needed out there in the wilderness of Box Hill. He would let you know when someone was about who should not have been there. An excellent rabbit catcher and anything else that moved. He would flush out any game the old man wanted to shoot, or should I say poach. As our bungalow was bordering Headley Heath, the old man would take us and Toby out onto the common, with his Belgian .410 shotgun. One day, Toby ran off after a small deer, out towards Headley Common. He just ran out of sight, he did not come back. So, the old man, Mother and us two young boys went out onto the common to see if we could find him, calling his name at the top of our voices, but to no avail. He was never seen again, maybe he chased a rabbit down into a borrow and got stuck. I cannot remember ever having another dog in his place.

Then there was my pet jackdaw Jackie. The old man had found him with a broken leg as a baby bird, it had fallen from its nest when trying to fly, maybe for the first time. The old man brought this young bird home. It looked very big to me at the time. He put the leg in a splint and Band-Aid, and we fed it chopped up worms with a pair of tweezers, often bread and milk (same as me). The best bit was the old man taught this bird to say a few basic phrases. It would call out 'Jackie', say 'hello,

Mum', or 'hello, Kenny'. It would swear a bit, and he would ask for food. Jackie the jackdaw would also follow us up to the village, flying free, while I caught the coach to school. Then when we got back, as I got off the coach, I would call out, "Jackie," and down from a tree he would fly. I say he, could have been a she for all I know.

Jackie used to come into the house and sit on my bed. Also, he used to take things and hide them, anything shiny. He'd take food off your plate, fly out the window. He would never stay in the house; he would always roost somewhere nearby, fly down onto the water butt we had outside, talking away. Then, one morning, a large flock of jackdaws flew into the trees around us. They were chattering away as they did and Jackie went up into the tree and joined them. As the flock started to fly off, Jackie came down onto my shoulder, where he often sat, pecked my ear, pretty hard, harder than usual, then flew off after the others never to be seen again.

Now, I was about six, possibly seven, years old, we had to leave the place in Box Hill. I am pretty sure it was because Mother was becoming too ill with tuberculosis, I believe she moved back to live with her parents at 2 Holmside Cottages, Mid Holmwood. Where the old man was is not clear in my mind. I do know that he once pushed Mother down the stairs at her parent's house while she was pregnant with Janet, but what happened after that incident I do not know, whether he was visiting, or living there again I do not know. Or maybe Granddad had him thrown out. It was not long after that Janet was born. I do know she was a very young baby, being looked after by my grandmother.

During the summer months we used to play out on the common, Gran and Grandad would bring out their armchairs and sit out on the grass of the common watching the world go by. I can remember, at this stage, my haircut, for when I was very young, I had a full head of tight blonde curls, nearly white. Until one day the old man cut my hair, with his blunt hair clippers, cutting out the curls. From that day on my hair grew straight. Mother went ape over it. The old man used to cut our hair to save money; well, he would pull two, cut one, very painful. When he had finished, it looked like he had placed a bowl on my head and just cut round it, or he had a vision of the thirty-nine steps, but he still managed to get a step effect. I looked like a monk on the run, the other children used to take the mickey, something terrible, being very horrible.

On arriving home from school one evening, Janet, my baby sister, was not there. She was very young, just months old how – many I cannot be sure. Mother was sick and in bed, not very well at all, I am sure we were at my grandparents'. I asked where Janet was, and told not to worry. "She's been taken to her new foster mummy. To be looked after, as Mummy was too ill to do it for herself." A new foster mummy? What's that, you've given my sister away? I started to scream the house down, I cried. I wanted my sister; I do not think the old man was there. Anyway, Freddie joined in the crying and screaming.

We were both calmed down by other relatives who had turned up. I can remember seeing a couple of bags packed, things had been put in places as if we were going to move again, and our things had been put into boxes. I could not understand what was going on, I was to soon find out. The very next day, out of the blue, we had a visit from this very well-dressed lady. She had a shiny black car, driven by a smartly-dressed man. She turned out to be a social worker. Miss Wright was her name. She had come to collect Freddie and myself, told us we were going off to a nice home to be looked after as Mummy was ill and couldn't look after us. I could not comprehend what was going on. Why should we be going to another place to be looked after by people that we did not know? Why could we not stay with Mother? My world was shattering, I was never happier than living on the common down at Holmwood. Once again, I could not control myself, because the old man had often threatened me with being put away in a home if I did not behave myself. I did not know what the hell I was doing wrong in his eyes, probably it was just my presence that turned him against me.

I was now only seven for Christ's sake! Freddie was just nearly three. I did not want to leave, I kicked up such a fuss, even running out of the house onto the common, only to be caught after a little chase. Both Freddie and I were scooped up by these two strangers, me by the bloke who ran after me, and Miss Wright picked up Fred. After a struggle, we were both put into the gleaming black car. Cars in those days only came in two colours – black and even blacker. Still making such a fuss, I think it was agreed that mother should travel with us to try and get us two to calm down. The year was towards the end of 1951. Bundled into the car, off we went, leaving Holmwood for the last time. I thought I would never see my grandparents, uncles and aunties ever again. Where were we going?

CHAPTER 7

RED LEYS CHILDREN'S HOME

We all set off not knowing where we were going, both Freddie and myself calmed down somewhat because Mother was with us, it took quite a long time to travel, in the mind of a seven-year-old. Eventually we arrived at this big house which was called Red Leys, in Glaziers Lane, Normandy, near Guildford. It had been built about 1925, initially occupied by Mr and Mrs Kirsch and subsequently by Mr and Mrs Martin, who developed Red Leys as a home for children with long-term illnesses in need of respite care, and later with some problem children. Like us two. Following the death of Mrs Marjory Martin on the 6th February 1983, the house was sold, demolished and the site redeveloped to accommodate four new houses named respectively Red Leys, Kenanian, Tahoe and Redlands.

The smart gentleman was driving and on our arrival we were met by this smartly-dressed woman, possibly about her mid- to late-30s, a no-nonsense person. She took hold of my hand, led me into the dining hall of the home, and there before my eyes were about another 20 children of all ages, from babies up to 13 or 14, all colours and nationalities. This was the first time I had ever seen a 'coloured' young boy and it was very strange to see such children.

Freddie and I were given something to eat, well, it was put in front of me, I cannot say whether I ate it or not. Meanwhile, Mother was shown around the house. When it came time for her to leave, Mother cuddled Freddie, gave me a kiss on the forehead, both Freddie and I cried. Mother just got in the car, gave us a wave and left. Left on our own with all these strangers all around us. Boy oh boy, did that hurt. Seeing that black car driving down the drive and out onto the main road, out of sight, leaving me and my little brother here on our own, I had a big question; what had we done for this to happen? I had tried to be a good boy for Mother, I must have been such a bad boy for this to happen to me, the old man said he would put me away in a home, but Freddie had not done anything at all so why was he here with me? Was it my fault that we now found ourselves in a home?

The staff at first tried to get us to eat something, but I was not having any of it, nor was Freddie; he was only about two or maybe three, still just a baby. Freddie and I did not know anyone, I just clung onto Fred, nobody was going to touch him, he was my brother. He was screaming for his mother and I doubt I was helping matters by holding onto him so tightly.

I remember a very small incident, very soon after arriving. Freddie and I were all sitting around the table with the other children eating dinner, when I inadvertently dropped some food and my fork onto the floor. A young lady helper made me pick up the fork. Her movement was so quick so I covered my head and cowered into my seat, ready to take a clout around the ear or head, as would have happened at home with the 'old man'. As quick as a flash, this elderly woman, who later I got to know as the matron, was next to me putting her arms around my shoulders, giving me a cuddle. She said, "Everything is alright, we do not hit children here." I think we both had calmed down enough although Freddie was still beside himself, for the young women helpers put us to bed in the same room. My thoughts after being settled down by the staff, were, *Who are these people, why are they being so nice to us?* Actually, what they were doing was looking after us, but most unusual was they cuddled us, speaking so nicely to the both of us, very softly and quietly. When two of the younger women who actually put us to bed kissed the both of us on the cheek, saying, "You are safe here now," what they were doing was showing Freddie and I love. It was a very odd feeling. However, Freddie did not stop crying all night, in fact he cried for the next three weeks, and it seemed like months. I had got used to the new surroundings a lot quicker than he did, well he was only three.

I got to know who the lady was who was now in charge of looking after the two of us. I started to call her 'Mummy Martin' as all the children, members of staff, and the local community also addressed her as such. I thought it was about time I toed the line, as it was sometime before I would call her 'Mummy'. Her real name was Marjorie (nee Boon), a very proud upright woman, always standing tall, but in essence not very tall in stature, just about five feet four inches tall. She had dark brown curly hair, her skin was that of a Mediterranean olive colour, always dressed very smartly, a very heavy smoker and had a very busy manner about her. She always had time for you; if you wanted to know something she would go to great lengths to explain the problem, making sure you understood what she was saying or trying to get across to you. 'Mummy Martin' was an extremely good listener and organiser of events. She had been married; regrettably Mr Martin died of a brain tumour in 1949. They had a daughter named Janet, who had been away at a girls' boarding school before going on to university. Mummy Martin was trained and qualified as a teacher in the Rudolph Steiner techniques of teaching, and Mr Martin, before his death, started a kindergarten at Red Leys for the local children. 'Mummy Martin' was a brilliant teacher and business woman. Following her husband's death, 'Mummy Martin' befriended and housed children whose parents were receiving long term treatment for tuberculosis in the Milford Chest Hospital, Godalming. This is where Cutts was treated for his condition. Mother was sent to the Charing Cross Hospital TB unit for her treatment. This information, I found out later in life.

Well, after a while, I started to trust the new people, and let Freddie go. He was put in a high chair like all the very young children, which he did not like at all, and he grabbed hold of me once again. The other staff I thought were very nice, there was another lady who always wore this white coat, she was the 'matron', an older woman with a fat-ish red rounded face, grey hair, very jovial at times, but, oh boy, could she be strict. A spinster, I believe, I never did get to know about her very well at all; she was a very private person. Matron was Elizabeth Turner, who helped with the running and working of Red Leys but during

1959, matron departed Red Leys, leaving to run another children's home in Rustington near Littlehampton. 'Mummy Martin' had set it up for children in care, effectively managing the influx of those children in addition to the running of the kindergarten. 'Parkie' Parker succeeded Elizabeth Turner in the running of the Rustington home remaining in service until 1972. Sadly, she passed away in 1977 due to cancer.

However, the service that 'Mummy Martin' provided for those children attracted the attention of the London boroughs. They saw in Red Leys the opportunity to satisfy their need to improve the health of the capital's children in the aftermath of the war years and to place children in need of special care, into a good foster home. It was still taking Freddie a long time to accept that Mother was not going to be around. To cap it all, after about three weeks, I heard this motorbike coming down the road. I froze, the hair on the back of my neck stood on end. I ran to 'Mummy Martin' saying, "My dad is coming."

Matron said, "No, don't be silly; he will not be coming for a long time."

I insisted they go and have a look; I knew exactly who it was, and I got to learn to hate that sound coming from his beloved motorcycle from a very early age. I knew every beat of that engine. To their amazement, they found that I was right. The old man decided he would pay us a visit, see how we were getting on. He brought this Mobo rocking horse (it was on four wheels with springs, so when you sat on it, you bounced up and down and it would move forward). It was for Freddie. Nothing for me. He stayed for about an hour, playing with Freddie and ignored me completely. As he left, he turned to me in a threatening manner and said, "You had better stay off that rocking horse, it's not for you."

'Mummy Martin' at this point showed him the door, telling him to stay away from now on, he then disappeared into the darkness, the sound of his motorbike going off into the distance, leaving poor old Freddie in a state of floods of tears once again. It was days, maybe a week or so, before Freddie really settled down again. We began to enjoy our new home, we made friends with the other children, and we had lots of brothers and sisters to play with.

Red Leys was a large house situated in Glaziers Lane, Normandy, near Guildford. It had quite large grounds. The house consisted of possibly four bed rooms on the ground floor, with possibly the same on the top floor. There was a large kitchen area built on the side as an extension, and on the rear of the house, the main building joined the out-buildings, and a large open-sided, glassed roof area which was called the loggia (low-ger, as it was pronounced). Attached to this was a very large single-storey hall, like you would get at a school, where they needed extra classroom space, a long single-story building, which was used as a dining area attached to the kitchen, for playing, schooling, nursery, everything really. At the far end were the toilets and cloak room. Going back to the main house, as you entered from the loggia, up a very short set of steps, immediately on your left you found the laundry room, which had two or three large washing machines and a couple of dryers. A few paces forward you came to a door right in front of you. This was the matron's living room, a very nice clean comfortable living room. Out of bounds unless you were invited in by matron. Immediately opposite, as you turned right into a very long corridor, was a toilet first, next the bathroom. On the left were two bedrooms with a couple of beds each. I think one only had a single. At the far end of the corridor to the left was a large bedroom with at least six to eight beds, where the large bay windows faced out onto the main road. It also had side windows facing out onto the unmade track. Immediately on the left was another much smaller bedroom – one or two beds. To the right was a very large, I mean large, 'cupboard under the stairs'. It stored all of our outdoors coats, boots and shoes, and it was big.

Passing the small bedroom on the left, you went up a small set of stairs, onto a small landing area where you found the front door. From the outside of the building one had to walk up a set of about ten steps to reach the front door. Turning right, leaving the front door to your back, you came upon a larger set of stairs; at the top was a sliding door. To the right a large bedroom with three or four beds, a girls' bedroom, next to that another of the girls' bedrooms with two or three beds. At the top of the stairs on the left was a large bathroom. Most of the bedrooms had bunk beds in them. In front of you after the bathroom was a door, which led to Mummy Martin's living quarters; a flat, very smart. 'Mummy Martin' had a garden area on a flat roof on top of the kitchen block.

To get into Red Leys, you turned off Glaziers Lane into an unmade private track called Strawberry Lane, which led into Oakland's Nursery. Only a few metres into this lane you came upon a driveway on the right. To the rear on the left of the building as you looked out of the kitchen was a large orchard, with a driveway, which came in at the bottom of the orchard. As you drove in through the drive, on the left were built three or four cabins where some of the staff would live, or stay for short periods. As you passed the cabins in front of you was a very large garage, more like a large barn or hanger. The drive bore round to the right, where you came to the rear of the dining hall, carrying on to the rear of the kitchen.

Going back to the main house into the loggia, looking out to your right from the main house steps you would see a large garden, with swings,, slides, and seesaws on the left. As you looked out into the garden was a large bank, formed by what was an old air raid shelter with six very large poplar trees; they must have stood anything up to 40 feet high. To the rear of these poplar trees was the large garage. Once again, looking out of the loggia to the right, towards the main road, was a line of medium-sized oak trees, nice for climbing. Right next door was a large unmanned telephone exchange placed out of bounds to us children.

Various staff helped Mummy Martin run the whole place. It is difficult to remember their names but I am sure these will come back to me as I progress with this story. First of all, I remember we had an odd job/gardener-cum-maintenance man. He looked just like Mr Pastry from the children's television programme of those days. In fact, we used to call him Mr Pastry. He used to laugh with us about it. He played along with all of it, he was great fun to be with. He must have been retired, a lovely man with white hair. When I could, I used to help him do some of his work. He lived in a bungalow a few hundred yards up the road from

Red Leys. I often used to go to his house with other children, listen to his stories. Some of the older girls would clean his house and wash up for him. I looked after his cats on a number of occasions when he went away on business trips or on holiday, he paid a little extra pocket money. All above board. He treated us all like one of his children. Towards the end of my stay at Red Leys, he passed away, it was very, very sad.

We had other local women. Who helped work at Red Leys? The first that I remember was 'Parky' Parker. I do not know what her real name was but she was always called 'Parky' by us, never as a nosey parker. Matron had her assistant who we all called 'Bridie' (surname was Hulme of Bushy Leas, Pound Farm Lane. She remained in service at Red Leys until 1972), who must have been in her mid-20s, very attractive-looking, who worked full-time. Again, she was a smashing person, always joking and laughing with us. I do not think I ever saw her without a smile on her face. Bath times were good fun with her.

Then there was Mrs Coomber the cook who was helped by Mrs Rose Warner, who lived in Normandy in a caravan with her family. She was a very, very large woman, not exactly fat, just big, six-foot-two, the same across the shoulders. The saying 'as big as a brick outhouse' comes to mind. She had a big red round happy face, a very good sense of humour, and she'd do anything for anyone. She had a large hooked Roman nose, always smiling, very dark straight hair tied at the back in a bun. She had large muscular arms, thighs like tree trunks, built like a Russian weightlifter, but a very nice, gentle lady. She was one of the cooks. Who also help around the place other than cooking?

Rose Warner had a daughter called Rosemary who was in her early teens; she would also come in and help look after us unruly children. Rosemary was also a big girl but not as I have described her mother; she was tall, but not exactly slim, but very well proportioned. Really nice figure, even at the age of eight. She was lovely. There were a number of other young girls who worked there from time to time; I fell madly in love with all of them.

Now there was als, 'Uncle Ron' Boon. 'Mummy Martin's' brother; a very nice man. He would visit quite often; he lived with his mother on the Thames near Windsor, near to the castle. He would take the older children out on 'treats' especially the older girls, the 14-year-olds. He used to take them skating at Richmond, then take them home for tea. The stories they told on their return of what they had got up to. Well, he was one for seeing young ones running around with no clothes on, or he would make a point of being around when it was bath time, washing the girls' backs.

There was Shirley, the other cook. Again, she was another lovely woman, lived up the road near to Red Leys, a blonde girl in her mid-30s maybe. I got on well with her, a lively character. The only miserable or disciplinarian one was a matron, but she was not always like that. She did have her moments. It was such a happy place, with so many happy people running the place, a real joy, especially for me having been knocked about so much before. If you did wrong you were punished in a humane and loving way. You learned the errors of your ways very quickly; you knew if you transgressed again you would lose any privileges. Janet Martin, 'Mummy Martin's' daughter, who was in her late teens, away at university most of the time, was a lovely girl like her mother, very cheerful. Another larger woman, not exactly fat, just well built, heavy-boned. When she came home things got really lively, especially on outings or visits to her grandmother's house near Windsor, boating on the River Thames and picnic in her garden. We had great fun.

While at Red Leys, we had to attend the local school, which was called Wyke First, about two miles and a bit of a walk in all weathers from Red Leys. You had to walk down Glaziers Lane, past a few nice large houses. There was a large field that often had cattle in, and on the right was the very large Elms Garden Nursery, with row upon row of greenhouses where they grew tomatoes, lots of them, amongst other things. Boxes stacked high with them. A little further on was another large fruit farm. Apples, plums, other fruits ready for scrumping, only for us to be chased off by members of their workforce. The owners were very sympathetic towards us and used to supply fruit and vegetables to Red Leys.

Walking on further down past a lot more of the nice houses, passing onto one corner the local newsagents on the left, on the right corner was the large village hall, at the bottom of Glaziers Lane where it met the main A 323, Aldershot Road. Opposite was the war memorial and Hunts Hill Lane. We turned left at the junction, walked past the petrol station, past the local doctor's house, Dr Webb. Further on was the Wyke church at the bottom of Westwood Lane, at the crossroads, known locally as Wyke Cross. We took the right-hand road into School Lane, then into Wyke School on the left.

I cannot remember any of the teachers or how good they were except I remember a new headmaster arriving, Mr Lewis. I also think that there was a teacher by the name of Miss Clegg, she must have been my teacher. I know I was told off more times than I can remember. One time after a heavy snowfall, we were allowed out into the playground to make a snowman and to have a snowball fight. I had to go that one a bit further than the rest by throwing snowballs at the teachers. I tried to hit one of them but she ducked – lucky for her because the snowball hit the classroom window, smashing a nice large hole in it. What I had inadvertently picked up in the snow to make the ball was a large stone. So I was in trouble. I had to stay in after school for detention, then when I got back to Red Leys, further trouble and punishment awaited me because Mummy Martin had to pay for a new window pane. Apart from remembering that we played football during one of the lessons, or it could be called kick and rush, I cannot remember much about my school days there; it is always a blur.

One of my favourite pastimes was to climb the trees in and around the main house, trying to see how many could be climbed. I had to climb the one that nobody else could climb, had to be the highest one. I had to be 'king' of the climbers. Then I thought about 'crossing over', in other words crossing from one tree to another without touching the ground. Squirrels do it, why can't I? This turned out to be a bit 'hairy' at times, as often the branches would not hold my weight. This would mean a visit to a matron with a bump on the head or a cut somewhere, followed by a good telling-off, or a 'flea in the ear' or a flick on the top of your head. Never any real violence, just something to let you know you had deserved it. Often when somebody or other wished to know where

I was or needed to speak to me and someone was sent to find me, they would miss me sitting right at the top of the tree.

It was during this period that we all heard that King George VI had died after his long illness. The news was full of the event, local churches rang out their muffled bells all day, everyone was wearing black. This was the first time I had watched a television or even seen one. All the children watched television for the first time as Mummy Martin had a television brought in just for the day so we had to watch the funeral. We all sat around this small television, some of the grown-ups were crying as we watched the parades going on in London.

There were really special times of the year at Red Leys, such as Christmas. In the weeks leading up to the festivities, we would be treated to a number of events. Our 'fairy godmother' would send us tickets to the local pantomime some way out of town, where we would have to ride in a coach or on the train to get there.

Six days before, a big Christmas tree (well it was big to us) would be erected in the dining hall, with lots of fairy lights; we would sit around, making various paper chains and other decorations to be hung up. The decorations always came down on the sixth day after as well. Then there was our nativity play. In the run-up to Christmas, all the women staff and helpers would have a number of children each and teach them their lines for the part they were to play. They would also make your costume. The first year, Freddie and I were both shepherds. The children would first have a performance in our dining hall. Then there would be Sunday school in the local church. This was followed by the highlight of our nativity; a visit to the village hall to perform for the old folk of the village, who would come along and watch, often leaving presents for us. Great fun was had by all.

Where the presents for all the children came from, one only knows, obviously from local charities and the like. Everyone got exactly what they wanted, well nearly everyone. The parties we had were so much fun, often people would come and entertain us, magic and puppet shows. The excitement on Christmas Eve was immense, everyone rushing around to get into the bath, collecting our stockings, which had to be placed on the end of our beds. Off we went to bed early. This was my first Christmas away from home; it must have been 1951. Seven years of age.

Me, being me, one of the bigger boys, a Mr Know-it-all, told my dormitory that there was not a Father Christmas who visited by coming down the chimney, it was only the staff who came around with all the presents who placed them in their stockings. So I laid there wide awake, pretending I was asleep. In came a staff member with the goodies, and I jumped up saying, "There you are, told you so, there's not a Father Christmas!" Killjoy. I was immediately grabbed by my ear, taken from the room, and placed in the punishment place – the large cupboard under the stairs. I was told to stay there until I was sorry for my prank, with no presents. After what seemed a long time, Mummy Martin came into the cupboard and gave me a strong telling off and told me to stop being a silly little boy. Back to bed I went with my tail between my legs. I had to help the staff with the very young ones all Christmas day but it was still fun.

While at Red Leys it was discovered that my ankles were a little weak, possibly due to the footwear that I had been made to wear prior to my arrival. This was mostly from wearing shoes that were too small for my feet; most of my clothes came from jumble sales, and some of it was girls' things. Mother would buy cheaply from these sales or from handouts or hand-me-downs. My toes were, and still are, a little deformed through wearing shoes that were too small for me, or the wrong shape. My feet were very small for my age, my toes cramped too close together from being restricted. So 'Mummy Martin' had me seen by a foot specialist. I had to be made to wear these specially made heavy, reinforced ankle boots. I had to attend a clinic in Normandy village hall every two weeks for about a year and a half, and it seemed to do the trick. Although throughout my life I have had slight problems with my ankles, mostly from twisting them, my toes have never been normal shapes, my little toes all bent up and squashed.

Easter was another really special time at Red Leys. On Easter Sunday, we woke up early in the morning to find that the Easter Bunny had been. There was a sizable apple orchard, and every tree would have Easter eggs on each branch like apples. In the early morning, with the bright sunlight and a little dew on the ground, it all looked so magical, and all the various colours were just like a fairy tale. How the staff managed to rig it all up without any of the children spotting them, Lord only knows, they must have been at it all night. All the curtains had to be closed, woe betide anyone who took a peek. Then, once we were all up, washed and had our breakfast, the atmosphere was palpable. The smaller children were led out into the grounds to find where the Easter Bunny had been. Those older members were allowed out, but we had to take it easy and help the younger ones. Best of all, and only at this time of the year, we were allowed to climb the apple trees to retrieve as many Easter eggs as we could.

'Mummy Martin' had some 20-30 children in her care who had to transport around. They acquired a very large old 1946 Daimler Black Prince hearse converted into a limousine with extra seating. She must have managed to do a deal with a funeral director and had rows of seats put into it. As I remember it, it was very comfortable. One year, Red Leys entered the Guildford carnival. We had great fun in converting this big old limo into Old Mother Hubbard's shoe. The men folk who often came in to do repair work around the place made up this large shoe shape to cover the limo, we all dressed up in oldie-worldly clothing. We looked great on the day of the parade. I was dressed in an old tweed jacket and cord trousers and a flat cap.

Another very exciting time was during the Queen's Coronation. Once again 'Mummy Martin' had a television put into the dining room. We all crowded around this big box with a small screen, with a big magnifying glass at the front to make the picture larger. I remember getting bored by it all as the event went on all day and into the evening but it was a wonderful sight to see it all on television. What a wonderful invention.

The older boys from Red Leys (which included me) were able to join the Cub Scouts, the first Normandy pack, which we attended every Tuesday evening. We were allowed to walk the mile-and-a-half to the scout hut on our own and back again. We would often have to do tests to get our badges. As an incentive,

'Mummy Martin' would let us go out on walks into the woods on our own, as long as we were back at a certain time.

One of our favourite places was an area called the Fox Hills, where the army had a tank training area and rifle range. What an attraction for young boys! We often would try to get as close as we could to the action. One day, four of us went out, taking no notice of any red flags that were flying. How were we to know what they meant? Until this day, we were in this forbidden area, red flags flying all around. We were crawling on all fours to get closer, when we bumped into a fully camouflaged soldier. Boy, did he give us a fright. Likewise, we must have given him the fright of his life. The whole platoon and others appeared from nowhere, rounded us all up, marched us quite a long way to a rather large tent where we stood before an officer who gave us the biggest telling off I had ever had since being at Red Leys. It was on the dangers of being in such an area with vehicles and tanks running about all over the place, especially when guns are being fired. Then he turned around to one of the other soldiers, saying, "Lock them up, Sergeant."

The sergeant, at the top of his voice, said, "STAND STILL." Then he bellowed, making us all jump out of our skins, "YOU BOYS! ATTENTION, RIGHT TURN, NO THE OTHER RIGHT, QUICK MARCH, GET INTO STEP, SWING THOSE ARMS." The sergeant did his job in scaring us witless. "Stop snivelling!" We were all crying our eyes out by now, having been marched along a road, and all the soldiers we passed were pointing and laughing. We arrived in a large area where there were lots of big army lorries parked. His next order, as we approached the back of one of these lorries, was, "HALT, now get yourselves into the back of this truck."

By now we were scared out of our skins. Helped by a couple of other soldiers, we all climbed up into the rear of the truck, then the sergeant instructed another soldier to lock us in the back of this big truck. Next the truck started to move off over this very bumpy ground, it must have been about ten minutes later when the truck stopped. The back doors were thrown open, and there stood a policeman. My chin hit the floor. All four of us were told to get out of the truck by the copper ,given another good telling off, read of the riot act, and given an explanation of the red flags that were flying everywhere and could not be missed. Then we were placed in the back of a police car, this time thinking we were all going off to jail. Four very frightened boys, huddled together, whispering to each other, trying to figure out what was going to happen to us now. Then the policeman shouted, "BE QUIET." We never said another word until we arrived at Red Leys.

Met by matron, boy, did we see her stern side. Her little podgy round red face was now purple. We were immediately sent to our room – the four of us lived in the same room – and given another lecture on the dangers of going onto Ministry of Defence property. All our privileges were taken away. For a short while anyway; we soon had them restored. The outcome from all this was that the army sent a VIP invite to Red Leys to their next Aldershot tattoo. Hooray! My thoughts on the incident now were that the soldiers and their officers were playing hard with us, giving us all a stern warning not to do it again, but made amends by giving the tickets for the annual show.

Bonfire nights were another exciting day of the year, come rain or shine we would always go to an organised bonfire party. Where, I haven't a clue, but it was always fun. It may have been to Windsor, where 'Mummy Martin's' mother and brother lived. Always bangers (sausages) and bonfire jacket potatoes. Lovely jubbly.

Talking of fire, on 26th June 1952, just after midnight, I was woken by the noise of a fire brigade engine's bell ringing. I looked out of the window and saw it turn into our lane, followed by another. Jumping out of bed, I ran into the loggia to find out what was happening. Lo and behold, the Red Leys garage roof was well alight. Anyway, it did not take long for them to extinguish the fire. A notice in the local paper reported that Red Leys had suffered a fire in an outhouse garage. The roof and a car were slightly damaged, but none of the pupils who were sleeping at the children's home were disturbed. Who said so? Everyone was out of bed cheering the firemen on. Both engines came out from Guildford station.

The second year at Red Leys was much the same. We had lots of trips out to various events, not always locally. We would go to the south coast, Bognor Regis, Littlehampton, and a few trips to Portsmouth to look around the ships on Navy days, or the *Victory*.

I had gained quite an interest in aircraft, being not far from Farnborough, and quite close to Heathrow. I used to do aircraft recognition, even at that early age I could tell you what type of aircraft was flying over without seeing it, just by the sound of its engines. Cannot do it today as nearly all aircraft have the same engine.

CHAPTER 8

ACCIDENT AT FARNBOROUGH AIR SHOW

The Farnborough Air Show was one of these shows that our 'fairy godmother' sent tickets for so that a number of the older children could go on the 6th September 1952. During the show, a very bad accident happened. Test pilot John Derry and his observer, Tony Richards, were flying in the new de Havilland 110 (later to be called the Sea Vixen), and were showing the crowd how to break the sound barrier, which they did on a low fast fly pass. Then the aircraft went into a steep climb but, unfortunately, the aircraft started to break up, killing both pilot and his observer.

The party of the older boys, me included, had a special treat to go to the Farnborough Air Show. As John Derry put his dH 110 through its paces, we decided to leave where we were standing on a hill and find an ice cream van. As it happened, those of us from Red Leys were very lucky as the aircraft exploded and broke up in mid-air. One of the engines crashed down onto the runway, the other flew into a hill near to where, a few minutes earlier, we had been standing. The second engine came down killing 29 people.

In total, 31 people died. All those from Red Leys were then ushered away from the area by police and other workers. It was a terrible sight and most of us were crying with fear. We were rounded up by the staff and taken back to a coach, everyone accounted for and all in one piece, no injury to any of us. Then we were taken back to Red Leys. It was lucky that we moved our position to get ice creams, as a lot of the aircraft debris came down.

Towards the summer of the second year, both Mother and the 'old man' turned up, they had come to visit us at Red Leys. We spent most of the afternoon with them. I think they took us both out for a walk near Red Leys, obviously to tell us what was going to happen to us. I cannot remember exactly what was told to us. On our return, both were shown around by 'Mummy Martin'. While they were having tea with 'Mummy Martin', we two children were sent out to play in the garden with all the others. Me being me, I was showing off a little bit, it had to happen to me. I went down the big slide – "Look at me, Mum" – and, lo and behold, I found the only protruding nail and tore my trousers on it.

This act was witnessed by the old git, my old man. He came flying out into the garden, got hold of me by my ear, and took me into the loggia. He laid into me something horrible, slapping my legs and backside in front of everyone. Not a nice sight and something that had not happened to me for the last two-plus years that I had spent at Red Leys. He was promptly grabbed by two female members of staff who he shoved away. It took 'Uncle Ron' and 'Mr Pastry', two much older men, to stop him. He was told to stop by matron and 'Mummy Martin'. I saw the anger on both of their faces as they shouted at him to stop what he was doing, "We do not do things like that here, Mr Cutts, will you now leave us." Shortly after, both he and Mother left, leaving us both there again, me with a sore behind and a thick ear, Freddie crying his eyes out once again.

About three weeks later we had another visit from my old man on his own. Once again I had heard him coming on his BSA motorbike from miles away. I ran to 'Mummy Martin' to tell her he was coming. This time she believed me and had a little time to get ready to receive him. Everyone at Red Leys was put on immediate alert and told who to expect. It turned out to be a very brief visit, in fact it turned out to be the one of the most upsetting times I had so far in my short life.

He approached the front door (not many people used the front door). He just turned up on that fateful day, unbeknown to anyone. Matron was waiting for him, arms folded, feet wide apart, in a stance that said 'you are not welcomed here, mate'. Two of the male volunteers stood behind her. He demanded to see 'Mummy Martin', saying that he had come to collect Freddie, in language which was not suitable for young children to hear, asking for his clothes to be packed immediately, then demanded she fetch Freddie.

After a short while, I think 'Mummy Martin' appeared and was trying to stall him in some way or another, which made him madder than ever. She may have been in touch with the police or some other authority. It was some time after when he then scooped Freddie up and put him in the sidecar of his bike. How Fred stayed in that sidecar, I'll never know. He was screaming his head off, trying to get someone to pick him up as he did not want to leave without me. It made no difference, the old man drove off with Freddie holding tightly onto the bike. He took him home, leaving me there all on my own, without a word of explanation. He drove off with me running down the lane after him, pleading. 'Mummy Martin' and a couple of staff were hard on my tail. She finally caught up with me as I fell flat on my face in the middle of the main road, cut and bruised. She picked me up as one of the locals had stopped in his car, not only to give way to a madman on a motorbike, but to give Mummy Martin a hand. He asked if he should drive after the old man. She said it would not do any good to do that.

I was so upset that Fred was not with us anymore. It took me some time to get over this episode, took 'Mummy Martin' and the staff a long time to get me to understand. Why was I not wanted, as I put it, was I so bad? The whole thing made me quite ill for a few days. The doctor was called in to see me, treating me very kindly.

Following the Farnborough accident, it was sometime later when another party of us were being treated to a day out in Guildford to see one of the latest films on 18th September 1953 at the Odeon, which, in those days, was situated at the top of North Street. This time we went into Guildford on the train, catching it at Wandborough station, a short trip on a steam train, which ran along the line that passes through Dorking. The train pulled into Guildford station, platform five or six. As we got off the train and were about to use the subway to get over to platform two where the exit was, our train had moved off so we had a good view of what happened next. It was very frightening. An electric train was entering the station from the Woking direction along platform one, which was a short platform, a dead end, or terminal platform. The train seemed to be going a bit too quickly to stop before the buffers at the end. The engines seemed to make a loud noise as if either trying to stop or to accelerate. There were a lot of screeches, then there was this almighty bang and a crash. The train failed to stop, running straight through the buffers, ending up in the ticket office building.

Panic set in amongst the people waiting for trains, clouds of dust and smoke everywhere. We were told to remain where we were. After what seemed like a long time, a member of the station staff led us out of the station in the opposite direction, away from the crash, out onto this walkway to the A31 Farnham Road. There were emergency vehicles coming past in all directions. We were taken to a small hotel on the Farnham Road and given drinks. We waited for some time until we had all calmed down, then we were taken back to Red Leys in a hired minibus. No cinema that day. Luckily there were not many passengers actually on the train, those who got hurt were the driver and a few rail staff. One of them lost their life but there were not many injuries to the public at all, thank God. Very upsetting for us young people. We did get to see the film eventually on another day.

CHAPTER 9

START OF MY ILLNESS. BEING BEDRIDDEN AND NOT ALLOWED TO DO ANYTHING

It was after this that I became a little more progressively ill, getting short of breath. I went to see the doctor, who examined me and said he would like me to see a specialist at St. Luke's Hospital in Guildford. Off I went with the lovely 'Bridie' and another young helper to accompany me. The doctor, I remember, was Dr Harwood (yes, I can still remember his name, I would recognise him anywhere today as well). He examined me saying that he needed a very important doctor to see me, so an appointment was made for me to see a specialist at St. Luke's. Dr Harwood's words as we left were 'Bridie'. "This young lad must now go back to Red Leys and be put straight to bed and must stay there."

"No, not me."

"Yes, young man, if we are to make you better."

It was not very long before the appointment came to see a consultant at St. Luke's Hospital. There, I had to undergo several tests and a lot of X-rays. As I understand it today, I was diagnosed as having a shadow on my lung (in other words, the first stages of the dreaded TB), probably passed onto me by my dear mother or old man – thanks a bunch. As it turned out, the old man was put back into hospital in Milford near Godalming after kidnapping poor Freddie, having succumbed to the dreaded TB once again. Thanks very much. Yes, I do blame him for everything.

At the age of nine years of age by now, I did not have a clue what was happening to me. My bed was moved into a single bedroom all on my own, and then I was told I had to stay in bed, at all cost, and must rest, but why me? Very hard for a little lad to take in.

Anyway, the girls who worked there looked after me very well. They gave me their special treats that the other was not allowed, giving me cuddles. There was always one of them sitting with me reading stories, helping me with my stamp collection and another hobby – collecting butterflies and moths, placing them under glass in trays for exhibition. During the summer I had to undergo what was called 'fresh air treatment'. My bed was moved out into the loggia, which was open to the elements but had a roof to keep the rain off. I could see the others playing. Apparently, I had to get as much fresh air as possible but remain in bed, often being left out all night, especially during the spring and summer months – something of an adventure for me out under the stars. I often got caught by the staff running about in my pyjamas in the garden, playing or trying to play football with the boys against all instructions; I used to get rather out of breath. During this time, while more or less confined to bed, I started my first stamp collection, ending up with three or four albums of King George VI, and lots before him. I had plenty of time to put it together. Albums were supplied by that 'fairy godmother'. Another hobby I had at the time was collecting butterflies, moths, beetles, and other insects. I used to mount them in glass cases by pinning them to the paper and writing underneath what kind of insect they were. I was also given a large collection of birds' eggs to look after – certainly it wouldn't be allowed today. I do not know what happened to any of my collections after leaving Red Leys.

So I had long spells in bed. I remember having been given a large Meccano set, loads of it, lots of nuts and bolts, wheels and motors, everywhere, in my bed and on the floor. Apart from making this great big crane with the help of some of the other boys and staff, it turned out to be the exhibit of Red Leys for a while. Anyway, I had a load of pieces left over so I got to building this rifle out of all this red and green metal. As it turned out, it was as big as me; the same size of a real rifle. I even made a bayonet to put on it. I was so very proud of this rifle. One day I jumped out of bed again against all the orders. I had fixed a sling onto it, put it over my shoulder, got out of my bed and ran down the corridor towards the loggia. At the end of the corridor I slipped on the shiny floor and fell, pinning my right ear to the toilet door with the bayonet – I still have the scar on my ear. All hell let loose as this had happened right outside the matron's room. She came flying out to see what all the fuss was about and found me screaming my head off, pinned to the door by the bayonet of my Meccano rifle. All she could do was stand there laughing, saying, "Serves you right, young man, maybe you will do as you're told and stay in bed!"

Then she got a little worried when she saw the blood pouring from my ear and with toweling wrapped around my head, I was promptly put into the old Daimler car and taken down the road to 'old Dr Webb', who put two stitches in my ear. He also had to give me a tetanus jab to stop the wound from going bad and causing lockjaw – but what was lockjaw? He rolled up my pyjamas to the top, exposing my thigh. Jokingly holding the hypodermic needle like a dart, he took aim, in a playful manner, for the top of my thigh, and drew back to launch the needle in the air towards my leg. I must have moved, or got frightened because his 'throw' never went anywhere near to my thigh but straight into my right kneecap, breaking the needle as it did so. The hypodermic, minus the needle, landed on the floor, with me once again screaming in pain. After another long exercise, the broken needle was removed and a dressing put on my knee. This time I had a sore bottom as he then put the jab in the right place – my left buttock, saying, "Serves you right, young man!" Where had I heard that phrase before? I was then taken back to Red Leys and put back to bed. The Meccano set was confiscated, never to be seen again.

It was not long after that incident that I had to go back to St. Luke's Hospital, obviously to see the specialist in TB. It was here that I had another shock of my so far short life. At the hospital I was put into a bay on a ward, and there were other children around, in bed or walking. The curtains were drawn around the bed where I was being examined, then I was left all alone in this curtained-off area while the doctors discussed my case. I heard them say that if things had gotten any worse, or if I remained in this state, things would get very bad for me, and that I would not reach the age of 19. Yes, I actually heard them say that. Serious treatment needed to be undertaken, and they were going to send me to a specialist hospital for this treatment. "But there's no sure cure for this complaint." Once again, I was in such a state from what I had heard. Back at Red Leys, I told 'Mummy Martin' who explained to me what was going to happen to me. Did I not really understand, not at that age.

The day came that I was to leave Red Leys; a very sad day for me indeed. I can still remember my whole world had collapsed. I was distraught and I could not be consoled. Once again, I met this smartly-dressed lady, Miss Wright the social worker, who arrived at Red Leys in her shiny black car. Once again, my heart sank thinking in the back of my tiny mind that I was going to go back home to Holmwood. But Miss Wright was so very kind. Having listened to a long explanation, I learnt I was to be going to a very special hospital for children to be made better. I was not going back to Dorking, but was being prepared to go on a long steam train journey. Miss Wright was so very kind.

I had to say all my long goodbyes to everyone. I was dressed in my best Sunday clothes. 'Parkie', bless her, held my hand while I was placed on the back seat of the car. She tucked a blanket around my legs to keep me warm, kissed me on the forehead, and shut the car door behind her. I could see that tears were running down her cheeks. All the children and staff lined the (I've a lump in my throat even now writing this) lane as the car pulled out; most were crying, waving. 'Mummy Martin' said, "We shall see each other again when you are better."

The car took Miss Wright and I to Woking railway station where we were met by two Red Cross nurses with a wheelchair and blankets; they put me in the wheelchair, putting the blankets around me, and then pushed me out onto the platform where a train which had just arrived from London was waiting.

I did not return to Red Leys as an occupant following my treatment but I did return from time to time to visit, spending a couple of holidays there and volunteering to help while at Sunnydown and when on the *Arethusa*, as I could not stand to go home to Dorking. I did miss my 'Mummy Martin' and all of her staff members very much indeed; she was such a caring person.

'Parkie' had stayed working at Red Leys for 35 years, retiring in 1972. Unfortunately she died of cancer in 1977. This is when other people, unknown to me, joined the staff. Kate West joined in 1966 and when she married in 1972, she inherited the 'Mummy' title from 'Mummy Martin', who in turn was then called 'Granny Martin'. She did not really like it at all and I will always refer to her as 'Mummy Martin'

Marjorie 'Mummy' Martin became very ill in October 1982 and died at home on the 6th February 1983, followed by a funeral service at Wyke church, then cremation at Guildford and Godalming Crematorium. There were no floral tributes, except I laid a single red rose on her coffin and cried my eyes out. Her death heralded the end of Red Leys Children's Home in Normandy, because the property had to be sold to provide financing of death duties. Her death also brought to a close an era of care in the community, directed by a singularly gifted and unique person who throughout her life was never anything other than a kind, gentle and generous person (X Sunny down X kisses). In September 1983, Red Ley was demolished. HAPPY DAYS. All gone forever.

Miss Wright was carrying my bags. I was put into a reserved carriage and made comfortable by these Red Cross ladies who left me with Miss Wright. She travelled with me down to Southampton; we had joined the London to Southampton Express, a good old steam train. About an hour or so after leaving Woking (which seemed like hours to me) we arrived at Southampton liner terminal. After seeing all the large ocean liners docked, I thought, *Blimey, am I going on one of them?*

No, was the answer, I was not about to sail off in one of the liners. I was again met by a couple of nurses and ambulance men, who came onto the train with a stretcher this time, I was to lay down on it, made comfortable, then taken from the train and put into an ambulance-cum-minibus. They were very kind to me, making me comfortable. I remember them telling me everything that was going on, every time I was moved they first told me what to expect. I remember they kept asking me how I was, was I all right, as we had a bit of a ride to the hospital. After about half an hour we arrived at the White House Sanatorium.

CHAPTER 10

WHITE HOUSE HOSPITAL SANATORIUM FOR CHILDREN

ATTENDANCE FOR TUBERCULOSIS, SIX TO NINE MONTHS OF HOSPITALISATION

A large white hospital standing on the cliff tops at Milford on Sea, New Milton. Overlooking the Solent and the Needles on the Isle of Wight. As I remember, everything in the White House looked to be very new, the beds in the dormitories and wards, the tables and chairs in the dining area. Everything smelt of very fresh cleaned floors and everything sparkled. It did not smell like a hospital. Several of the windows in parts of the building were round, just like those of a ship's porthole. I later found out that I had been placed in this hospital for children because I was suffering with what was called a 'shadow on the lungs', or the dreaded tuberculosis.

Miss Wright stayed with me until I was put to bed in a ward of six other young boys of about my own age. I was around nine years old, maybe ten, on our arrival at the hospital. The ambulance was met by a couple of nurses in very smart light blue uniforms, starched white aprons and very stiff large, winged headdresses. It looked like they had big birds sitting on their heads. Boy, did they look smart. I remember them being very kind to me. We were taken to a dining hall, it had very high ceilings with these large lights hanging down, lots of big paintings all around the walls of large ships and flying boats. I was sat down and given a meal; I think it was about teatime.

Then I was shown around the house (or hospital). There were several wards with various aged children, one ward was full of girls, another had older boys or young men. The treatment started almost immediately, after about an hour of being on the ward,

Miss Wright said her goodbyes, saying she would come and see me sometimes, then turned and left. My heart once again hit the floor. Here I was, once again left all on my own with all these strangers.

Next I was visited by the matron wearing a navy-blue uniform, with different head gear from the nurses – it was more like a cream bun sat on the top of her head, with starched ribbons hanging down the back. She told me that under no circumstance should I ever get out of bed without permission. A nurse had to be present if I needed the toilet or bathroom. There were plenty of young nurses on duty at all times.

Then the matron summoned a nurse who was nearby and she was told to look after me. She checked my temperature and other vital signs. The matron left me with the nurse, some moments later returning with a large round-faced balding man in a long white coat. He was to be my doctor. He started to give me a thorough examination, all the time the matron was relaying notes to a very young good-looking nurse. I haven't a clue as to what it all meant.

Anyway, the treatment started that day. First, I was given an injection in the arm, given a few pills to take, which was to be the routine every day. One test they carried out on me was I had to sit in a chair and roll up the left sleeve of my pyjamas. The doctor then had this needle sticking out of what looked like a cork and proceeded to scratch a small area of my upper left arm with this needle, then he dropped a very small amount of liquid from a pipette onto the scratched area. Then I had to sit still for a while, with this area he had scratched stinging like merry hell. After a while, a nurse dressed the area. I was told not to rub or scratch it at all. All the people were wearing face masks; all you could see was their eyes, very frightening for a very young man.

After a few days, the patch on my arm that was scratched by the needle started to weep, it was also getting very sore, and after a few more days later it started to form a scab, becoming very pussy and very painful. After a couple of weeks, it started to get better, leaving what looked like a small hole in my arm. Apparently, it was a test they had come up with to tell whether or not you had tuberculosis. Anyway, after a few weeks, it went away altogether.

When the weather was good, not raining too hard, and mostly when the sun came out, our beds were wheeled out into the fresh air for 'fresh air treatment'. I was still taking all of these pills and having regular injections. After a few weeks I was allowed to get out of bed and walk around with the aid of a nurse, always accompanied by a wheelchair in case I became out of breath. Remembering it was difficult for me to walk, I got rather out of breath, coughing a lot.

There were classrooms for some of the patients to go to school; at this time I was not attending any schooling at all. After a while, as it was summer and the weather was fine, I was allowed to sit out on the lawn, which had great views of the Solent across to the Needles. I watched the coming and going of all the ships, some were big liners but the biggest ones went out around the other side of the Isle of Wight, out of our sight. I got to know what ship was what, what shipping line it belonged to, what type of ship they were. I also learnt a lot about the bird life around the coast, identifying what species they were. Generally, I took in whatever was in front of me.

As the White House was situated right on the coast, facing south, when it was windy you nearly got blown out of your bed.

It was just down the coast from Calshot which was where there was a flying boat station, the Sunderland and other classes of seaplanes would fly over quite regularly. There was a Naval air station at Lee-on-the-Solent, quite close too. All these aircraft used to fly up and down the Solent. Then one day this very large seaplane came thundering by – well, making a nice sound like a whistling propeller – it had six engines, three on each wing, which actually housed ten engines in all. The two inside housed two engines each, the outer one had just one engine, all were turboprops. It came up the Solent so low it made it a little dark. What a sight! What I had seen was one of the first flights of the Princess flying boat. Britain's largest aircraft of the time, as big as today's jumbos. Bigger than Howard Hughes' Spruce Goose. I saw it fly maybe half a dozen times after that, apparently it flew a total of 46 times. There were two others built that did not fly at all because air travel was becoming more popular from land-based airports. The Princess did not fly much after that and it was taken out of service, broken up in 1967. Notice it was also a double decker, which the Airbus A380 is today.

After I had been at the White House some time, maybe about five months, I started going to school classes for a very short time each day. I must admit, I did not get on very well, but my health had improved immensely; they were curing me of this dreadful illness. I was often allowed to go out with some of the other children, mainly for walks along the clifftops, or playing games which I could not play at the time so I just had to watch. I was still so very skinny and looking rather sickly, and still getting rather out of breath so very quickly. I was being watched every second of the day by the nursing staff.

After about nine or ten months, one day, Miss Wright turned up unannounced. She had visited me twice during this period to bring me things from Mother and home. She entered my ward saying, "You are ready then; you are going home today." What a surprise that was! I shot out of bed and started packing my little case which she had brought with her, and she had these nice new clothes. Smart long trousers – I had only worn long trousers once before and that was to go to church on a special day – a smart new shirt and a tie (I had never worn a tie before) and a tweed jacket, plus new shoes. When I got dressed, I felt and looked a million dollars, a right dandy.

After a long goodbye to the staff and nurses, finally the matron said, "Now you are going home, don't forget now, you must not do any running about, you must only walk, and then rest or you'll be back in here." Thanks a bunch. I was not allowed to partake in any physical activities; no sport, no football or anything. When I left the hospital all the nurses who were on duty lined up outside, with the doctor and matron standing by the car. I shook hands with the doctor and thanked him for looking after me (like all gentlemen did), then the matron kissed me on the cheek. As we moved off, the nurses blew me a kiss. I could not help it but I cried my eyes out. It was just like they did in the movies.

Off we went in this big black car, leather seats, me sitting in the back with Miss Wright holding my hand, down to

Southampton Docks Railway Station, past all the big liners lined up at the quayside. We boarded the express train to London. As we sat down in our reserved compartment, I asked Miss Wright if I was now going back to Red Leys, to which she replied, "No, you are going to live with your mother and 'father', in their new house."

It saddened me somewhat to be told I was now on my way back to live with the 'old git'. Miss Wright could see that my mood had changed and tried to explain to me that things would be different (little did she know, 'worse' was the word I had in mind). The train stopped at its first stop at Woking where we got off and were met by a driver in a black car again. Instead of going to Red Leys, we drove all the way to Dorking, which I had not seen for some three, nearly four years. It must have been 1955.

CHAPTER 11

BACK HOME AFTER THREE OR FOUR YEARS AWAY

Things started to get really bad for me after returning to the person – Charles Frederick Francis CUTTS – I had to call my father, or 'Daddy'. Arriving during the early evening, still very light, we pulled up outside number 29 Nower Road, in Dorking. I was met by Mother, no loving greetings as such; she may have kissed my forehead. Freddie and the old man did not come out to greet me, and no Janet as she was still with her foster parents in Leatherhead. I was ushered into my 'new' house. It looked very nice, but I remember it as being very dark inside, almost as if it were nearly always nighttime. The old man would switch off all the lights and gas not being used. I soon got used to it though.

Mother and the old man had been given this council house due to them both having had this dreadful illness, tuberculosis, which they were both still recovering from. The old man was as grumpy as ever, I think even more than before. This time he had an excuse, or so he thought. He had undergone an operation to remove both of his shoulder blades – he said without anaesthetic. He had two dirty great scars on his back. This was due to having pleurisy on top of the tuberculosis. Serves him right, the animal. All he did was grunt at me just like a pig whenever I entered the same room as him. I felt really bad about this place, this time he may have had an excuse, or so he thought. That was why, after taking Fred from Red Leys, he had to go back to the hospital in Godalming, so all the time I was in hospital, so was the old man. No sympathy there then.

I moved in, sharing a small bedroom with Freddie. The house was lit by gas lights, these were fed by pipes coming out of the wall, where you had to put a filament, or mantle, turn on the gas cock, and light the gas, which gave off a yellowish light. Everything was gas-fed. This proved a problem for Mother, the old man and I, as it affected our breathing, making it difficult.

It was a rather nice house situated near to the Nower, in Dorking; also close to the 'new' Sondes Place School which had not long been built. I had to attend school, so I started at once again at St. Martin's school which was situated behind the old fire station on West Street. This turned out to be pretty good, I had to walk down the struggle, down Vincent Lane. By the time I got to school I was out of breath, still not allowed to partake in any running.

At lunch time we used to have to walk hand in hand down Church Street, to what is now the Christian centre by St. Martin's Church, Dorking. I can also remember having to sit my eleven-plus examinations in the same hall in the Christian centre. It was during this period that, due to me being classed as very underweight, doctors of the day prescribed a pint of full fat milk, which Mother obtained through the milkman, as she got it free. I was also given a powder type of milk to take, coupled with a tablespoon of a malt extract twice a day and deep concentrated orange juice. Mother got all this free from the clinic in Dene Street, right next door to the adult learning centre.

I remember having to go to the chest clinic at the same place in Dene Street every fortnight to start with, having an X-ray, and to see Dr Hunter, a specialist in tuberculosis Then, after a while, my visits to the clinic were changed to once a month, then to every six weeks and so on until it was every six months. This was an ordeal I had to undertake with Mother.

For some reason, during this period, we were moved by the council from Nower Road. I think it was because of the problem with the gas. So off we went to 217 Chart Downs. The house was a little larger, and a much bigger garden. We were on the bus route to and from Dorking as we still had to visit the chest clinic and have regular visits to Dorking Hospital for various tests.

However, we settled into the necessary routine, which for me fell back to prior Red Leys days. The old man once again would take it out on me. Whether I got things right or wrong, I got a belting. I just had to be in his sight, or within reach of him. I would get an awful beating, it just did not stop. As I was now older and had grown somewhat, I turned out to be a bigger target for him. Things were getting worse than before, it did not matter to him.

I agree that sometimes I deserved some of the telling off as I did try to buck the system as much as I could, especially if it meant annoying the 'old pig'. Because I was not allowed to do this or that, I would sometimes go out of my way to see how far I could get before I felt his wrath. But there should not have been the brutal beatings, it was endless. It was here that I first became really physically and mentally abused. I became extremely scared of the dark. I was sent to bed most times without any tea for some small or trivial thing, such as coming home from school with dirt on my knees and on my clothing, having been playing on grass. That was one of his favourites. Or if there was a new scuff on my shoes. I would get a good hiding, and I mean a hiding, often with his belt, which was ornamented with various army regimental badges all around it (which he had a large collection of), a wide leather belt. Or he might use his army webbing belt, the type with two buckles on the back with clips to the front. Boy, did that one hurt.

You may not believe any of what I am now saying, it may seem impossible to you reading this today in this 'modern era', but believe me, hand on heart, it happened. It was brutal. I could do nothing to stop him; nor could Mother. If she intervened, she also got the back of his wrath. One time he had me on the kitchen floor, kicking me, trying to hit me with a broom. Mother tried to stop him as she walked in on him when returning from working somewhere or other, so he then laid into her. I jumped up trying to defend her; he just grabbed me by the throat and threw me out of the back door, straight into the shed door. My thoughts went into how I could kill him, to stop this horrible man. No, he was not a man, but a beast.

When sent to bed early, especially in the winter when very cold with no heating or double glazing, we slept under greatcoats or overcoats. The old man would always come up to my bedroom, threatening that if I did not get my head under the bedclothes he would belt me, which he did very regularly. Thinking he had left my room, I poked my head out to see if he had gone but he had not. He would stick something like a straw in my ear and blow in it, which hurt, then he would roar or make some sort of animal noise. If Mother had gone to work or had gone out for any reason, he would creep (that was what he was: a creep) into my room all nice as pie and praise me, then fondle me under the covers, all the time swearing and telling me what he would do to me if I said anything to anyone at all. "I'll get you sent away to borstal, you won't like it there, it's like prison." I hated the bastard.

On at least two occasions, I did try my best to kill him, knowing exactly what I was going to do and what it might mean if I did – I'd be sent to prison. Me, a frail nine or ten years old by now. Once I took a large carving knife out of the kitchen drawer, tip-toed into the front room where he was in 'his' chair, thinking he had fallen asleep while listening to the radio. I crept into the room (must have made some noise or moved something) just as Mother came home through the back door. She saw me through the open front room door with this knife above my head as though I was going to stab him in the chest. She screamed, he jumped out of his skin and flew at me. I dodged him and ran into the bathroom which was on the ground floor, locking the door. I was still holding on to the carving knife. He started banging on the door, shouting and swearing, Mother still screaming. I do not know where Freddie was or whether Janet was around. Crash, the door flew open, kicked from the outside, lock broken. Whoosh, I was hit by a bucket of freezing cold water, which Mother had thrown at me. She pushed past him, tried to grab the knife, and with the feather duster, her favourite weapon, in hand, the bamboo stick handle, hit me everywhere. She was in a frenzy and just kept on hitting me. I would react by raising my arms above my head, trying to ward off the blows she was raining down on me, then she tried whacking me around the legs until I gave up the knife.

I do not know exactly where Fred was when this was happening but he got very upset. I believe that Janet was also in the house, on a trial period, to see if she could live with us or not – if she could not then she was to go back to the 'Lush's in

Leatherhead, which did happen in the end. Janet, I think, enjoyed her foster family, mind you, it was the only life she could remember.

The old man was shouting that he was going to call the police, to take me away and lock me up, Mother was trying to stop him. They were shouting and swearing at each other and me. Eventually she got me out of the bathroom, but I got cut by the knife which left a lot of blood on the floor. After putting a Band-Aid on my hand and her cuts, I was put in my bedroom and told not to move by Mother, saying she had to clean up the mess that I had made in the bathroom.

While she was downstairs, the old man crept upstairs behind her back, came into the bedroom and told Fred, who was scared out of his wits, to go downstairs and play in the front room. Then he started to thrash the living daylights out of me again, with his bloody belt once again, shouting, "I'll teach you to pull a knife on me!" I really thought he would kill me this time. Mother heard the commotion, came running upstairs, grabbed him by his collar and dragged him off me. Another argument and fight went on the landing and he was calling me her bastard. Eventually it all went quiet. I was so scared, the silence was dreadful. I could not hear him or Mother anymore, what had they done to each other? After a while I just fell asleep.

The next time I tried killing him, I think I very nearly succeeded. He loved listening to this large radio; there was not any television in our house in those days, just the radio for entertainment. At six o'clock, if we were in, we had to be especially quiet for the six o'clock news.

One day he went through his usual routine. His beloved radio seemed not to be working properly the first time he tried. He accused me of having fiddled with it, giving me such a clout with another back-hander, knocking me off my chair where I was trying to be so very silent. He was in the process of trying to find the fault and to fix it; he had taken the back off the radio, started pulling out valves, checking that they were working properly. All the switches worked all right but he could not get a sound out of it. It was electric, plugged into the light socket in the centre of the room in a ceiling rose. The flex went along the ceiling and down the wall beside the fireplace, then into the rear of the radio. He thought he had found the fault which must have been in the ceiling rose light fitting. He grabbed a chair and as he was standing on it in the middle of the room, he turned to me. "Don't you dare touch that switch while I am up here," he shouted at me. I saw what he was about to do – he was going to push his finger in the socket to test the springs on the connector. As he did so, I jumped up out of my chair, then threw the switch to the 'on' position. In a flash, I was outside running straight out the front door, I heard him scream followed by a loud thud as he hit the floor. Remember, I was still under the medical clinic for the illness I had earlier, still not allowed to partake in sports, do any running. I did not wait to see what had happened or what I had done. Crying, I ran in my slippers out onto Chart Lane, down past the Royal Oak, still running, not looking back. I ran and ran, down past Inholms Lane on towards the Plough public house where I had to stop as I was rather out of breath. I looked behind me to see if anyone was chasing me but could not see anybody. I could hardly breathe at all. There is a public footpath situated right opposite the Plough public house, which I knew eventually led out onto the Holmwood common. So, after a short rest, I could not see anyone coming after me, so I ran down the long footpath, onto Holmwood common, having lost one of my slippers in the process. Still not looking back, I ran across the common, coming out by what is now Pearce's garage, which was next to the Norfolk Arms.

At Mid Holmwood, I had run up the common which was a long way, even for an adult, to my grandparents' house. I fell into their kitchen, Gran and Grandad came running from their front room, Grandmother screaming like a banshee, trying to find out what was wrong with me this time. I could hardly speak, I could not catch my breath, all I could say was, "Killed him, killed him." I was so exhausted I just collapsed. Nothing on my feet. They were bleeding, Gran and Grandad cleaned me up and put me to bed in one of the spare rooms. Next thing I remember was waking up some hours later, the next day, I think. Uncle Bun, Granddad and Mother were looking over me, and I thought I was in for it. I got a good telling off from Mother, Grandad told me how stupid I had been to run all that way, followed by Uncle Bun. What a relief when they told me I had not killed him, he had just burnt his hand badly. *Serves him right,* I thought. I stayed with my grandparents for a few days before being taken back to Chart Downs. I wished they had not because I got another prompt good hiding as soon as Mother turned her back and went out to the shops, telling me that was the last time I would disobey him. He was going to have me put away. The threats kept coming, every which way I turned, he was always on my case.

One other chore I had to do regularly was the washing and drying up after every meal. If it was done with a moan because I wanted to go out to play, I got, "You know the drill by now, straight to bed," and a flea in the ear, or worse. As we were hard up for money coming in, we had to watch what lights we could put on so we often had to move about the house in darkness. He took the electric bulbs out of their sockets where he said they were not necessary. My bedroom was one of the places. As I've already said, I was so scared of the dark. Because he would always have a go at me when the curtains were drawn, the room in pitch darkness, when he came into my room, he would stand silhouetted by the light that came in from outside. This ghostly shape scared the wits out of me; he used to make horrible noises. Sometimes when doing this, he would shake the end of the bed, saying, "I am coming to get you, your mother's little bastard."

All our heating was from a stove in the kitchen, which also gave us hot water through the taps, a round stove at the bottom, which housed the ash can. The top half was square, with an opening on top where you placed the fuel, coal or wood, a round tube, went up through the kitchen out into the open air. There was always a hot kettle on top, steaming away. If it was not there when he wanted a cup of tea, it would always be my fault as it was my duty to make sure the kettle was always kept full of hot water.

In the front room was an open grate fireplace; this would heat the front room, burning coal but mainly wood. Where did the coal and the wood come from? Well, you see, the 'old man' had made this trolley/wheel barrow out of four old pram wheels, build a large box on top of the wheels, then made two handles out of two pieces of two by four wood, bolted onto the sides of the box, shaving off the handles to form a grip. Guess what he had made this contraption for. Well, it was made so that I could go out and collect wood, fallen wood along the road towards Inholms Lane, past down towards the Plough, picking up branches and logs, I had to fill it up before coming home. It took me a few trips to realise that it would not be such hard work if I started picking up the wood from Holmwood Common and pushing the barrow back towards Chart Downs. Then it was my job to cut or saw the wood up into manageable sizes to fit the kitchen fire or the front room fire, which took the larger ones. I had to cut them on a sawing horse, then, using an axe, I had to split the larger one to make them into logs.

Sometimes the old man would take the barrow out late at night – remember, he was still supposed to be recovering from his illness – he would go out with this barrow and come back with it full of coal. I still wonder where he got it from. There were a few coal depots around, as coal was one of the main burning fuels. The closest one was out in North Holmwood by the Brick Company – not too far for him to go 'nicking'.

This homemade 'barrow' was also used for a number of other things. One of them was for me, again, sometimes with Mother. We would go up into the Glory Woods to collect leaf mould to be put onto the garden, to break up the clay, they used to say. This turned out to be hard work for an adult let alone a young feller of ten years of age, still suffering. Mother used to love her garden, especially out the front, which is where I learnt a little about flowers, and what were weeds. Again, weeding was carried out against my will as I could see all the other children playing on the grass in front of the community centre, and riding their bikes, which I did not have.

Talking about the old pram wheels, Chart Downs community centre had just been built. My second cousin, Brian Chandler, who is a carpenter and builder, had put a lot of work into building the community centre. To celebrate its opening, they put on a carnival, during which a soapbox race. A soapbox car was made out of soap or orange boxes – the larger wooden ones – with two larger pram wheels at the back and two smaller wheels at the front for steering, which you did by either your feet resting on a wooden bar, or by using a rope tied to the wooden steering bar. Well, we, meaning a couple of friends, the Ropers, Colinsons, and myself, got to work on making a soapbox racer. We placed a seat on the rear wheels, fixing them properly, then placed on a centre beam to which the seat and front steering was fixed. Old Man Roper got involved, showing us how to make it safe and sound. Then we had the brainwave to try to make it look like a racing car, so we got some old plywood and cardboard to make a fairing. We painted it red and blue and took it for a test ride, from the top of the 'slight hill' on Chart Downs. It started with a couple of pushers running as fast as they could, just like you see in the Olympic Games bobsleigh, to get you started. Off you went down the hill, round at the bottom was a right hand bend, passed in front of the shops, and the finishing line was outside the grocer's store (which is not there today).

Come the day of the celebrations and the opening of the community centre, the soapbox grand prix was started. I remember it was a very hot day, all the soapboxes were paraded in front of the committee of the community centre to be judged. I cannot remember if we did win anything in the parade – there were 20 to 30 cars. Then the drivers of the various soapboxes were put into different groups according to age and size. There were several races to be run, nearly all afternoon. Several heats took place and I did get to ride in our racing car, in about the third race of the day and the third race for our car. No firsts were recorded but one of the Roper boys came second in his race. Then it was my turn. Get ready, set, go! Two of the bigger boys gave me a running start and off I went. I was flying. That right-hand corner was coming up fast, with the cardboard fairings flapping. I hit this bend at uncontrollable speed. I forgot that you slowed it by pulling on a handbrake bolted to the frame next to the back wheel. Well, I was going too fast to get around the corner, hitting the curb at a fast pace and over I went, wrecking all the good work which had been put into building this soapbox. I was devastated, a bit bruised and battered, this time at my own fault (not the old man's). I was broken-hearted that I had broken our cart. The other boys came rushing down the hill, picked me up, telling me it was all right, it was only a bit of fun and what fun we had making it and testing it. We could get it mended anyway and still have fun with it.

Do you know, I just broke down in tears. Why, because I thought that I had done something so very bad in breaking our pride and joy. To be praised for doing it and not getting told off for it was such a release. It was great fun for as long as it lasted and when I was allowed to go out to play with them and our cart. The boys used to gingerly come around to ask if I could come out to play with them, only to be chased off by the 'old man'. I think they did it in the end to wind him up, make him angry; I always got a telling off from him. He was known as the 'grumpy old man at 217'. Fair game for the kids when he went out, they used to chase after his motorbike shouting silly things at him, which I doubt he could hear anyway through the noise of the bike and his leather flying helmet he used to wear, before crash helmets were made compulsory.

During the same summer, Dorking Hospital put on a garden fete with a fancy dress parade; the band of the guards turned up and did a marching display. Mother dressed me up as a street newspaper seller, in an old tweed jacket and trousers that she had sown newspapers all over, with my granddad's flat cap on sideways. I had a bundle of newspapers under my arm, with a news board tied around my neck. I won first prize. My picture appeared in the local *Dorking Advertiser*.

Mother used to go to a lot of jumble sales, as I have already mentioned several times, to buy clothes for us. It was the cheapest way as we had hardly any money. I never got any pocket money like all of my friends, most of the clothes she bought turn out to be girls' trousers or blouses, rather than shirts. Often the shoes would have straps with a small button to fasten them. Yes, I had to wear whatever I was given and wear it to school, even trousers that did up along the sides. So you can see that if there was to be any mickey-taking – today they call it bullying – I got it in the neck. Believe it or not I used to take off the blouse or the shoes and go to school in bare feet. I often pleaded with Mother to wear whatever she had got for me but without any joy at all. "Wear it, there is nothing else." I often took the 'nothing else'. After a while, the school took pity on me, but that did not help in any way at all. Then there were the old man's haircuts; that was just as embarrassing. He insisted that he would cut our hair as he could not afford to have a barber do it properly. He had his own haircutting kit, but he did not know how to use it properly. He used to 'cut one pull two' and it didn't half hurt. It looked terrible with the 39 steps up the back, really short, and as if he had put a bowl on my head and cut around it.

CHAPTER 12

SOCIAL SERVICE CALLED INTO ACTION

(Things started to get really bad for me was an understatement – my whole world collapsed)

The biggest shock in my short life was still to come. One Saturday morning, Mother took me to one of her jumble sales in Dorking, and we walked all the way into town from Chart Downs – there and back, no money for a bus. I remember I had quite a good day, really happy, up until the time I arrived home.

It was at the time that Janet had been allowed to return to the family, on a trial period. I remember I was about ten years old, Fred was four years younger, so he was only about five, not quite six. Janet was six years younger than me, meaning she was three, nearly four years old. Janet had only been back with us for about a week or two to see whether she could get on with living with us. Remember, Janet was the old man's daughter.

I returned home this Saturday afternoon with Mother and I walked in through the back door of the kitchen, full of beans in a very bouncy, skipping, happy mood, having been into town with Mother. The bastard flew at me, barging past Mother, grabbed me by the throat, one hand around my windpipe, smacking my head with his free hand. I could hardly breath, everything went black, flashes of stars in my head, then he threw me into the middle of the front room floor, flat on my back, my head hitting the floor with quite some force. Fred and Janet were screaming and crying in a chair in the corner. Standing over me, he shouted, "I'll bloody well kill you, you bastard, if you ever interfere with my daughter, your sister, again."

What was I supposed to have done? Mother was screaming and shouting, asking what the hell was the matter with him this time. She started to intervene; but she was pushed to one side, told not to get involved. He carried on ranting and raving, he was kicking me in a frenzy. "This little bastard of yours (emphasizing the words 'bastard') has interfered with my daughter." Then he turned to Freddie, saying, "Tell your mother what you saw."

I don't think Fred could say anything properly as he was out of his head with fear. Apparently, while I was out, the old man got the two of them together, threatened them to say that I had sexually touched Janet. Me, I was only ten, maybe just turned 11 if that. What did he mean 'touched her sexually'? I did not have a clue what he was saying. Well, from then on, Mother took his side, asking me why. My whole world exploded, here I was, a ten-year old boy, being accused of this very bad act. I could not understand what was going on.

In the meantime he had told Mother to go to the phone box across the road and phone for the police. After the police left, saying it was for social services to sort out. I was taken off by them, to Surrey county council offices in Reigate. Now Fileturn House, situated on Reigate Hill, and it is now the registry office. Here was where I was questioned by two older men and a large woman; a child psychologist. I could not understand this 'sexual act' I was being accused of. I knew nothing of sex. let alone a 'bad act' or why had I done it, but I kept telling them I did not know what they were asking me, I could not understand all these questions. What did they mean? They kept on telling me my 'father' and mother had given them the full story, there was no use in telling lies, it would not help me. This went on for what seemed like hours and I was not allowed to see anyone. I was so frightened, getting very hot, at which point, the woman who was in the room said, "If you are feeling hot, then take your jumper off."

At this point, I tried getting my jumper off, which was a little tight or too small for me, and I was in pain from the beating I had received. The lady stood up to help me, but as she tried to pull the jumper over my head, it must have pulled my shirt and vest up with it. She exclaimed, "Oh my God, what has happened to you, have you been in an accident or something?" Not knowing what she meant, I just shrugged my shoulders, there for all to see were the welts and bruises that the monster had inflicted on me. There was still a little blood on my vest from my last beating.

A man appeared with a camera and asked me to undress. The lady nearly started to cry, saying, "Who has done this to you." Then the gentleman started taking photographs of my body, as some of the marks and scars seemed to be a lot older. They then took off my trousers, by now I was naked so they could see the effect of his beltings on my back, buttocks and the back of my legs.

Another visit from the police, who were called, asked more of the same questions of how and why I had all this bruising and cuts on my body. All I could say was, "Don't know," remembering the old man's words echoing in my head: *You tell anyone and I will kill you.*

The course of the questioning then took on another tack, the change was out of the blue. People around me became a lot 'nicer', offering me sweets and chocolate. Always at the back of my mind was the phrase 'don't take sweets from strangers'. I felt so scared that if I said anything else about how I got all these marks on my body, I would be taken from home and placed in a borstal, as the 'old man' had always threatened me with.

I believe a doctor was called to look at me or to treat me, he must have given me a sedative, or something to make me sleep. I then was taken to another small room in the building, which had a bed in it, their first aid room I think, where I was put to bed. I do not remember how long I had been there, or if it was the next day or not, but next Miss Wright appeared from Epsom social services and was sitting on my bed. She gave me such a loving cuddle, telling me everything was going to be alright from now on. I broke down, once again uncontrollably I cried and cried so hard. I could not catch my breath until she put a brown paper bag over my mouth, which again sent me into another frenzy. I breathed in and out until I could breathe properly again. Once I had calmed down, and got myself dressed properly in clothing supplied by Miss Wright, she took me to a waiting car. She said, "I am taking you home." At this point I was hitting the roof again, she could not get me in that car. I broke free, ran out of the grounds of the house as fast as I could and started to run down towards the Reigate train station. I was going to run away, get on a train to London, but after some time the two men caught up and found me hiding behind some dustbins. Then both of them carried me back to the house, kicking and scratching. They put me back in a room where Miss Wright tried to calm me down again, she told me that I was not going home to Chart Downs but she was taking me to my grandparents' house where as she said Mr Cutts was not allowed to go. It was then I started to feel a little better.

We arrived at my gran's and I was greeted by a hug from Granddad. How I remember that smell of the tobacco that he smoked; he used to roll his own, it had its own smell. I often got sent to Bondie's grocers to get his quarter of 'Digger Shag', a very dark tobacco, not unlike thick black treacle with strands of tobacco in it. Boy, was it strong, as I found out later in life. I just let it all out on him, crying my eyes out again, he did listen to what I had to say. He kept saying, "I know, I know, you're safe now." They gave me a meal and put me to bed. I was quite ill for a number of days. This was not the end of the incident by a long way; I had to return to the Surrey County Council social office in Reigate, put through more and more questions and what I now know were psychological tests.

Like before, the nature of the questioning, which I could not understand, changed. Out came the chocolate and sweets, from now on the questions were not of what I had allegedly done, but what was being carried out on me and by whom. I had to mention being sent to bed without any tea or a beating, telling the people who were questioning me (or counselling me) what the 'old man' would do once Mother went out and what he would do after, dark in my bedroom, or when Mother had gone out for her evening work.

I had to tell the people all sat around in a circle, Miss Wright was next to me, they all had notepads on their knees and when I said something their heads would go down and they started to write things down on their notepads. I let it all go, telling them every moment which was engraved (and still is, as you can tell) on my mind. I felt so good that someone else now knew what I had to endure from that 'animal'.

I eventually was sent back to live at Chart Downs. Dreading every moment until it happened. I was greeted by the old man's words, "I told you, you little bastard, that you would end up in a borstal. That's where you're going, my boy, I'll make sure of that." To which he added another few choice words.

In the meantime, I was still going to St Martin's School in West Street. It was around the time that I had to take my eleven-plus examinations. The day came, off we went in twos, holding hands to the St. Martin's church hall, which is now the Christian centre. When we arrived, we were each given a single desk to sit at, there were three long rows of these desks. I was placed in one at about the middle of the hall. I remember that the teacher drew the curtains which made it dark, until someone put on the lights. Next, another teacher came around and put our examination papers on the desk. We were told not to look at them yet. The teacher, who was standing at the front, stopwatch in hand, told us what to do and that we only had an hour for the first examination paper. On his command we were to start by putting our names at the top of the page. Well, off we went, the clock was ticking, I tried to do a few of the sums. I had a good reasonable knowledge of fractions and how to divide, etc., but why should I try, I was going away in any case. It came to the time to hand our papers in, forming a line to hand in our examination papers as we left the room. It was my turn, standing in front of the teacher, scared out of my wits because I had not answered very many of the questions. He pulled me to one side as he saw the empty paper. "What do you call this? You have been wasting your time and ours, and you'll not get another chance."

I replied, "Don't care."

He clipped me around the ear, saying, "Report to the headmaster when you get back."

The headmaster was a large, bald-headed man, very stern. As I stood in front of him, my knees knocking, nearly wetting myself, I got the biggest telling off from anyone other than the bloody old man. I ended up telling him I did not care what he said to me, and he gave me detention. I replied, "I don't care, I am going to borstal anyway."

He produced a ruler (not the thin plastic ones of today, the type made out of hardwood) and told me to hold out my hand, gave me three whacks across the fingers. Boy, did that hurt. "Now on the other hand." Oh my God, did I scream. I could not hold any writing implements for a couple days.

The beginning of the next term it was off to the Sondes Place School for a very short time as I had failed the eleven-plus, big time. Sondes was situated not at the new building (as it was in the process of the build being finished) but at Dene Street in Dorking, which is now the Adult Education Centre. We used to have to walk hand in hand down Dene Street to what is now the Christian centre for our lunchtime meals and march back. I had to walk to school each day from Chart Downs, up the hill of Chart Lane South, along the bypass, down to Dene Street, but to get to Sondes Place, the larger 'new' school, situated off West Bank, it was a lot further.

However, it did not do me any harm at all. I did not get on very well at school, always having the mickey taken out of me as some of my clothes still turned out to be girls' ones Mother had bought. In those days I looked very thin due to the illness I was still trying to get over, not being able to play any sports still, yet it was open season on me as far as the 'old git' was concerned. Mother did not do much to stop him, often, in my opinion, taking his side.

As I have already explained, I had to attend counselling, being met by a friendlier atmosphere, to undergo more and more counselling for what I had gone through, I had done nothing to anybody, I later got to understand once I had got much older why I had to attend these meetings every Friday. I had to leave school in the afternoon after having had my free school dinner, walk to the bus station, down the footpath which was called the 'struggle' as it was so steep. To go over to Reigate for these counselling meetings I had to catch the 414 green country bus from outside the then bus station on Horsham Road to the Red Cross in

Reigate, making sure that I had my free bus pass supplied by the social services. I was often feeling travel sick when I got there, getting off the bus and walking up the road, over the level crossing by the train station to Fileturn House and have my sessions. Afterwards, I had to do the journey back to Dorking again.

I often thought of going the other way towards Croydon and running away. I did on one occasion but instead of going towards Croydon, I did take the bus back to Dorking, getting off at the bus station, but instead of getting the bus to Chart Downs, I boarded the bus to Guildford. I was going to go to Red Leys and 'Mummy Martins', but my plan fell foul when an inspector boarded the bus at Shere, where it was found that not only did I not have the fare or a free pass for this route but I was also being rather sick due to too much travel that day on the bus. The inspector did question me as to where I lived and where I was going. He said, "Are you running away from home?" I had to tell him the truth that I did not want to go home. Anyway, he took me off the bus and we waited for the returning bus going the other way back to Dorking which came along some minutes later. Back at Dorking, the police were called and they took me home the short distance to Chart Downs, which caused another ruction, every neighbour having a look at what was going on.

The bus station was a very big place in those days, situated in Horsham Road, opposite the Queens Head public house. It took up all the space from the corner of South Street to St Paul's Road. There was a large area where the buses came in or terminated, with a very large garage area, outside of which there was a large parking bay where all the buses were parked.

If you thought the old man was strict on me, you haven't seen anything yet. Still ten or 11 years old, remember, I had to do all the housework, except most of the cooking, I had to dig the garden, heavy old clay, which stuck to everything. He would give me jobs to do if he ever went out. One day, I had to dig up the potato patch, which I had planted some months earlier. Over time, I had hoed them up into long mounds (called drills) so that the taters could grow nicely, then it was time to dig them up before the weather turned. His instruction was he wanted them all dug up and placed on sacking to dry. There were about ten rows, each about ten yards long, quite substantial even for a grown up. I was not even allowed to leave the garden, to play with the other boys in my street. If I asked to go out all he did was call me all sorts of names. He said I was an animal, and he called me such, no holds barred on him at all now, he had said he would see me suffer for what I had allegedly done. Anyway, doing as I was told, I set about digging his potatoes up. He had gone out on his motorbike and sidecar to have a drink and meet some friends as he could not work anymore and was on social security benefits.

After a while, I got fed up with digging up all these potatoes, trying to keep the sticky old clay off the fork, which was very hard work for a skinny little chap. I needed a rest. So I slipped out of the back gate, going over to the swings to play with the other kids. I was having a great time, losing all timing, then I thought I had not dug up all of those darn potatoes yet, I had not even managed a couple of rows. I saw Mother coming home and about to enter via the front gate, so I sneaked back into the garden through the back gate, back to my digging. Mother brought out a drink for me and a biscuit, then I heard the dreaded sound, that bloody BSA motorbike coming down the hill on Chart Lane. I picked up the fork and started digging like merry hell, potatoes were coming out of the ground like popping peas. However, I was so concerned that I had not done what he had instructed me to, I was petrified at what he might do.

He came around the back of the house, parked his bike, as he walked down the path he grabbed my upper arm, dragged me down to the back door, saying he would teach me a lesson on how to do as I was told. But this time Mother screamed, pushed him off me. "Leave him alone, look." She pointed to a trail of blood on the path. What I had done in my haste to try and dig up his bloody potatoes, I had put the fork right through my right foot without knowing it until Mother pointed it out. Only then did I feel anything, it hurt. I had filled up my Wellington boot with blood which was coming over the top. I had gone through an artery in my foot. I still got a thrashing for putting him and Mother through a fright. Mother took me to the bathroom, stood me in the bath, took off my boot, and cleaned up my foot. Next morning, we went down to the doctors and got my foot looked at and dressed properly, for my pains I got an injection in my bottom. Luckily, apart from being very sore for a couple weeks, it healed nicely. The injury did not excuse me from digging up the rest of the potatoes. It took me all I think three days of digging and being helped by mother and Freddie to get them all out of the ground.

During this period, Mother put me in the St. John's Church, North Holmwood choir so every Wednesday evening I had to attend the church for choir practice. I had to walk from Chart Downs through the brickyard footpath to the church, doing the same again every Sunday morning and again in the evening, for evensong. During Sunday afternoon I had to walk to Hampstead Road church hall for Sunday school and back again. Now this again became a bit of an ordeal. Why, you might ask. Well, you see the shoes I wore were either too small and hurt my feet, or the 'old man' used to think himself a bit of a cobbler shoe repairer or 'snob' and would put extra leather on the soles of the shoe, which I wore with Blakey's on the front tip of the shoe and one on the heel, often putting hobnail suds in the sole, which sometimes would poke through the inner sole, pressing into my feet. Every time I wore my shoes he would inspect them for any of what he called undue wear; or marks and scuffs. Well, you know now what I got if he found any was a good hiding. So, as I said before, I would take them off and walk in my bare feet. Put them back on when either reaching the church or the house on my return.

CHAPTER 13

CHOIR

St. John the Evangelist Church. Practice, mid-week, and Sunday School

On some Sunday afternoons and a few evenings, a 'funny man' would often visit Mother but only when the old man went out. He was there within minutes of the old man leaving, funny because he had two 'funny feet' – he had two very badly clubbed feet, but he would ride his push bike or his moped. He would bring us extra food, fresh fruit and vegetables, which he grew in his own garden. He seemed to me to be a very sad man, because every time he set eyes on me, I could see that he was crying or had tears in his eyes, trying very hard not to show it. He would always put a shilling coin in my pocket when he left, putting his finger to his lips as if to say be quiet. A shilling was quite a lot of money in those days, especially for a youngster who had nothing. I often saw Mother kissing him on the cheek, closing her purse, as if having been given money.

Sometimes, on a weekend, I was allowed out to play on the green with the other children. We were playing 'touch he', one of the kiddies shouted out, "Last one to touch the telephone box is it," and off we all rushed. I ran across the road obviously without looking to see if any cars were coming, there were none on the road in those days which was normally OK as most people on the estate could not afford to drive a car, so cars were quite rare anyway.

What happened next? Wallop! Clumsy me, I tripped on the curb, heading head first for the telephone box. I put out my right hand to stop me hitting the telephone box or falling flat on my face but unfortunately my arm went right through the glass, as I fell, I got hung up on a piece of the broken glass. Some of the other children started screaming, while a couple of the bigger boys got hold of me and stood me up, then I saw what I had done. My right arm was open in four or five places, pouring blood, bleeding like hell. As I moved my arm up and down, the muscle would pop in and out of my arm. I thought this was great, bleeding profusely, off I went running into the house, shouting, "Mum look what I've done!" I moved my arm up and down, showing her what the muscle was doing, she hit the floor, fainting for a few moments.

Another lady, one of her friends, was luckily in the house at the time and quickly wrapped my arm in a towel, got Mother up on her feet. Whack! Another one around the ear. "What the hell you playing at?" she cried.

Off we went to Dorking hospital on the bus, yes on the bus, with my arm now wrapped in two towels still trying to stop the bleeding. There was blood everywhere as it was still coming through the towels. The bus reached the bus station in South Street, then we had to walk up to the hospital, so you can imagine that by now I was feeling rather ill having lost so much blood, and traveling on the blinking bus.

On reaching the hospital I was taken to the emergency children's ward where the doctor stitched my arm up. They kept me for a couple of days just to see if my fingers and tendons were working all right. That turned out to be a bit of a treat for me as I did not have to see the 'old git', coupled with the fact I was being looked after by some very nice nurses.

I was still attending the Dorking chest clinic in Dene Street (next door to the Adult Education Centre) at least once a month to see a Dr Hunter, a specialist in chest and TB, to have my chest X-rayed. The doctor prescribed an extra pint of full fat milk a day, and I had to take a malt extract – two tablespoons a day with an extra orange juice and cod liver oil every day, so I was still on these horrible tasting things, because they thought I was underweight and needed building up.

I was still attending counselling over at Reigate, it was at another one of these sessions that Mother and the 'old man' had to attend. When we arrived, met by a couple of social workers,

I was shown to a sideroom, while both the 'old man' and Mother were shown into another room with Miss Wright and another person. A long discussion took place; obviously my future was being discussed. The 'old man' would often be heard to shout and swear saying, "I don't want the little bastard in my house." I think he was told to leave the room while they spoke to Mother on her own.

Anyway, the outcome was that I was to be sent away to a special boarding school as soon as possible, as it was put, for my own good. They had found a place for me at a school in Guildford. As it was again stressed for my own good and protection, I was not to go back home to Chart Downs, the 'old man' must not come within a certain distance of me without someone else being with him. Until I was placed in the school, he was to stay away from me. In the meantime I was to stay for a short time with my grandparents once again. As it turned out, it was a matter of possibly one week. Miss Wright once again turned up one morning in this smart black car, but inside was my 'old man' with Mother. My gran had packed me a small case, which was put in the rear of the car, then I caught sight of him sitting in the front seat of the car. I threw a very big wobble, at first I would not get into the car but after a few minutes, my grandmother took me to one side, told me not to be stupid, or words to that effect, or make things worse than they already were. After a quick cuddle from her, maybe my first ever which surprised me very much, then an even bigger surprise – she gave me a kiss on the cheek – I got into the back of the car with Mother, in between her and Miss Wright. Off we went to Sunnydown boarding school, just off the A31 on the Hogs Back, in Guildford.

I did not have a clue where I was being taken. I was scared out of my wits, my thoughts were that I was now a very bad boy and was off to be locked up in some borstal or prison for boys as the old sod always threatened me with if I told anyone of what he did to me. All these thoughts kept rushing through my mind. I had not told anyone but I may have said something during the interviews or counselling periods I underwent over in Reigate every Friday and now I was going to pay for it.

CHAPTER 14

SUNNYDOWN SPECIAL BOARDING SCHOOL FOR DELICATE AND PHYSICALLY HANDICAPPED BOYS

INTRODUCTION TO THE SCHOOL, 1954-1956

Sunnydown, on the Hog's Back, in Compton near Guildford, was purchased for the use as a private preparatory school in 1900 and continued as a private preparatory school until 1941. During the Second World War the building was let out to St. Thomas's Hospital was a training centre for nurses and afterwards the Royal Surrey County Hospital used it as a hostel for nurses up until the Summer of 1947. In 1948 the building became the property of the Surrey County Council. Sunnydown Boarding School for Delicate and Physically Handicapped Boys opened in March 1949. Mr Francis (Frank) Bevis had been appointed headmaster for the school in the autumn of 1947 and continued in the post until July of 1970. In 1983 the school was closed and was moved to new premises at Portley House, Caterham.

Sunnydown Boarding School for Delicate and Physically Handicapped Boys motto: 'Venimus Vincire' (we come to overcome or to conquer).

An early history of the school and its situation within the area. There was a wooded area to the right of the school and a wooded path which ran down the left-hand side of the grounds towards Compton, which was not part of Sunnydown property. To the top of the picture but not in the picture was the main road A31 which was at the start of the Hog's Back, with a B road leading off to the left which was the road into Compton.

As you entered Sunnydown, there was a large house called 'Peddars Way', built by Mr and Mrs Howe following their retirement from the earlier preparatory school and was occupied by Mrs Howe until her death and after that, by a Miss Davies.

The land with a large greenhouse (top centre) subsequently became two classrooms. There were a number of buildings to the left as you look at the photograph (obscured by trees). There were situated two or three cottages which included a large garage, the cottages housed the cook and handyman, Mr and Mrs Wilson (in the 1950s) and the gardener, Mr Brown.

The building and small courtyard, to the upper right of centre, was I believe originally built as a sanatorium for the preparatory school, and was later divided as a house for Mr Gordon Murch (Bursar) and his wife, Doreen, and son. The other half of the building provided two dormitories for senior boys. The white attached to the main building by a corridor was used by the staff accommodation but during the '50S was the home of Mr Francis and Mrs Ella Bevis and their daughter, Elaine.

Shown at the lower centre of the picture is the school swimming pool, which was built during the mid-50s helped by the school inmates, including me, by digging out the hole in the ground, I think it took us and the builders a number of months to complete. Below the swimming pool (not in the picture) about 30 yards away was a smallholding in which the school kept a few pigs, chickens, plus three goats, called Snowflake, and the kids, Snowdrop and Snowy. When Snowflake passed away, the kids, now rather large, were moved to their own paddock. This is when the smallholding was run down and closed, the pig sties were left empty, a nice play area, which was frowned on by the masters, placed out of bounds in the end as it was a little unsafe.

The school was called *Special School for Delicate and Physically Handicapped Boys*. I do not or did not count myself as being 'handicapped' in any way, or 'delicate', maybe a little in that I was still getting over the illness of the previous two or three years. I was a little weak, and way behind on my education, so maybe that was a good enough excuse for my 'parents' to have me put away at boarding school. I was classed by them as being uncontrollable, as I often heard the old git saying. This was not only to build me up but for me to catch up with my schooling as it had been affected for almost three years now, so I had to start to work hard to pick up again, which I found extremely hard to do.

Arriving at Sunnydown, I am not sure when the exact date was, but I do know it was midway through the year of 1954. I was not yet 11 years of age. Miss Wright, my mother the 'old man Cutts' and myself were met by the headmaster, Mr Francis (Frank) Bevis and his wife, Ella. This boarding school appeared very stark and formal and my thoughts went back to the days of Red Ley's and the White House Sanatorium; the school was nowhere near like the place that I had just left and lived at, my home.

On my arrival, all were ushered into the headmaster's study where a maid (who turned out to be a young lady called Sheila, who helped to clean the school and helped with the cooking) supplied tea and cake for the whole party, while Mr Bevis explained about the school. After this, Mother and the 'old man' were shown around the school, while I was taken by Mrs Partington (I am not too sure whether that was her name) the matron to my dormitory where there were three other beds as well as what was to be my own bed. I remember asking the matron, "Is this a borstal or prison for bad boys?"

She replied, "Most certainly not, young man, why do you say that?"

I replied that the 'old man' had said that he would have me put away in a borstal or school for, as he said, bastards who cannot do as they are told or behave themselves.

The matron broke into saying, "Firstly, we do not use that language here, young man, secondly, we look after boys who have been unwell, thirdly, we build them up again, make them well again."

So, I replied, "But I am not ill anymore, why should I have been brought here then?"

Matron then replied, "Oh yes, you were very ill about a year ago, so you have been placed here to complete your recovery."

I could not control myself, I just broke down in tears, sobbing my heart out in relief, trying to say, "I am not a bad boy then."

Taking my little suitcase from me, Mrs Partington showed me to what was to be my bed space. I was given a little bedside locker for my personal things, which were not very much at the time. She helped me unpack what I had brought along with me, then lay out my pyjamas on my pillow.

After this I was taken back down to the headmaster's study where I was confronted by the 'old man' who was being rather loud and trying to stamp his authority. I had to stand and listen to a lecture from him telling me what I could do and what I was not able to do, until Mr Bevis interrupted him, saying, "It's now my job to see that Kenneth understands what is required of him while in my care."

At this point, the 'old man' lost his temper with the headmaster, telling him to keep out of his business. The headmaster asked him to be shown to the door by a little squat man with dark balding hair, starting to go grey at the edges, wearing a pinstriped suit. He turned out to be the secretary of the school, a Mr Murch. He tried to show the old man the old man lost it again. Mrs Bevis said something like, "What a totally rude man."

At first, he kept arguing with the headmaster, then Mr Murch stood between the 'old man' and the headmaster's desk, saying, "Please follow me, Mr Cutts," pointing towards the door. He was shown out to the secretary's office.

After a few minutes the old man had calmed down a bit and was allowed back into the headmaster's study, when I had to say goodbye to Mother (to my recognition, it was not as loving as it might have been, *or should have been*). When it came to the 'old man', I just stepped back, pulling away from him. The headmaster then said, "Now Kenneth, young man, at this school we shake hands and say thank you as all gentlemen do." I was made to shake the 'old man's' hand and say thank you to the bastard who had now got his own way in getting rid of me.

I must say, it did not take me too much time to settle into the daily routine of the school. I must admit I did not feel homesick at all, not really too much of a hardship as I had been away from home now on and off for up to four maybe five years now, getting quite hardened to it by now, so I was quite used to it. What did come a little hard for me was the schooling, as I was now about two years behind in my school studies. However, the routine was quite strict but very fair. I would not say that it was exactly paradise but it was absolute heaven to lie asleep, knowing I did not have to listen to the ranting and raving, the drunken clumsy footsteps of the 'old man' climbing the stairs to drag me from my bed and thrash me for no reason, just for his pleasure and gratification. The food was not a bit like Mother made, but I soon got used to that too. There were early morning calls, about 6:30am, to get up, wash, get dressed and get your dormitory cleaned before breakfast. I was now settled in with 39 other boys of my own age.

I began researching Sunnydown. During 2009 at the Surrey History Centre in Woking. When going through some of the documentation, I came across a register of all the names of the boys, who were at the school at the same time as me, next to each entry was a parent's contact details with names and addresses. On inspection of the list, lo and behold, I came across an entry of a Ken Chandler (not that of *Kenny Cutts)*. Next to the entry for the contact there was a blank space, no details at all for me. It was only a couple years after I had left Sunnydown that I was told that my name was indeed Chandler and not Cutts. So why did my mother keep this from me? And why didn't the school authorities tell me earlier? To carry on calling me Cutts when they knew I was a Chandler is mind boggling.

The school had two 'houses', Swallows and Hawks. I myself was placed in the Swallows. Aach house had a house master. Swallows' was Mr Hartley for a short while as he left not long after I came to the school to be replaced by Mr Hughes. Hawks' house master was a gentleman by the name of Mr Chester, a very large man, said to be an ex-Royal Marine captain, could have been true. A head boy was placed in charge of each house as 'house prefect' with an assistant each, who were house 'captains', and there was an overall head boy, Colin Beckford, or head prefect of the school.

I was placed in a dormitory with three other boys. There was Michael 'Spud' Sullivan, Sidney 'it hurts' Payne – both were suffering from asthma. Michael 'the professor' Beecham, who was handicapped all down his left side, but to make up for this he was so extremely brainy. It did not take me long to make friends with him plus the others in my dormitory. The proof proved to be a godsend when it came to extra school work, like maths. He was a wizard with homework, especially when it came to examination revision. There were 40 boys in all when I arrived but later the numbers were increased by two to 42. Mainly boys suffering from various chest problems such as asthma or other breathing difficulties. I was so skinny, built like a racing snake, and placed on a special diet of plenty of full fat milk, at least a whole pint a day, lots of malt extract to build me up, having to take two tablespoons of the sticky stuff a day, one in the morning, another in the evening. Now look at me, I have extreme trouble in trying to keep the weight off.

John RAWLINGS, 73, Lion Lane, Haslemere, Surrey.

Douglas RUMBOL, 4A, High Street, Redhill, Surrey.

Archie BROWN, 41, The Homesteads, W   Green, Normandy.

Charles Winter, M 'C' Svala, Weybridge Marine, Thames Street, Weybridge

Alan Hare, 49, High Street, Carshalton.

Robt.STANBRIDGE, 4 Wandle Road, Hackbridge.

Ken CHANDLER,

David BALL, Oak Park, Alton Lane, Four Marks, Alton, Hants.

Raymond RADWELL, 42, Hawden Road, West Ewell.

Richard Radford, 30, Carshalton Place, Carshalton

John EVES, 26, Huston Avenue, Surbiton.

Ian WOOD, XXXXXXXXXXXXXXXXXXXXXXXXXXXXXXXXXXXXXX 4, Brrook Close Rochford Essex

Christopher BEWLEY, 211, The Greenway Epsom, Sy.

Chris BINTON, Littlethorpe, Furze Hill, Kingswood Sy.

Part of the Register showing my name without any address or contact details.

107

CHAPTER 15

SUNNYDOWN BOARDING SCHOOL COOK – MEALS AND OUTING POINTS

The food was basic and often quite bland, with such dishes as potato cheese (one of my favourites), cheese with this, cheese with that, or corned beef, fried, boiled or mashed potatoes, bakewell tart or bread and butter pudding for sweet, but I survived. The dining room was set out like a small restaurant of about eight or nine tables, where five or six boys would be assigned to each, one of the boys from each would be the 'duty boy' for that table and would serve such things as drinks, or hand out the bread and butter, and sometimes looked after the toast. To get your food, each table in turn got up and formed a line at the serving hatch, after all the staff had been served the same food by the maids or kitchen staff. Two favourite dishes were potato cheese and corned beef hash (bully beef).

The suggested one week's menu for Residential School for Senior Children (Calories Approx., 2700 Total Protein 100 grams. Per day

MENUS

BREAKFAST

Mon   =   Bacon.

Tues   =   Poached eggs on toast.

Wed   =   Bacon and tomato.

Thurs   =   Bacon and fried banana.

Fri   =   Scrambled egg on toast.

Sat   =   Bacon and egg.

Sun   =   Boiled egg.

Daily =   Cereal or porridge with milk. Wholemeal bread or toast, marmalade or honey. Tea.

MID MORNING. Daily = Milk and bun.

DINNER

Mon   =   Braised steak, carrot, parsley, boiled potatoes. Rhubarb sponge and custard.

Tues   =   Boiled ham salad, jacket potatoes. Canadian gingerbread and maple syrup sauce.

Wed   =   Steak and kidney pie, spring greens, cream potatoes. Stewed apples and custard.

Thurs =   Liver and onions, peas, boiled potatoes. Lemon meringue pie.

Fri   =   Russian fish pie, grilled tomatoes, creamed potatoes. Semolina and rosehip syrup.

Sat   =   Hot Pot Cabbage, Chocolate Gâteaux,

Sun   =   Roast lamb, mint sauce, roast potatoes, spring greens. Pineapple flan and custard.

HIGH TEA

Mon   =   Rice and cheese scuffle, green salad, brown sauce.

Tues   =   Meat cake, tomatoes. Fruit cake.

Wed   =   Scotch egg and salad. Queen cake.

Thurs =   Stuffed tomatoes on toast, cheese scones.

Fri   =   Cheese stuffed potatoes, watercress. Date and walnut loaf.

Sat   =   Sausages and chips, coconut cookies.

Sun   =   Soused herrings and salad. Cherry cake.

Daily =   Brown or white bread and butter, jam, honey or Marmite. Fresh fruit. Tea.

BED TIME = Milk.

Cook had many and varied recipes, but none would turn up on the plate quite as often as these ones.

Burnie's recipe for sponge for 40 people.
2½lbs.= Flour, 1¼lbs.= Margarine, 1 lb.= Sugar, 2 oz =Baking Powder 8 oz. = Dried egg
To Vary: Add 12 oz., cocoa + extra ¼lb sugar or vanilla essence or 1 lb dates, figs or mixed fruit or 3 lbs marmalade or 6 ozs of ginger and 2 ozs mixed spices.
This sponge can either be baked or steamed. For baking plain sponge – when cool, spread top with jam, syrup, lemon curd or marmalade.

Fish custard (for 4/5 settings).
2/3 fillets, 3 eggs, ½ pint milk (approx.), salt and pepper.
Method. Grease casserole dish, put in raw fish, beat eggs and milk together, season and pour over the fish. Bake in a moderate oven for ¾ to 1 hour.

Other such menus were used like one I found in the archives in Woking:

SCHOOL MEALS SERVICE

Recipe of the Month

Coconut Tart – 100 portions short crust pastry with 4½ lb. flour, 4 lb Jam. FILLING: 2¾ lb. margarine, 2¾ lb. caster sugar, 12 eggs, 3½ lb. coconut, 1lb. flour, 1 pint water.

Make the pastry, line shallow tins and spread with jam. To make the filling cream margarine and sugar, add the eggs and beat well. Stir in the coconut and flour and sufficient water to make a spreading consistency. Bake in a moderate oven until lightly brown on top and the pastry is cooked through.

Prunes would often appear, mainly at breakfast. Sometimes we would have steak pie, braised mutton (not lamb), savoury mince.

Cornish pasties and fish cakes did appear from time to time. To gain any privileges at the school, particularly for the weekends, such as being able to go out on Saturday afternoon outing into town or Sunday afternoons out with parents or relatives (which never happened for me the whole time I was at Sunnydown), a points system was in place. You had to work, doing various tasks. This could be domestic chores, like washing floors, helping in the kitchens, doing the washing and wiping up, helping a teacher with some odd job, doing your school work correctly. We did not get homework because we were not going home, but we did get what was called 'house work' – school work to be done outside of normal working hours, which you might call 'prep'. You could also have points deducted just as quick if not quicker than when earning them.

Each boy was issued a weekly white card, which you had to carry on your person at all times unless you were playing sports, so that the staff could deduct points for a misdemeanour or to give you a bonus point or two. At the end of the week, you had to have reached a certain total depending on your age or standing within the school. Each 'house' also had to gain a minimum point as decreed by the headmaster or house masters. After Saturday morning clean up and inspection, all pupils had to assemble in the assembly hall to first find out if you had passed the Saturday morning inspection or not, whether you had to clean your particular cleaning station again or not. There were three-week periods or rotas where we had special tasks or jobs which had to be done; these were rotated after every period. During the week, one had to earn one's 'freedom' for the Saturday and on Sunday following church parade.

During the week, we had to earn a set total of marks depending on your age, or if you had a 'disability', (being placed on the sick list) you could also earn bonus points. I found the best way to do this was to offer to do the domestic jobs for the lovely young maids (well they were a lot older than us but I fell in love with one of them in particular, Shelia, she was a lovely girl of late teens or early 20s with bright ginger hair) but not all of them were so nice, I certainly had my favourites. This meant doing the washing up and wiping the dishes, or scrubbing a floor or two. These bonus points went towards your house marks. Depending on whether he had received the correct number of points meant different amounts of time you were allowed out; the system was a bit complicated, but you soon got used to it. If your house had gained the most overall points, you had even greater privileges. A pupil who failed to gain the required points would not be allowed out at all, he was classed or called a 'criminal' and had to undergo extra work and work harder the next week. Everywhere you went you were called a criminal, gaining the wrath of all his other house mates, or got a beasting or beating from the head boy of that house. This did happen to me on more than one occasion. If your house had won the week's contest, you were allowed to go out as soon as the assembly had finished around 11am, remaining out until 9pm, plus you got a cake for Sunday tea. Then if you were in the losing house you would start your leave at 1pm, back by 7pm.

Before anyone was allowed out, the third and best part of the Saturday morning ritual took place. Pocket money or pay day. This was sent in by your parents (and 'banked' if your parents sent it in). In my case, I did not get much, in fact I got nothing from my parents at all, but did get pocket money of sorts. Where it came from, I am not sure). This was also carried out in stages: age, bonus points earnt, or again your standing within the school. Also, 'criminals' could have their pocket money deducted depending on how bad they were, some of us could be classed as bad. The television came into the equation, so if you did not want to go out, you could maybe watch television. This could mean the same as if going out, how long you were allowed to watch depended on your marks tally at the end of week.

Every Sunday morning meant church parade, after breakfast and the cleaning of your dormitory. Everyone except Roman Catholics had to fall in outside the main entrance to the school and march in twos in all weathers down to the village, to Compton Church about two or three miles away. On our arrival at the church, all the boys had to stand on the edge of the pathway facing inwards while the local village parishioners entered the church. Some of us were made to sing in the choir. I tried the old chestnut one week soon after joining Sunnydown in an attempt to get out of marching down to Compton Church, by saying I was Roman Catholic. Unfortunately this did not work as the staff knew everyone's religion – only cost me deducted points and a 'criminal' that week. The Roman Catholics had to go down into Guildford for their church service in a minibus.

On our return march from our morning's worship, around 12:30 pm, those who had parents or relatives who might be visiting the school would be able to spend time with them, or spend time around the school. Those of us left (I never had a visit from any relative, for the whole two-and-a-half years at Sunnydown) would be allowed out into the local countryside, left to get up to all sorts of mischief, it was great fun.

While at Sunnydown, we were encouraged to partake in all sports, freedom at last from the restrictions that were placed on me after my illness. I could run, join in anything I wanted to do, or told to do, it was part of our upbringing and being 'built up'. It was not long before I became fit again. I found other sports like cricket, football and of course hockey. I could now play at the same level as the others of my age. We were actually encouraged to play games. Most afternoons were set aside for these activities.

CHAPTER 16

FINDING CRICKET, INTER-DISTRICT SCHOOLS FOOTBALL COMPETITION

I found that I was not only allowed but was encouraged to play cricket, by accident really. Why? Because I thought it to be too slow and a boring old game. This was due to the fact of not knowing anything about the game, or how to play it; I just thought all you had to do was stand in front of these three sticks while someone else threw a hard ball at you and you had to try to hit this hard ball.

One day I was pushed into it by one of the teachers, Mr Cheshire, housemaster of the Hawks, who was not very sporting himself, a rather large bespectacled gentleman. His attitude was that you must do it or else you will be letting the side down. It was not long after the order was given for me to take part that it became my turn to bat. I took up position, in front of the stumps. Not taking a guard (did not know what a guard was or what it was for at this stage), the first couple of balls were bowled down at me. I swung my bat as hard as I could at the ball, but it missed by miles.

Mr Hartley, who was housemaster of the Swallows and also a cricket coach, moved towards me saying, "You have not got a clue, have you, boy." He took the bat out of my hand, stood me to one side, showing me how to hold the bat, how to stand, made a few forward strokes telling and showing me and the rest of the class how important it was to keep a straight bat and the follow through the line of the ball, keep your head still and get it over the ball, always watch the ball from the bowler's hand, follow it right onto the bat. Not easy by any means. What a lot to do. First of all, keep a straight bat, follow through the ball, get your head over the ball, how the hell do you do that? And keep your head still, watch the ball coming from the bowler onto your bat; I thought, that's all right for you, 'Gunga Din'. Well, I was given the bat back and told, "Now do it properly." Do it properly was his order, you had to obey or else.

First ball came down, yes, I watched it from the bowler's hand straight back past my bat, hitting me hard on my leg, even with the old style of pads on it bloody well hurt. Well, I did as he had told me, next ball down. Was my bat straight? Before I had thought about how my bat was, it came again and I missed it, played straight like I was told but still missed. "Try again," was the teacher's comment. "Watch the ball out of his hand." Yes, I know, I had already done that and it hurt.

Next ball, I decided, right I'll watch the ball but I'll go and meet it. I stepped out of my crease (at the time I did not know what a crease was), took a pace or two, with a straight bat, and whacked it! The ball went off the bat with a crack, stinging my hands and went over the boundary for four, the master had not told us anything of a bat stinging your hands. He said, "That's nearly the right way to do it." What does he mean, 'nearly the way'? I had done what he had asked of me. "Now do it again."

The sports period went on for the rest of the afternoon, stopping from time to time to repick sides. Just having fun, I found that I really enjoyed playing it, in fact I was hooked. Having hit the ball hard on a number of occasions, the stinging in the hands, I started to get used to it. I had a bat and bowl, which again came to me pretty quickly, by no means fast, just slow plodders and fielding a little.

We were lucky enough to have a sports master who not only knew his job but could also spot potential in a person, then coach them to do it right. At Mr Hartley's suggestion, I joined his after-school cricket club as he called it, where we would have more time to practice in the nets. Mr Hartley left the school soon after setting up his 'cricket club', which was taken over by Mr Hughes, who was as equally as enthusiastic. We had a lovely sports ground, and a separate football pitch, cut into the hill on which the school stood, a lovely flat pitch, then below this was a very nice hockey pitch, with an excellent cricket pitch with nets to practice in. When the weather was good about a dozen of us would go down the hill to the sports ground after school to the nets, often Mr Hughes would be there coaching, he helped me a lot.

As time went on, near to the end of my two-and-a-half-year stay at Sunnydown, I found myself in the school cricket team, normally batting at number four or five in the batting line up, sometimes as opening bat but not that often. I did bowl a little from time to time, I liken it to spin bowling, but with my stubby fingers I could not make the ball spin that well, so I really turned out to be a slow to medium bowler, nothing fast. We played quite a few matches with other schools or boys teams from local schools and clubs, sometimes winning a few but mostly enjoying the game.

My only claim to fame in the sport of cricket at this tender age was during the annual school prize-giving day, in the mid-summer, where parents and the board of governors would be paraded. The highlight of the day (a Sunday) was a cricket match, boys versus the parents/old boys, followed by the actual prize-giving. This particular year was 1956. When Surrey County Cricket Club had their Guildford week, one of the Surrey County Cricket players, Peter May, the captain of Surrey, who were doing very well in the County Cricket Championships, was invited as guest for the annual prize-giving. He accepted, bringing with him three or four of the playing staff of the Surrey team to present these prizes.

The prize-giving was always followed by the annual cricket match between boys versus parents and old boys. The parents and old boys had won handsomely as they always did. After, the Surrey cricketers, instead taking their leave of the school, stayed to put on a bit of an exhibition, Peter May along with the younger players of the Surrey squad, a young Ken Barrington, Tony Lock, and Peter Loader. They suggested that a little exhibition cricket match be played. They would put a ten-shilling note (50p – a lot of money in those days) on the stumps, each time one of us boys took their wicket, we pocketed the extra ten shillings. I came away with having bowled both Tony Lock and Peter Loader once each (others did it too), but not only that. I, like several others, also scored a number of runs against them – 20 to 30. A very good day was had by all.

A few days after, towards the end of summer term, the headmaster, a really old-fashioned Victorian type of headmaster, Mr Frank Bevis, sent for me and four other boys. 'Spud' Sullivan, Terry Lincer and his brother 'Johnny', and Bob Collins. I thought, *Hell, what have we done now? I have not been caught smoking, or bunking off lessons.* The only time you normally went to the headmaster's study was if you were in trouble or your parents were in the school. That would never happen as far as I was concerned. We were lined up outside the head's study by 'old Murchy', the little bald-headed, round-faced school secretary. We were all asked to go into his study together.

Mr Bevis said, "Be at ease, there is nothing to be afraid of, just relax, boys."

There was another gentleman sitting opposite the head's desk. All smart in his pinstriped suit, he was introduced to us by name. It now escapes me but it turned out he was on the Surrey County Cricket youth coaching team and had been with the guests of our prize-giving. He was looking out for youngsters for their Surrey Colts or Young Amateurs team, as they were known then, and he was at the school to invite us to go along to the Oval Cricket Ground for a day to partake in a few trials.

The next weekend off we went with Mr Murch (again), him driving the school Bedford Dormobile to the Oval. When we arrived we were met by a number of other young cricketers dressed in their 'whites', we were shown to a large dressing room, which was full of other boys from other schools, mostly private schools and other boarding schools. There must have been more than 50 boys all crowded into just this one room. We were put through our paces with a lot of other boys of our age from all over Surrey. As things happened, I did not make the grade but the two Lincer twins from our school did make it, but I do not know what happened to them, they were extremely good at all sports, especially football.

The outcome from this day's work was that I and two others from school were invited to join the 'Colts Classes' to get coaching through and from the Surrey and Guildford Cricket Club staff from time to time down at the Guildford Cricket Club, which proved very useful later on in my life.

As doctors said I needed building up, I was on the final road to recovery. I slowly but surely worked my way back to normal health. After a time, being a great relief to me, I was allowed to partake in sports once again as already mentioned. One of the greatest thrills of my life was to put on a pair of brand new 'real' football boots. My parents could not afford to buy them, so who had sent them to the school for me? It was put to me by the headmaster, Mr Bevis, that they had been sent by my fairy godmother. To this day, I do not truly know who she was but I am pretty sure it was that lovely lady of Red Leys, 'Mummy Martin'. Those boots, as I remember them, had dark brown toe caps, hard as a rock, with light brown uppers, which covered high on your ankles. When you put them on you felt as if you had two clubbed feet, toe caps were hard as concrete. With layered leather, nailed in studs, when wearing these boots, it was like putting on a pair of ice skates (not like the slippers now worn by the professional players and footballers of today). You were not able to keep your footing on the tiled dressing room floors. After every game we had to clean our boots thoroughly and apply this horrible thick dubbing.

Back to playing football. This time I was tried at right back (some people would say right back behind the goal). I was not keen on the right back position, I preferred to be like Stanley Matthews (I had his style of boots) flashing down the wing, but I was not built for that sort of speed. Some bright spark during one of the games suggested I go in goal as there were not the players who were very good at goalkeeping. I was prepared to throw myself around a bit, so the job became mine. After a season of matches, I got a little fitter and the hang of this goalkeeping. Apparently, I wasn't too bad at it, being picked for the school first team at the age of 12, but it did not last.

We were in the Guildford and District School's Knock-out Cup Competition, quarter finals, playing another local school team from Compton at home. Sunnydown were firm favourites, we had beaten them twice during the season, along with Stoke Rovers, Onslow School, and Shackleton Primary School. We were out to win the cup for the second year running. It was November of that year. Why did I not last? Well, it was like this. One of my dormitory mates, John Reed, had some couple of weeks earlier been rushed to St. Luke's Hospital in Guildford wit appendicitis, which he had removed. Having spent two weeks in hospital, he chose the day of the match to return to the school. Who did he come to see on his return? Yes, that's right, me. I was at the time doing very well with my team of keeping Compton out, until one slack moment while play was up the other end of the pitch, which was near to the end of the match. It was Sunnydown (2)-Compton (1) with a few minutes left, the Lincer brothers had scored a goal each. John Reed, not satisfied in telling me all the gory details, had to show me the scar. He pulled up his jump so that all around could see his scar.

I can picture it now, me, leaning on the goal post oblivious to what was going on at the other end of the pitch, totally engrossed in this scar. Suddenly, everyone was shouting my name. I turned to see what all the fuss was about; too late, the ball was in the back of my net. Oops! Scores levelled, two all, the incident put me right off my game, having been set upon by the whole of my team for not paying attention. The headmaster on the halfway line was having an apoplectic fit. To cap it all, in the last seconds, I lost my nerve following the first incident and rushed out of my goal line, bringing their number nine down, giving away a penalty awarded by our sports master, Mr Hughes, who was the referee. We lost. Sunnydown (2)-Compton (3). That meant we were knocked out in the quarter finals, and did not even reach the final.

I was dropped. I never did play for the school team again. For a few weeks that followed I had the mickey taken out of me, something chronic, sometimes even being pushed around a little as it was my fault that we had lost the match. In fact, I lost all interest in playing football. Well, for a little while anyway. Instead, my interests began in supporting Portsmouth City FC (Pompey).

I also learnt how to play hockey after receiving tuition from the sports master. I became very proficient at it, playing for the school team when a fixture could be arranged. Far better than playing in goal at football, my position as it was in those days, was at inside right. As stated earlier, my interest in soccer now turned to being a spectator. So after the school Saturday ritual, six or more of us, with a member of the staff, normally the school secretary Mr Murch, ex-Royal Marine bandsman, if we had gained the required marks, we would rush around to get ready in our 'Sunday best'. It certainly helped a lot if you were in the winning house for that week, so a little strategy came into the equation into the final score. For if 'Pompey' were at home that week, you worked even harder to get top marks to get away earlier; it did not really matter if they were playing away.

Mr Murch would organise a visit to Fratton Park to watch Portsmouth if they were at home. So on the Saturday following assembly, if you were within the winning house, you would rush around frantically trying to get ready in your best clothes. We would gather together those who were going to Portsmouth and catch the bus down to Guildford railway station, and catch the fast train to Fratton Park. The great 'Pompey' as they were then, well maybe on the wane a little after their great run in the early- and mid-50s, but they always had large crowds, they are the team I have supported up to the present day.

CHAPTER 17

ANIMALS, PETS, BOWS AND ARROWS, AIR GUNS

Sunnydown had other things going for it. I found it to be a very friendly school, and nearly everyone got on with everyone else. They had quite a few farm animals, such as a small pig farm, three goats, a pigeon loft or dove cote, rabbits and other small mammals, all of which needed looking after. We all took it in turns to do the jobs of looking after them, these are some of the tasks we had to undertake to gain marks for the end-of-week total.

I normally got the goats to look after, they were the big white type, very placid really. I only got butted once, which did hurt. I was cleaning out one of the pens and bent down, turning my back on the billy, Snowy, wrong thing to do. Wallop, he had me full on the backside, only because I was not giving him the affection he was used too. I had paid the price for not greeting him properly. I had gone in to let them out into their paddock, forgetting to close the door behind me, without stroking and making a fuss of him.

I also had a long stint at looking after the white fantail pigeons in their loft, watching them breed, laying eggs and hatching them. I looked after the squabs (young birds), feeding them. We also had a number of racing pigeons and other varieties such as red checkereds.

Another pastime of ours was to climb the trees around Sunnydown, often staying up in the trees for most of the day, especially on weekends when we did not go out. I also learnt how to make bows, arrows, French arrows and 'pug sticks' out of hazel wood, which we would use for two or three things such as hunting birds or playing 'cowboys and Indians' for real. The French arrows were fired by a single length of string with a knot in one end. I would pass the string around the shaft of the French arrow, pulling it as tight as possible then throw it like a spear; it used to go for miles. The pug sticks were used to launch a round plug of clay, which you stuck to the end of the pug stick, flicking it hard and it would act like a catapult.

We managed to get hold of a couple of old air rifles and an old Webley air pistol which would take small dart-type ammo. The Webley air pistols were so old that when you pulled the barrel forward to cock, then slammed it down again, it would go off without pulling the trigger. These 'weapons' were smuggled into the school by boys returning from the school holidays, and were hidden in the ground of the school in some of the chalk caves, which had been dug out in the woods of the hill. These caves were not big enough to hold more than one boy who would have to stay on his stomach. Other weapons which we made were catapults out of the hazel trees, the rubber or elastic was purchased from a shop in the high street of Guildford on one of the trips out on your own.

Playing 'cowboys and Indians' for real could be a bit dangerous as you did not know where the weapon was pointing; anyone could have lost an eye or two. One or two came very close to it. We used to pick sides, the 'cowboys' had the air guns, the 'Indians' had bows and arrows. Off we would go, the Indians into the woods to be found by the cowboys and have a battle. Those who had the air rifle would actually shoot at you, at first just pulling the barrels as if to load them, then fire them without placing any slugs up the barrel. This would make the sound of a slug or air leaving the barrel.

This soon got boring, so to spice up the 'games', on one afternoon when allowed out into Guildford, a few of us pooled our pocket money to buy a few tins of .177 pellets and some of the darts which had feathers to help in their flight. The air guns were hidden while not being used in a chalk cave which we had found within the ground and enlarged for our own purposes. I cannot believe that we were never ever found out while I was at the school, but the matron did get a little concerned with the number of 'accidents' which needed treatment.

One afternoon during the weekend, a gang of us went down in the woods, picking those to be the 'cowboys' and those to be 'Indians'. I became an Indian, and off we went to lay our ambush. The cowboys counted up to 100 before they could start out after us. I managed on this day to climb a large tree, bow in hand with a quiver of arrows and sat ready for the cowboy's posse to come and find us. I sat there waiting to catch one of the 'cowboys' who I could hear approaching, bow drawn. Then, thud, I got hit around the left breast with one of the dart pellets, it went through my shirt. I screamed out that I had been hit, nearly falling out of the tree. On reaching the ground, blood had formed on my shirt, everyone was in a panic, what should we do now, there I was with a hole in my shirt and blood coming out. One of the older or more senior boys, Collinson, shouted for us to calm down, taking a pen knife out of his pocket. He undid my shirt, saying we've got to get the pellet out, so he told two other boys to hold me still while he got the knife and literally dug the little dart out. Boy, did I scream. Well, it was back to school and quickly with my handkerchief stuck over the wound, leaving me with a little scar. I then reported to the matron, saying I fell over or something like that, or that I climbed a tree and slipped and fell on a stick.

We never at any time while I was at Sunnydown got caught with the weapons, we hid them. For all I know, they may still be hidden in the wood, or in one of the chalk caves that we dug out of the hillside. On another occasion, one pellet entered my forehead just above the hairline (now receded) and another went in the second joint of my right index finger. What we had to do if we got injured was to dig out the pellets with a pen knife. The bows and arrows could be just as dangerous, as we used to make them into sharp points. I remember a boy called Kerslake who met one of my arrows with his nose, went straight through the other side, and that took a lot of explaining to the matron. Did she believe us? I don't think so. We used to have battles with 'pug stick', a long straight hazel stick, very whippy. We used to make ammo for them out of balls of clay, stick them on the top of the stick, then throw them, they didn't half go a long way.

There was a large hay barn at the bottom of the hill, on the same level as our sports ground. Sunnydown House was on the top of this hill, part of the Hog's Back, with very large grounds, which stretched for about half a mile to the bottom of the farthest sports ground. The large barn was where all the hay was kept for the animals. It had a pitched roof, and on the front it had a flat roof or shelter or overhang, made out of corrugated iron sheets. We used to climb a tree which was overhanging the pitch roof, transfer to the top of the roof then slide down as if doing ski jumping. By spreading out the hay we tried to see who could travel the farthest, great fun until someone actually fell through, cutting their leg. I had one or two scrapes.

How we never set the hay alight I'll never know, because this turned out to be a lovely smoking den. Oh yes, a number of the older boys did smoke, which in turn led to us trying it and getting hooked. We didn't go behind the bike shed, there wasn't one, ours was the hay barn. It was also a great place to meet some of the local girls, as it was situated right next to the public footpath which leads down to the village of Compton.

CHAPTER 18

SCHOOL OUTINGS

I still had a great interest in aircraft of all sorts. During 1955, a lot of boys were asked if they might like to go to the Farnborough Air Show and I was one of them. One of the best sights I have ever seen was the Black Arrows, a formation of 22 (yes 22 in number) Hawker Hunters, painted black (doing what the Red Arrows do today), 16 of them flying in this large diamond formation. They were joined by another six aircraft doing loops, changing shapes. Also, a lovely sight was two white Vulcan Bombers, flying with four or six Fairey Delta 1s, they called it the 'mother hens with her chicks'.

It was also during this time that I got really interested in the wildlife around the place. I learnt how to identify lots of birds. We would often stray onto a farmer's land, mostly on purpose I might say, one or two of the farmers would at first chase us off but after a while we got talking to them. Then they in turn would invite us onto the farms to help pick soft fruits and to help in cutting the hay and the corn in the summer months.

While at Sunnydown we had lots of things going on, like concerts. We actually had Slim Whitman, the singer, and Bert Weedon, the guitar player, come to the school to give a concert. These were great nights normally around Christmas time. Often we had trips out to the Farnborough Air Show, to Portsmouth Navy Days, or school trips to Portsmouth just to see the Royal Naval ships, or Southampton to see the great ocean liners. I remember the whole school going to the Odeon in Guildford to see Kenneth More in *Reach for the Sky* and other historical films such as *Richard III* and *Henry V*. In 1955 the whole school was taken to the Royal Tournament at Earls Court, a great spectacle for young men.

During June of 1956, a number of us went on a trip to HMS *Mercury* (signal school) to see the sailors learning Morse code. We had a go at sending a message to each other, after which we were taken to lunch in their canteen where we sat down to fish and chips. After lunch back, to the coach for a further trip to Portsmouth dockyard.

We had a visit to HMS *Victory* to be shown where Lord Nelson had met his death by being shot on the upper deck, then taken below decks to see where he actually died. When this finished, we were shown around the battleship HMS *Vanguard*. Two or three (Spud Murphy, Bob Starkey and myself) broke away from the main party who were being shown around the ship. We needed to see how the engines worked, so off we went down a few ladders (stairways) going lower and lower, trying to find the engine room. We were found by this sailor far down in the ship looking around the mighty engine room, who took us by the arm and returned us back to the upper deck. Then it was on to see the cruisers HMS *Swiftsure*, *Cleopatra* and *Dido*. Then back to Sunnydown.

During the '50s, Guildford Cathedral had still to be completed, still a lot of work until it was finished. All of those who visited the cathedral had their name put onto a brick, this was on the 12th March 1956. Somewhere within the cathedral is a brick with the name of Kenny Cutts.

There was this particular gamekeeper, Joe, who caught us looking for partridge and pheasant eggs. He took a very dim view of this, taking us back to the school and complaining that we were upsetting his game birds. Having been told off by the headmaster, and the field we had been caught in being placed out of bounds, several of us took it upon ourselves to go out onto his land again. Having been approached once again by him, we started talking to him and he got interested in us. We got invited to a pheasant shoot as beaters. What a great day that was; wet through, but very good fun, even the teacher who came along with us enjoyed himself. We actually went out one night with Joe the gamekeeper, with the consent of the headmaster, shooting rabbits from his Land Rover, catching them in his headlight, or the beam of a very bright torch. Bang, you're dead, 'Mr Wabbit'.

CHAPTER 19

OUTBREAK OF GERMAN MEASLES AND VERRUCAS

There was an outbreak of German measles within the school, and me being me, I did not get it until most of the other members of the school had been clear of the illness. So when I eventually caught it, I was put into a dormitory on my own and had to stay in bed isolated from the rest of school. All my meals were brought in by the Sister and my class work had to be done on my own in the dorm.

I found I could entertain myself, having made a catapult earlier, prior to falling sick. I kept it under a short loose floorboard, under my bedside locker, with a couple of large bags of marbles – very good ammo for a catapult. I would open the window which overlooked the front lawn of the school (not a weed in the grass, it was immaculate thanks to Mr Brown, the gardener), the swimming pool, and a very good view of the rest of the grounds. It also overlooked a very small enclosed courtyard, where there was a glass enclosed passage, or corridor, with a pitched roof, which joined to the classrooms and the dining hall.

I would take a shot at whatever turned out to be a good target; I would try to hit it with a marble. I got to be quite a good shot at using a catapult. One lunchtime I saw a wood pigeon near our dovecot. Wood pigeons do not mix with prize fantails. In my rush to hit the pigeon, I failed to hold the catapult tightly, pulling back in my haste, I let go of the leather pouch with marble in it. Wallop, the marble hit my thumb, the catapult flew out of my hand, clearing the enclosed courtyard, clearing the pitched roof. It went over the enclosed glass passageway, clearing the flower beds, landing on the edge of the newly mowed lawn, in full view of the dining room, which had everyone sitting down for high tea. Did anyone see my weapon landing on the grass or not?

Oh my God! I thought, or words to that effect. If the catapult was found by any of the staff, there would most certainly be an investigation into whose catapult it was, restrictions or other punishments would be put onto fellow boys and if found to be mine, I would be for a very high jump, maybe so high I would not come down. *What should I do, I must get the catapult back, but how?* I toyed with several ways of trying to retrieve my weapon, there was no other way than to go and get it by the same way as it had got onto the lawn.

So I climbed out onto the window ledge on the first floor, I was young and I was fearless of even falling, trying very hard to see if anyone else was about, such as a teacher, but they were all sitting down to their high tea. Then, leaning across a gap of about two to three feet to a drain pipe, I shimmied down it, to the next to the window (ground floor), then down into the enclosed courtyard, Now if anyone had seen me, I would be trapped with no other way out. Other than through a picture window into the corridor. Still, I had not been seen so now I had to get over the passageway, nothing else to do but to climb up another drain pipe, onto the pitched roof of the corridor/passageway, slide down the other side of the pitched roof. I found another drain pipe in the corner, which took me down onto the flower beds in front of the lawn. My position now was right in the corner where two parts of the building joined, but it was a blind corner if I stayed still. The flower bed could be seen from the dining room windows, so I had to stay very low to the ground by lying on my stomach and keep as low as possible, crawl under the windowsill for a couple of yards, grab my catapult, turn around, returning by the way that I had come. I was hoping to hell no one had seen me.

I managed to get back up the drain pipe in the blind corner, over the pitched roof, back down into the courtyard. I was a little out of breath so took a little rest to get my breath back, then started to climb the drain pipes back up to my dorm window. Luckily, I caught sight of a head of fair hair. Blimey, the sister who was looking for me as I could not be found in my bed, she had already checked the toilets. *What do I do now?* I thought the young brainwaves started to work overtime. If anyone else had seen me doing my covert climb all hell would have been taking place, but everything was quiet, so I jammed the catapult out of sight, behind the drain pipe, trying to stay out of her sight, hoping she would go away and look for me elsewhere.

No such luck. As it was a little dusty on the drain pipe, a little dust got up my nose, as she turned to walk away from the window, I could not hold off a sneeze, which slipped out, echoing around the courtyard. Looking out of the open window, and to one side, she saw me holding onto the drain pipe. I could hear her foot tapping on the bare wooden polished floor, arms folded across her large (lovely) chest, breathing deeply, her face becoming a bright purple colour. Christ, I was in for it now, I have to think quickly again, what was I doing on the drain pipe...

I pulled myself onto the windowsill, swung my legs in, and jumped onto the floor, saying, "Oh! That's better, poor little bird."

She said, "What the bloody hell do you think you are doing, what do you mean 'that's better, poor little bird'?"

Sorry, miss, there was this great tit, got caught up in the wire up there on the roof, just below the gutter above my window, it was making a lot of noise so I had to rescue it, so I climbed up there." I pointed to the guttering on the opposite side to where I had hidden the catapult.

"Where is it now then?" she asked

"I saved it and let it loose, it flew off."

Sister was gobsmacked, lost for words for a few moments. After composing herself, she let fly at me. "What the hell do you think you were up too, that was a very dangerous thing to do, you could have fallen and lucky you were not killed, now get yourself to the bathroom and wash your face and hands, get cleaned up, and change your pyjamas, we'll say nothing more about it, for if the head finds out you will be for the high jump."

"Thank you, miss," was my reply, nearly fainting with fear, my knees and legs felt like jelly about what she might do.

On my return from the bathroom, she put me back to bed, giving me a little kiss on my forehead, saying that it was a very brave thing to do. I'll never forget that little moment, someone had shown me a little affection, she was a smasher, even to an 11-year-old, lovely body, later to marry one of the masters and leave the school.

During my stay at Sunnydown, I was to come under the care of the Sister a number of times. A watch was obviously put on me because of my record of illness a couple years earlier. While at the boarding school, I came out in the dreaded acne, I was covered from head to foot. One day I came out in boils all over the back of my neck and on the back of my legs behind the knees, ten on my neck, seven on the back of one knee, 11 on the back of the other leg, a very painful period for me. It got so bad I was actually admitted to Guildford General Hospital, situated on the Farnham Road, by the railway station (not there today). The worst treatment was for me to have hot poultices placed on the affected areas, very, very painful but did the trick in the end. I do not think I have ever had another boil since. Part of the treatment was to take a medicine, which was called a blood mixture, to help clean the blood, or so it should have done. It may have been because by the time I left Sunnydown, the acne had all cleared up; to have this treatment I had to visit the Sister's surgery every day.

There was one occasion where nearly all the boys at one time went through an epidemic of verrucas, obviously caught in the open tiled floor of the shower room or the swimming pool area. So we had these people from the council medical team come along and treated the whole area. It never occurred again while I was at the school. However, my plight was that both of my feet were infected, like at least six of the other boys. I had 11 of the blighters on the left foot and nine on the right (yes, believe me, I did have that number). Again, a very painful affair which went on for many weeks, no sport, no swimming, no showers. The treatment for these in those days was not as easy as it is today. First, they tried burning them out with an acid type of fluid, by little drops being dabbed on by the Sister, which turned them black, hurting like hell; you could hardly walk with the pain. That did not work, so we (I say we, there were about six other boys who were badly affected or as bad as I was) had to visit St. Luke Hospital in Guildford to see a specialist who treated them with something akin to a soldering iron, but this had a fine red hot needle on the end. He tried to pick out the verrucas, as if taking out a splinter, hell, it was so painful. After this treatment we had to walk back to the minibus, the pain was out of this world, which stayed for a number of days. This did not work either. So it was back to the hospital, same consultant, with his sidekicks fussing around us. Then one of them suggested they be frozen off. Thoughts went through our minds about what they were going to do with us next, put us in a big freezer? No, what they did was to place a phial, taken from a nitrogen gas container, which formed a cloud of mist when opened, then they placed the phial on each verruca, leaving it to get very cold. Again this was very, very painful to start with.

I remember them having to wait for quite a time for each spot treated to form into a blister, then the doctor would come along with a scalpel and cut around the skin of the blister, then with twisters would pull on the skin which he had just cut, and out popped the verruca, roots and all. It was amazing to see how much was under the skin of each one, leaving a nice clean round hole. Painful for a few days after, but I never had another visit from a verruca ever again. Maybe because I was now so aware of how one came into contact with them, I must have taken much more care of my feet.

Another stupid thing we used to get up to was to play 'chicken', on a bridge, which was just outside the main gates of Sunnydown. It carried the Hog's Back or A31 and it crossed the A3. Rather high, with concrete struts, we tried to see how many times we could climb across a ledge on the outside of the bridge without falling (thankfully nobody ever did fall, if they had they would have most likely been killed) or we used to hide high up in the bridge struts and just sit above the traffic. Sometimes we were caught by the police because someone had accidentally dropped something down on the cars below. If one did get caught, you knew you would get six of the best from the headmaster.

CHAPTER 20

SUMMER HOLIDAYS, SHEEPHATCH OR STAYING AT SCHOOL

(TIME TO LEAVE SUNNYDOWN. 'WHAT IS TO BE DONE WITH ME NOW?' AUSTRALIA)

Oh yes, then there were the various school holidays, Christmas, Easter, long summer holidays and half terms. We got half a day off school at half term, to be increased to a whole day off where most of the boys went home to their parents during their holidays. I would often stay at Sunnydown, especially during the long summer, only going home for a few days. While on my first holiday, I went home catching the train from Guildford to Dorking, a good old steam train. I loved, as everyone did, to lean out of the window, letting the wind through your hair until a hot piece of soot got you in the eye. Arriving at Dorking Town Station (now Dorking West), I got off the train, looking up and down the platform but there was nobody there to meet me, so I walked all the way from the station to Chart Downs carrying my suitcase. When I arrived home, I was first greeted by Freddie who was in the garden playing. Janet had been sent back to her foster parents, the 'Lushes' in Leatherhead.

The next person I saw was the 'old man' who greeted me with, "What the bloody hell are you doing here, you've escaped, you've run away, I am phoning the police." He took off his belt. "I'll teach you a bloody lesson not to run away again." Grabbing the collar of my shirt with his left hand, laying into me with his belt in his right. Mother was not in. So, I left, dropping my case where I stood and off I went once again, across Holmwood Common to where Auntie Hilda lived in Vine Cottage. I told her

132

what had happened, that no one was around to meet me, so I walked home to be confronted by him. I gave her the full story in floods of tears.

I stayed with her that afternoon, then Auntie Hilda accompanied by Peter, Valerie and Michael, went round to my grandmother's. I spent the rest of that holiday with Gran and Grandad; Mother had been informed by the school to expect me home for the holiday period. She knew exactly the details of my coming home. Apparently, she saw my suitcase and went a bit mad at him; it did not help me in any way. All I wanted to do was to get away from him.

From then on, I would only go home for short stays, because the school actually shut down on most of the holiday periods. The next time I came home, Mother and the old man had moved from Chart Downs, to Stubbs Hill on the new Goodwyns Estate, having swapped houses with my Uncle Don and Aunty Marg. It was a nice place; I thought it was much better than Chart Downs. Unfortunately, nothing changed in his attitude towards me.

However, going back to Sunnydown was now always looked forward too, sometimes I would come home for a weekend, but life was made hell for me. The air that I breathed, he owned, the chair I sat in was his, the ground I walked on was his also. I could not sneeze or cough in his presence for fear of him saying, "If you cough once again, I'll send you back as being ill and passing on your foul disease you brought home with you." It got so bad that when the holiday periods came around, I literally refused to go home, I could not bring myself to get ready to go home, so social services were asked to get involved again. During the Christmas and Easter holidays, I stayed at my grandparents' house, either going back to school earlier or before the holidays were to finish, always traveling on my own, aged between ten years old and 11.

Come the summer holidays, which lasted six lovely weeks, a place was found for me to go to; 'Sheephatch' Boarding School, situated out in the countryside at Tilford, a village near Farnham in Surrey. It was a large school, laid out like an army barracks, long wooden huts, with bunk beds on either side of the huts. The dining room was one of these long huts, with long tables with long

benches to sit on. Sheephatch housed hundreds of children, so
when their summer term came to an end, the residents had all
gone home on their long summer holiday. We, the like-minded
children from Inner London and children in care were sent there
for their summer holiday. Six weeks of adventures, freedom, and
activities, to be looked after by a band of happy volunteers who
enjoyed our company. When the summer holidays arrived, I was
sent home to Dorking, where the next day, Mother had to make
arrangements to get me to meet a coach in Guildford, which took
me onto Sheephatch.

There was every activity imaginable, a large swimming pool,
numerous sports playing fields; we were allowed to do almost
anything we wished to do, as long as there was a member of the
volunteer staff with us. We used to go out to Frensham Ponds for
swimming, or long walks all around the heath. I went there two
years running and had the time of my life. I even became a member
of a skiffle group. I played the base which was made out of an old
tea chest, with a broom handle through the middle with a string
attached which you plucked to the rhythm of the music. Singing
the latest Lonnie Donnigan songs in the hit parade.

Mother and the 'old git' did not remain long in Stubs Hill
before moving to The Oaks, still on Goodwyns, near to the shop.
A ground floor flat, because the old man had trouble going
upstairs. Pity he didn't fall down on them. I was made to return to
my parents on a number of occasions by social services. When I
sat down to eat at the table, he would watch everything that went
into my mouth, cursing every mouthful. I remember once, Mother
gave me a piece of toast which had butter and jam on it, he
jumped up, slapped her across the face, grabbed the slice of toast
out of my hand, which she had presented to me, he then scraped
all the butter and jam from it. Then he picked up a used tea towel,
wiped the toast with the tea cloth, then stuffed it painfully into my
mouth. "Now eat it." He turned to Mother. "Don't you ever give
him 'my' butter and jam ever again."

So I always had bread and little jam, I mean a little jam spread
on it, no butter or margarine. I was lucky if I got some 'dripping'
of fat from the roast the previous weekend, under this dripping

normally formed a 'jelly' which was very tasty, if there was any sign of the jelly with my dripping on my toast, he would snatch it back, either throw it away, or eat it himself. He was an animal, and tried treating me as one.

It was at this address that one time I came home with a very bad cough and cold, which I dreaded because I knew he would not let up on me. I just could not stop coughing. Do you know what the bastard did, put a gag over my mouth, sent me to my bedroom and locked me in? Yes, he locked me in with a key. I was to remain there until, as he put it, I could control or stop coughing. I could not get out, or so he thought. He had even thought of the windows, by screwing them up so that they could not be opened, but the silly old sod forgot the small window, the one at the top, thinking it was too small for me to get out of, little did he know. So I climbed out, first throwing all my belongings that I could onto the grass outside, squeezed through that little window, climbed out onto the ledge, jumped down onto the grass, collecting up all my things, legged it around the corner to my Auntie Hilda's place, which was now 16 Glory Mead on the estate. Auntie Hilda put me up for the night, me sleeping on the floor in Peter's room. The next day it was arranged for me to go back to Sunnydown early. Do you know that bastard never even knew that I had got out, until Auntie Hilda went around to see Mother and told her later the following day after I had left to return to the school? This happened again later in my life, he did not learn.

So I got to stay at Sunnydown. I enjoyed staying behind on holidays, there were about six of us lads with similar home lives, who like me would rather stay behind as we got treated like kings, compared to my experiences at 'home'. Even Mummy Martin got to hear that I was still having trouble on my holidays, so she invited me to spend a few of the holidays at Red Leys. Now they were good times. I was given a little chalet to live in, with the young female staff and I with some of the older boys had some fun playing the top records of the day, Elvis, Cliff Richards, etc. with the girls who worked at Red Leys, who were a little older but very nice to me. I fell madly in love with one of them, Dawn, she was a young lady a few years older than myself who was employed by social services or Mummy Martin to look after the very young children. She was accommodated in the next chalet to me. Dawn eventually left Red Leys soon after and moved down to the village of Wolverton near to Kingsclere.

I was soon to leave Sunnydown, towards the end of 1956. My social worker, Miss Wright from Epsom, had sent for me sometime around September 1956 to find out 'what I wanted to do with my life' after Sunnydown. Miss Wright had said I was to be given an option to go to a sheep farm in Australia. This would mean leaving England for good, possibly never to see any of my family or England again. I did for a short time think about how nice it would be to leave these shores for good and go to a new life 'down under'. I would be taken to Liverpool, put on an ocean liner and have this wonderful boat trip to the other side of the world. My mother had indicated I might like to be given the chance of going to Australia. When she asked me if I would like to work on a farm, I said yes to the question, thinking of a farm near Dorking or at least in this country. No, what she was about was to join this sheep farm in Australia for good. Do you believe that, to be put on a ship at Liverpool and sent out to work on a farm at the tender age of 13? It would be like going to Sunnydown; I would still go to classes to finish my schooling, and live in houses with staff/ teachers to look after me. It was put to me that I would love working with the animals.

Having had a lot of time to think things through, anyway I did not much like the idea, but there was the thought of a nice hot country, working with animals, but I would not be coming back home to Dorking anymore. I did not give an immediate answer to her question, I was told to think about what Miss Wright had said. I would be going to see a film somewhere in Surrey about life on a sheep farm in Oz, with a lot of other children from various schools from London and the home Counties.

Before this happened, on one of my Saturdays out, I took a journey down to Guildford Railway Station and took the train a short way to Wanborough. There I got off and walked down Glaziers Lane to Red Leys and told 'Mummy Martin' what had been said, and asked what I should do. 'Mummy Martin' gave me all of her time that afternoon. We had a long talk, she gave me some very sound advice, and one or two options, telling me I should stay at school and do a lot of catching up as I had lost a lot of school time having been ill. However, 'Mummy Martin' went down the line that, as she had known me for quite some time, I liked the sea and ships. If I was interested, she could find out about me joining a training ship, rather than going to Australia if I did not want to. That evening she drove me back to Sunnydown, only a short distance of about five or six miles by car.

In the meantime, I remained at Sunnydown until the end of the year, but not before I got another visit from Miss Wright. She once again tried to get me to go to Australia, however, 'Mummy Martin' had obviously got in touch with Miss Wright and my mother, and they had agreed that if I would say I wished to join a training ship, then the Australian idea would be dropped. I agreed. I had to first take an entrance examination to join a training ship or nautical boarding school. Well, true to form, I failed the entrance examination. Once again, I was threatened with Australia. What did I do but run off again? Yes, I was so upset that I ran away ('escaped') one evening from Sunnydown because I thought I was so bad for failing the examination. They were going to send me away, so off I went to Red Leys. 'Mummy Martin' once again came to the rescue, she obviously contacted the school to let them know where I was, we had another long chat, still not yet 13. Anyway, the outcome was that Mummy Martin came and collected me every time I was now allowed out.

'Mummy Martin' had somehow got hold of the examination papers for the *Arethusa* training ship. We went through the questions time after time until it was impossible for me to fail. I sat the next entrance examination, passed not with flying colours, but by enough for me to be accepted. Meanwhile, while waiting for my joining date for the *Arethusa*, I was sent for by the headmaster of Sunnydown, who had a large brown envelope in his hand. It was the papers for my transit to Australia. I was to go and prepare myself to travel to Liverpool by train where I was to meet up with other children from all over the country, for a six-week passage to Sydney. After a few days I was instructed by the matron to pack a small suitcase, which had to be labelled, and a label was to be fixed to the collar of my coat. I also had endured a course of injections against different tropical illnesses. I expressed my feelings towards my social worker, my mother, 'Mummy Martin' and the headmaster, for going back on what had been agreed, that I was to join the *Arethusa* training ship situated at Upnor, near Rochester in Kent. But this episode was proved to be wrong in that the communication had broken down slightly, the instruction to go to Liverpool to join a ship for passage to Australia had 'crossed in the post', so all was well in the end.

Unbeknown to me, 'Mummy Martin' was still working hard to keep me in this country, she must have pulled a few strings somewhere along the line. I received a date to join the training ship *Arethusa*. I could not believe it, she did this and got a result just two days before I was to join all those poor children in Liverpool. What timing, enough for me to be accepted. Boy, I loved that woman of Red Leys.

At the Christmas holidays of 1956, I left 'Sunnydown'. I was now an old boy but still not quite 13. I went home for Christmas with the 'old man', Mother, brother Freddie, and sister Janet at The Oaks Oakridge, one of the worst Christmases I have ever had. All presents I had received were taken away from me by you know who, that bastard, as he would say you won't need that where you are going. Christmas 1956 gone, the new year arrived, but I could not go back to Sunnydown as I had now left, so I begged my Auntie Hilda if I could stay with her, but the 'old man' came around, accused her of taking me away from his family. So I had to stay with him and Mother until I was to join the *Arethusa* towards the end of February 1957. Life was so very miserable then. I was thinking I should have got on that ship out of Liverpool for Sydney, Australia.

I was now 13 years old so I had to go to school while waiting to go to the *Arethusa*, so I was back to Sondes Place for a very short time. The school was not too bad, I started to enjoy it, something new. When school had finished for the day you went home, something I had not done for two-and-a-half years, my home was the school.

Things did not change at home, I was cursed day after day by the 'old man' on everything that I tried to do. For anything on the table, I had to wait until everyone else had got what they wanted, yes, believe me it is true. Mother seemed to do nothing much to help in my situation. Her version may have been a little different, she hardly ever stood up for me, she was so very scared of the 'old man'. He had such a hold on her, but why? I even tried to get on his good side by doing jobs for him, but alas this did not work. He had blinkers on and would not recognise anything, just bullied me incessantly.

One day I got to the *Daily Mirror* before he had read it. Holy Christ, you would have thought I had robbed the bank of England. Once again, I was locked into my bedroom until the morning, this time he had screwed all the windows shut, he had said to keep out the burglars. I could not find anything like a screwdriver, so stayed locked up this time. I soon learnt what to do with the *Daily Mirror* or *News of the World,* his favourite papers. If I read them first, I would set up the iron, a heavy thing, which had to be put onto the gas cooker ring to get it hot, we could not afford an electric one, then I would iron the papers flat again 'as if new'. Nothing got past that git, I still used to get a belting from him still. One day I threw the iron at him, hoping to hit him but missed, thank God, or who knows where I would have landed up.

I was allowed out to play with some of the lads on the new estate as there was only Goodwyns Road, Oak Ridge Flats, all the buildings were on one side of each road, down to Stubs Hill, again only one side was built, and the other was that of Glory Mead. Talk about mud, there was mud everywhere, you could not help but get muddy if you were out playing, especially with the other boys on the new estate. We did have some fun running about the 'new' buildings until being run off by one of the workmen. Our other stomping ground was up in the Glory Woods, climbing trees. All this led to yet another good hiding because I had to be in by 7:30 in the evenings, but leaving as late as I could to get in, the inevitable would happen. Some of my so-called friends, both boys and girls, used to crouch down under our front room window to listen to him laying into me.

Once on my return to Sunnydown before I actually left for good, I got called into the headmaster's office, where I was told the police had been in touch to say that a number of buildings on Goodwyns had been damaged overnight, and that my name had been given as being one of the boys who had committed the offence. Luckily for me, on this occasion I had been back at Sunnydown for some weeks and it had nothing to do with me. As the headmaster said, "How could it have been Kenny Cutts, he's been in our care for up to six weeks prior to the events in question."

This happened several times while I was on the *Arethusa*, and even when I was in the Royal Navy – my name would be mentioned in investigations into petty crime in or around Dorking. Obviously, it was not me as I could prove exactly where I was. It did become a bit of a nuisance, I kept being named when I was not there and could prove it, so when I did return home, it made me more aware of where I went and who I was with.

The history of the emigration of children started soon after World War Two. For two years no ships were made available to take migrant children to Australia. Meanwhile, social changes meant that few British children were available for child migration. Youth migration to Australia was much more popular. However, the Dreadnought Scheme did not survive the war. In 1947, the first post-World War Two child migrants arrived in Australia. The majority was placed in Western Australian institutions and about half now came under Catholic auspices. Big Brother Movement, New South Wales and Tasmania, renewed its youth migration to Australia and during the 1950s brought some 400 young men per year, 15 to 18 years of age, to Australia. Overall, some 12,500 teenagers were sent to Australia under this scheme since its inception in 1925.

In 1952, John Moss, retired Home Office inspector and member of the Curtis Committee, toured Australian child care institutions. In general, Moss remained sympathetic to child migration for certain deprived British children. In 1956, the Home Office Fact-Finding Committee visited Australia to study Australian institutions taking child migrants as the Commonwealth

Settlement Act was due for renewal the following year. The Committee's SECRET report to the Home Office was very critical of some Australian institutions and cold to the whole idea of child emigration. British Catholic care institutions terminated all plans to send further children to Australia. But children from other social services were getting much younger, deprived children were still being sent to Australia. In 1957, the Commonwealth Settlement Act was renewed by the British Parliament, but few child migrants still arrived in Australia, although small numbers arrived under Barnardo's and Fairbridge auspices. In all, some 3500 to 4000 migrants were sent to Australia during this period. In 1967, the last nine child migrants were sent to Australia by air with the Barnardo's organisation. In 1973, the New Labour Government ended preference for British migrants to Australia.

Oh, happy days at Sunnydown. The life at this Special Boarding School for Delicate and Physically Handicapped Children did what it said. I left there very much better off, health wise, with a lot of 'brothers' in the same situation as me. I had been built up enough to take on the next chapter of my life.

CHAPTER 21

LIFE ON BOARD ARETHUSA

I was known for the majority of my time on board as boy Kenny CUTTS 207, 21 mess, quarterdeck starboard, from February 1957 to September 1959. Life on board the *Arethusa* was harsh, beastly, sometimes humiliating, often humorous, most of the time happy. I was to find out what real *discipline* meant.

The two years, seven months that I spent there was all of the above. The reasons why I was sent to the '*Are*' are still not clear to me. I do believe that my stepfather (the pig), Charles Francis Frederick (the bastard) Cutts, hated me so much. Mind you, the feeling was mutual, if I could have killed him myself, I would have done during my time with him. I had a couple of goes. Luckily, I was very unsuccessful in that respect. Another reason could be that my mother could not manage to look after me, or maybe, in their eyes, my behaviour was that of an out-of-control child. The 'old man' often said that he would have me sent to borstal. Or my mother put me on the *Are* to get me away from him; I would like to think the latter was the real reason.

However, towards the end of February 1957, with a little brown attaché case given to me by Grandfather in my hand, with all that I owned in the world within it, Mother and I arrived at 164 Shaftesbury Avenue, London, WC2. Big blue imposing doors; we went up to the second floor, where we were greeted by civilian staff who tried to make us feel welcome. After a few minutes we were shown to another room where, sitting at a large mahogany desk, was a rather large gentleman in naval uniform with two and half rings on his sleeve – a lieutenant commander. I cannot remember who he was but he may have been a Mr Townsend, the second officer of *Arethusa*. In the same room I think there were four other boys sitting near to the desk with their guardians/

parents, plus another boy dressed in uniform with lots of badges on his jacket or top, looking very smart. Again, I am not sure but I believe that this smart boy was none other than Petty Officer Boy Gutteridge (he later became the Chief Petty Officer Boy, gold badges and all). I was not the last to arrive, a couple of boys came in after me and I wish I could remember their names, but alas I cannot for the life of me.

At last, the final boy arrived which made our little lot up to its final number. When we were all present and correct, the first thing we had was a medical examination followed by an interview with the first officer who told us the routine of what we were going to do. All this information went straight over my head, a bit too much to take in at the time, telling our parents what was expected of us, and what the parents could expect from the *Arethusa* in return. He spelt out a few dos and don'ts. We were given light refreshments. Then we had to go singly to another office where the first officer again asked us one-to-one questions. What did we as young 'gentlemen' wish to do, go in the Royal Navy or the Merchant? I can recall I wanted to be a steward on the Cunard liner *Queen Mary* or *Queen Elizabeth* as they were the biggest and best ships on the sea at that time Mother's idea was far different from mine. "Oh no you're not, your grandfather wants you to go into the Royal Navy." The way she phased the answer, made me wonder why she had said it like that. So that was that; Royal Navy for me.

My grandfather had done all he could to encourage me to join the Royal Navy. He had been in the Royal from the start of the First World War and joined at the outbreak, aged 27. His first training was on HMS *Vivid* during 1914. He himself had served right through the First World War, at Jutland and in the Falklands. He served on HMS *Iron Duke*, HMS *Benbow*, and HMS *Valiant* – all battleships – as a stoker, specialising in steam turbines. A very hard life. A very proud man.

I had, while at Sunnydown, visited Portsmouth Navy Days several times, having tours around a couple of cruisers like HMS *Cleopatra, Dido,* and *Swiftsure,* and other small destroyers, which were tied up forward of the battleship HMS *Vanguard*. There was no doubt in my mind about what I wanted to do when I grew up, and that was to go to sea.

Well, after a while, we said our goodbyes to our parents at Shaftesbury Avenue. After they had gone, Pete Guttridge took charge of us. I cannot say what he said to us, I am sure it was something quite horrible like 'do as you're told from now on or else', or words to that effect. Off we marched, somehow arriving at Charing Cross Station and boarded a train, which took us part way along the Thames where you could see the ships working, then on down through the Kent countryside until we arrived at Strood Railway Station. Some form of transport conveyed us to the village of Upnor.

In 1932, the training ship *Arethusa,* lying off Greenhithe in the Thames, was condemned. She had been moored there for 60 years and previous to this she had seen 20 years as a 50-gun frigate in the Royal Navy. It was during this time that she became famous as the last wooden warship to go into action entirely under sail. When under the command of Captain WR Mends, she bombarded the forts at Odessa in April 1854.

The Shaftesbury Homes and *Arethusa* training ship, to which she then belonged, were faced with the problem of finding a suitable ship to replace her when they heard of the four-masted barque, *Peking,* being up for sale. Negotiations were begun, and the ship was purchased and brought back to England for just under £7000. On top of this, the cost of converting and equipping her for training purposes came to over £15,000. Renamed the *Arethusa,* she was then moored off Upnor in the River Medway where she continued the excellent work of turning out a splendid type of lad for the Royal Navy and the Merchant service.

It is interesting to recall that the Shaftesbury Homes and *Arethusa* training ship was originally founded in 1843 by a young solicitor's clerk, William Williams. He was so appalled by the sight of youngsters being deported to penal settlements that he devoted all of his spare time and money to forming a ragged school to keep slum children out of mischief, and his first establishment was in a cow shed in Streatham Street in London.

CHAPTER 22

ARRIVAL AT UPNOR AND NEW ROUTINES

There we got our first sight of this big, I mean big (to us anyway), black and white sailing ship, big, tall yellowish masts sticking up into the sky. There she was anchored out in the middle of this big river, the Medway.

The ship was a four-masted barque. This vessel was built at Hamburg in 1911, of steel, and was one of the famous German Flying 'P' fleet, employed mainly on the South American to Hamburg nitrate trade. She was a fine ship, and her dimensions were 322 feet long, with a beam of 47 feet and she had a gross tonnage of 3,191 tons.

When we finally arrived on the foreshore, she looked huge. To get on board her, we had to pass through an arch, with the word 'ARETHUSA' in brass at the top of the arch. At either side of the arch were two field guns. We had to walk across this very long causeway. As I recall it was very cold, in fact it was sleeting or snowing, the wind was blowing down the river. So you can imagine the sight, this band of motley little boys, heads down fighting the wind and sleet, thinking, *What have I let myself in for?* Once we got to the end of the narrow causeway, you came across the ship's brow, or gangway. The tide was in so it was quite a steep climb to get on board. PO Boy Guttridge went first, stood on the top of the brow, eyes left and saluted. He then instructed us on what to do. As we stepped off the brow, he ordered us to look over our left shoulder in the direction of what we later learned was the quarter deck. This is a Royal Naval custom; you always salute the ship's quarterdeck when entering or leaving a ship, if you did not have a cap on then you would salute by smartly turning your head towards the quarter deck. Wearing a cap, you saluted in the proper manner.

We were met under the beady eyes of Lieutenant 'Ferdie' Farrington, the second officer, he had two rings on his sleeve. He greeted us, having a few harsh words for us. A tall man (couldn't call him a gentleman at the time) and he was immaculately dressed. He wore long shiny black gaiters. His boots were just as shiny. A frightening sight of a man who immediately told us that we were the 'sorriest-looking bunch he had ever set eyes on or who had ever joined the *Arethusa*'. Apparently, that was his welcoming speech to all new boys.

Reality set in rather very quickly, as the vast strangeness became apparent. I had survived what discipline was thrown at me during my time in the children's home and at boarding school, so as far as being homesick, that did not matter at all to me. In fact, I was once more very glad to get away from my 'old man'.

On that very cold overcast day, snow in the air at the end of February, we were all issued with new uniforms. We were shown how to dress correctly in those itchy new clothes, but I felt a million dollars. As one of our groups had spent time in the Sea Cadets, he spent time showing us how to wear our uniforms correctly.

All of us new recruits were then met by a load of other young faces, eager to greet us by shouting, "Hallo, nozzer," as new boys were called. They all wanted to know where we came from.

"Where yer from? Anybody from Birmingham? Any Brummies?" was heard.

Another voice shouted, "You'll be sorry! They've got yer now."

Some of the 'old timers' were trying to find out if they had any 'townies' (a person who came from the same town as them) amongst this new intake.

The first thing on the agenda was to be introduced to the first officer. We were also soon to learn that Ferdie Farrington rarely found anything, or anyone, 'up to the mark'. We soon learnt to keep out of his way when he was on the war path with his persuader, 'Herbert' or 'Herbie' (which was a length of black electrical flex approximately 18 inches long), or one could find themselves receiving the end of it across the back of your legs. Soon we were shown down below to the regulating office where we had to turn over all our pocket money to the officer in charge who then recorded the amount in a ledger. I personally did not have very much money on me at all. It would be doled out after Saturday clean ship and captain's rounds. Pay day; given just enough to buy your toothpaste and maybe a few nutty bars (sweets or chocolate). The petty officer boy shouted out to us all, "Stand still, pay attention to the Chief Petty Officer." At this point he turned to the chief petty officer boy and said, "New intake present and correct."

We were then told or detailed to our divisions and mess decks. A chief petty officer boy (I think he was Matysiak) would call out our names. You had to step smartly one pace forward, as the petty officer boy had instructed us, give your name back in return as acknowledgement, standing to attention. My turn came.

"Kenneth Cutts."

"Yer."

Stepping forward, I thought I had done it smartly, just as the others before me had done. I did not realise that when a leading boy or upwards told you to 'stand still' during any type of muster, he meant completely still, you did not move a muscle.

"What do you mean 'yer'?" was his answer. "Answer properly; 'yes, sir'. Cutts."

"Yes, sir."

"Your number is 207, your mess will be 21 mess, your division will be quarter deck starboard, and your divisional officer is Mr Fuller. Follow your petty officer boy (again, I cannot remember who he was, possibly Mahe). He'll show you your mess."

We had arrived just in time for evening dinner, well meal anyway. I was quite hungry. I was placed at the top of the table, next to the leading boy (name escapes me), he sat at the end of the table. Then the most senior boy of the mess would sit next to him and so on down the table, until you reached the bottom, where the mess 'nozzer' would sit. On this first occasion, the new boy sat at the top. The leading boy introduced me to my fellow messmates. Then the questions started to flow: how old was I, what you were sent to the *Are* for, where you from, got a 'muvver and farver'.

The food arrived by way of the 'duty cooks' of the mess, carrying a number of aluminium trays of cheese and potato pie, runny spaghetti, a slice of bread each and margarine. I was given mine first, served up on a shiny aluminium plate; I thought at the time this plate looks like a mirror, it was so shiny. I was given a white enamelled mug, filled with what turned out to be called 'gnats', which it certainly was, a very weak tea. At the time it was needed as we had travelled down from London without any refreshments. I was so hungry, but the taste of the spaghetti, well that was something I had not tasted before, it had a sort of diesel taste to it. Having been used to eating meals that had been bulk-cooked, having just come from Sunnydown Boarding School, the food was more or less on the same lines. Cheese and potato pie were a favourite at Sunnydown as well.

I was soon to learn the reason for the 'senior' boy of the mess sitting at the top of the table. He got first pickings of the food, and then so on as the food was passed down the table, until finally the 'nozzer' or new boy got what was left. More often than not, it was not enough but that was the rules. You would only move up the mess when one of your messmates either got made up to be the leading boy, or he left the ship, so everyone eventually got to become head of the mess deck, and got first pickings. This system worked with all meals but at least as time went on, we all became 'top enders' then we got the big shares.

.After the evening meal, we 'new' boys had to muster again outside the regulating office. We were then taken down to the tailor's shop and kitted out with more clothing, some washing gear, toothpaste, pyjamas, our clothing, more uniforms, shoe-cleaning material, towels (two), gym gear, a comb, and all the other bits and pieces that would, for a long time, be all of our worldly possessions.

We were moved onto another compartment near to the tailor's shop and given our hammocks, a rough blanket, a thin mattress and a very lumpy pillow. 'Sproggy Mayne' 209 was detailed to be my nurse or winger or 'sea daddy' who showed me what to do with it, how I was to make it up, ready to be slept in. Where and how I should 'sling it'. The hammock is made of canvas. Before this happened, you had to be shown where and how to 'sling the hammock' by securing one end lanyard to the inner hammock bar overhead so that the ends of the nettles hang at the level of your chest. Pass the other end lanyard to the outer hammock bar. Then distribute the bedding evenly over the length of the hammock and tighten up the slack nettles, if necessary (still with me?) The hammock should always be tied well up to the 'deck-head' (ceiling) to allow passageway below. Hammocks should never be slung in a gangway. Once I had mastered this part of making up a hammock, once done properly, it stayed made up so you would not have to go through all that routine again, unless you had to replace or wash your hammock.

I was shown to my locker space; it was right down in the bowels of the ship, right arft, where the sides met the keel, so it was like standing on a steep slope. Below the 'tiller flat'. The lockers were about two by two by two feet, you could not get much in there, but somehow we managed to stow all our kit and personal effects inside them. I was given a quick tour around the ship, shown the various places I could go, and where I could not.

"Oh, by the way do you smoke, got any fags on yer?" was my guide's next question.

I replied that yes, I did smoke, but not much, but no I did not have any cigarettes on me. Then I was told to be careful to not get caught smoking. The punishment for doing it was bad!

CHAPTER 23

SHOWER TIME – TURNING IN

Then we were instructed to 'fall in' forward of the mess deck outside the communal shower, dressed in only a towel wrapped around our shivering bodies for toothpaste inspection, and woe betide any boy who didn't have toothpaste! We had to remove our towels and march into the showers. The sight of naked young bodies, I had never seen the like of it before, not on this scale anyway while at Sunnydown. But what did surprise me was the number of boys' buttocks which were covered in raised angry red welts, most of which were the handiwork of the second officer's 'Herbert'.

The water was not exactly hot, more like lukewarm if you were very lucky, or even cold – remember this was late February. Showering over, we had to then get dried, then parade in front of the duty officer to be inspected before being ordered to get into our pyjamas, fall in back at our messes, to our hammocks, and made sure we paid a last visit to the heads (toilets), then turn in before last post.

Then came the time to turn in. I was to hear the Last Post sounded on a bugle for the first time. Wherever you were, you had to stop what you were doing (if not already in your 'mick') and stand to attention until the Last Post had finished. Lights out, no talking, silence except for the occasional soft footsteps of the night watchman doing his patrol, telling those who were whispering to 'keep silent'. This was the very first time I was to sleep in a hammock and what a strange experience that was, not only to get in and out of the blessed thing, but one soon got used to it.

The next day, shock horror, 'call the hand', 'reveille' (there goes that noisy bugle again), whatever you wanted to call it, 'Charlie', 'lash up and stow'. It always came at 0600, some

Sundays, depending who was 'officer of the day', you might get a 'lie in' until 0630 or 0645. One had to jump out of our 'mick', get dressed in shorts and shirt. I started to put on my pair of shoes but my 'winger' quickly told me to take them off.

"We do not wear shoes during the day."

"But it's bloody cold out there!"

"No, take them off."

Everyone was only allowed to wear any type of footwear – boots or shoes – on a Sunday or when going ashore. But, as I found out, that was not always true. Footwear was only worn when you were told, if there was a parade or you had to visit someone or go to a place away from the ship then footwear was worn.

Everyone had to quickly muster for a wash, the washroom being the farthest away from my sleeping area. They were situated right up in the bows of the ship. Two rows of metal sinks, 240 boys had to wash and shave. Yes, I did say shave, you did whether you needed to or not, in a matter of minutes. If you were one of the last to the washroom, unlucky the water was now stone cold. Then quickly we returned to our sleeping billet to make up our hammock in the correct manner. You were shown once, the next time you had to do it yourself correctly. Woe betide you if you had to be shown again.

To lash up a hammock, first you had to distribute the bedding evenly over the length of the hammock leaving a space of about six inches at each end, to prevent bedding sticking out of the ends when it is lashed. Lower the hammock until it is about breast high, and stand on the left side facing the head. Take the coiled lashing from the head nettles of the hammock, adjust the first turn around the head of the hammock, and draw it taut. The succeeding turns are taken as follows (now stay with it, you may learn something; all this I had to do myself on the first day). Coil the lashing up and pass it up and over the hammock with the right hand and bring it under the hammock into the left hand, then over its own standing part and haul taut by swinging back on it; this hitch is called a 'marline hitch'. Six turns are taken in this manner. The seventh and final turn is taken round the neck of the hammock

151

at the foot and is secured on its own part by a half-hitch; the end is then passed neatly along the hammock under each turn. The clews are stowed by twisting the nettles round right-handed and tucking them with their lanyards under the turns of lashing along the hammock, should look like a trusted-up sausage, if done properly, really tight, could act as a life buoy if needed.

Then back to our mess-deck table, with a long bench either side of it. After the little interlude of breakfast, once again I was put at the top of the table, just for this one last time. It often consisted of a slice of bread (or a 'slicky'), a little bit of margarine (or 'slide' in the shape of a flower), accompanied by a dollop of jam with it on the odd occasions, a slice of bacon, fried to a frazzle, or an overcooked sausage (small).

At the instruction of our petty officer boy, accompanied by my 'winger', we had to get our hammocks down. Strip the hammock down and learn how to put it all back together again, how to lash it up and how and where to stow it, in the correct netting. Then we had to do it all over again, making sure that it was extremely tight this time, the correct number of turns and hitches, nothing hanging out, a nice tight bundle.

The biggest shock was to follow. The officer of the day and the duty petty officer boy's next orders to the new boys was to fall in up on the foredeck (where was the foredeck? What did that mean to us 'new boys'?). What, in this weather? Dressed in only your shirt and shorts, nothing on your feet? In the snow and ice on the deck? I thought, *You must be joking*. Nobody was joking, it was for real, and it was freezing, absolutely bloody cold below, let alone up in the open air where the temperature was below freezing point. Ice and snow lying on the deck.

The duty officer ordered the Petty Officer boy to show us how we should climb the mast (funny thing, he had his boots on) then one at a time we had to climb the mast dressed only in flimsy blue shorts and a blue No.8 shirt, no footwear of any kind. We had to go up and touch the first platform then come down again. I thought to myself, *They must be mad*. I was all for climbing trees and other things, in good weather, but this was madness. I took a look up, this was to be higher than anything I had climbed. I had more than butterflies in my stomach, it must have been a herd of elephants running around. This was a bit scary to say the least, the ratlines (steps or rungs) were covered in ice and were a nightmare. When it was my turn, I managed it after a while. I was not only shivering with cold but with fear. Many poor frozen boys had to be brought down, not only frozen with cold but frozen with fear. The instructing petty officer boy made no secret of the fact he resented losing his free time to guide us through this stage of our induction into training ship life.

After having gone through the routine as I have described, we had to return to our mess, clean our ship station, then it was quickly inspected all before 0845 hours so that you could be properly dressed in the dress of the day, fell in on the main deck, ready for 0900 colours. This was when the flag of the ship would be hoisted, followed by a short prayer from the padre (just like assembly in schools but a lot more discipline). The first time I witnessed this daily ritual, all the 'new boys' had to fall in at the rear of the main companion ladder housing as we had not yet been shown how to fall in, stand to attention, or march.

The next thing on the agenda, the duty petty officer boy took us to visit the ship's barber. We were all lined up on a bench to receive a training ship haircut. It could not be described as a hairdressing, but more 'it's all coming off, like it, or not'. We literally got scalped. Talk about the 39 steps, that is what the back of your head looked like from behind.

The duty petty officer boy proceeded with a tour of the ship, accompanied with dire warnings about what would happen to us if we were ever caught 'out of bounds'. Then we were shown where the 'heads' (toilets) and washing facilities were and told when we were allowed to use them. There was not much privacy in the heads, cold wooden seats, not much of a door, anyone could watch you going about your business. Nothing to protect you from the very cold wind whistling down from the upper deck.

Much of the first day was spent in how to do this, how not to do that, you can go here, but not there. The chief petty officer boy and petty officer boy's quarters were out of bounds, unless called for (mainly to be punished). You needed to be given permission to enter.

Before going to or being 'turned in' that night, it was shower time. I had no problem there, having just come from boarding school. Got undressed, got my piece of hard soap in one hand, toothbrush with paste in the other. In I went straight under the water, bloody hell the water was freezing – last ones in got what was left in the hot tank – quickly jumped out again, only to be met by the officer of the day. It was the physical training instructor, Mr 'Shacks' Shackleton. An ex-'Bootneck' (Royal Marine) always immaculately turned out. "What's up with you, lad, don't you like water?" A swift smack of his 'stonockey' (a canvas tube of about one inch in diameter, about one to two feet long, filled with sand) across the cheeks of my bottom. "Get back in there and wash yourself properly, boy."

When we had finished washing ourselves we had to undergo the indignity of Shack's inspection. "Fall in out here, single file, legs wide apart, arms at shoulder height." Then he would walk along the line looking under your armpits, pulling your ear lobes to look behind your ears, lifting your 'John Thomas' with the end of his 'stonockey' while he made joking comments about the size of your private parts paraded before him. Then he gave the order, "About turn, face the bulkhead (wall), now bend over." Then he proceeded to inspect our nether regions. As he passed you, you got a swipe from his ever-present 'friend', on your backside (his strip of canvas filled with sand) and told to return to your pit (hammock) and get turned in. At the double.

He was not the only joker in the pack around that night. Having returned from the shower room, dried myself off, and got into my pyjamas, ready to turn in, I made to pull myself up into my hammock, by holding onto the hammock bar and then swing my legs up into the hammock followed by my main torso. Next thing I am flying through the air, landing flat on my back on the deck. I had come down some six or seven feet, crashing down with a wallop. Every man Jack around me broke out into fits of laughter; I did not think it at all funny. This mishap was not due to my poor rope work, I knew I had tied up both ends of my hammock with the correct 'round turn and two half hitches' before going to the showers. No, this was the first step of the initiation process all new boys had to suffer. The lads of the mess thought they would have a little fun at my expense. One had to keep his cool. Don't say anything. Nothing that you might have broken your back in doing so. Boys will be boys, anything for a laugh! JUST GRIN AND BARE IT.

CHAPTER 24

EDUCATION – SCHOOL ROUTINE

The following day we were taught how to lay out our kit and equipment for inspection. Everything had to be rolled up correctly, tied with white ribbon, with your name and number upward clearly showing. Also, we had to learn how to fit all of our kit into our locker properly, once again how to put your hammock together. We went through it over and over again, until you could do it blindfolded and correctly.

After doing all this we were enrolled into the school and shown to our classrooms. When I first met Mr 'Willy' Wightman, another tall, upright, not exactly skinny officer, he was one of the education teaching instructors. I think he was an ex-Merchant Navy. He had a long jovial face, and a large hooked nose, and he lived in a flat over the swimming baths. His special subject was science, he had a room or laboratory layout which was designed by him. Mr Wightman was also, as I remember it, responsible for woodwork, craft and art work. His classroom was very large and took up most of the upper deck housing.

In the evenings, after the day's work routine was done when the weather was not too good on the upper deck, the classrooms were opened to the boys for, as it was put, time to 'express' themselves artistically and manually, a godsend in the winter months.

While on the subject of education on the *Are*, I remember there was a library with a various number and range of very good books about every subject you wish for. If my memory serves me correctly, the library was run by our padre or ship's chaplain, the Rev Simms-Williams, a very short man, but stocky, with a 'full set' (a beard). He did have a disability in that I believe as a youngster he had poliomyelitis, which affected one of his arms and hand, but this did not affect his ability to do things or teach in any way. He also taught other subjects, I know he passed on his knowledge of model-making and wood-carving. He also spent a lot of time on the river showing us boys the art of sailing, in whaler and 14-foot dinghies during part of school periods. Later in my stay on the *Are,* this helped me to qualify and pass as a coxswain of small boats like the 32-foot cutter, and 27-foot whaler, while under power, sail and oars, along with the 14-foot sailing dinghy.

The headmaster was, I believe, at the time I joined, Mr WA 'Himmler' Wallace, with the deputy head, Mr Eric Orme, a not-so-tall and squat man with a wrinkled round face. He hardly ever smiled, a very stern man. Then there was Mr Toms, another instructor. There were also a few rooms on the *Glen Steathallan,* a large motor yacht, or a small steam ship, moored alongside and used as classrooms or accommodation for staff. More of her later in this story.

The next joy was to be given our work or cleaning stations. Mine was the good old aft locker flat, which was situated right at the bottom of the ship, right down on the keel, which had high sloping sides. This had to be cleaned twice daily, scrubbed on hands and knees every Saturday for Captains rounds. The locker fronts had to be cleaned and polished shiny so that you could see your face in them.

Every day the upper deck had to be scrubbed clean, in whatever the weather come rain or shine, frost or snow. This was done with open ended fire hose, each boy had a long hard headed broom, teepol, (a soap product), which gave a froth; the water was pumped directly from the river Medway through the fire system, to the upper deck. Freezing cold, you nearly always got wet through, with the wind whistling up the river Medway you soon got very cold indeed, you learnt what cold could be.

The next thing was to meet up with Mr Fred Hartree the Gunnery Officer and Parade Instructor, also the Swimming Instructor. He was a short man, very fit, with an elongated face with a huge, hooked nose. Our afternoon was spent with him on the after-well deck, where we learnt how to stand at ease, come up to attention, how to turn about, where and when one should 'fall in', how to 'dress' when in ranks, who, and when, to salute. Followed by mustering to meet the captain, Commander MH le Mare. He told us at some length what would be expected of us as *Arethusa* boys. Smoking. He pointed out that smoking was in his words a serious 'crime' on board the ship. Telling us that a number of boys had already been caught and severely punished, but many more had escaped. His main concern that the practice of smoking would result in the ship catching fire, apart from the fact that boys under 16 should not smoke.

Another point the captain made was that our standard of the English language was still very low generally. Boys were not allowed to read any comics other than the accepted decent ones of which he rattled off a list, such as the *Eagle, Hotspur, Marvel, Wizard, Hornet, Lion, Magnet, Rover* and the *Victor*. All others, if found, would be destroyed. So this encouraged covert, contraband trade in 'tuppenny bloods' (comics).

Each boy was to be paid two shillings six pennies (2/6 or 12 1/2 pence in today's money) a fortnight. I had to send about two shillings of this home to my mother. Uncanny really, because she was possibly sending some of the money anyway. It was to be spent at the canteen bar, situated on the mess deck at the rear of the regulating office, adjacent to the main companion ladders that led up to the upper deck, also down to the lower classrooms, where the 'Wiz' had his seamanship classes and his communications school were, where those learning signals would be taught to type to music and leisure rooms, where the snooker table was located, and the lower locker flat.

Visitors were allowed on board. Only on a Sunday after 1pm (1300 hours). The boy must be told of impending visits so that the boy in question could apply to the captain for permission on a Thursday, to leave the ship up until 7pm on the Sunday.

Portable radios were not permitted, it was found that too many became a nuisance in the ship, several being played at once. He told us that there was a first-class television set, one situated on the stage in the gymnasium, which had a very large screen, on which we used to watch the BBC *Lone Ranger* on a Saturday evening. Everyone crammed around to watch, and the gym would become full. The captain pointed out there was a very good radio system with loudspeaker on the mess deck.

My background, of being from an unstable family home and having spent most of my time in homes and boarding school, had prepared me for some of the hardship I would be experiencing. I knew how to obey an order when given, and how to do as I was told, but I have to admit the first couple of months on board really tested me to the limit, both physically, and emotionally. So much so that it often got me into trouble, or trying to wear the 'old green jacket'. The 'old green jacket' is an expression used within the Royal Navy, meaning that if you were wearing it, you did not conform to the regular routines, you were bucking the system.

Looking back, the food was pretty poor. It was served regularly and on time, but I had been used to that in my previous environment. I have never been keen on getting up early in the morning. To leave a nice warm bed, or hammock, to hit the deck on a bitterly cold winter's morning to wash in equally cold water, then stagger to the heads. Then on non-rainy days, climbing up the starboard rigging, up and over the first platform, back down the portside. With duty officers or petty officer boys with rope ends waiting to land one on your backside if you were moving too slowly for them. So, you see, at first I was a bit slow off the mark when getting up in the morning, making up my hammock, getting it stowed away in the proper place then off to the washroom and back to the mess before breakfast had finished. Doing things 'just on time' – I knew how to buck the system a little bit. Which meant that I was nearly always too late for my porridge and bread, but believe me, after a few mornings of being hungry I soon speeded up my routine, to the point that I was nearly always the first on the mess for breakfast.

As I said, the food was poor, the menus for the main meals were the same for each day of the week. Every Saturday you might get a pork pie, mash, and gravy, or you might get 'UNOX' – deep fried luncheon meat in batter. When you pressed it a squirt of fat would pop out, the fat just dripping out of it. Or there were the old favourites, corned beef hash, or potato cheese, the same day every week. I don't think Mo and Stan could cook anything else; that's not fair they did surprise us from time to time.

Dhobi day (or laundry day) was another experience. You would have the mess dhobi bucket, bar of 'pussers hard' (soap) between about ten of you from the mess. 'Senior boys' got first use of the dhobi bucket and the soap. So, when it came down to your turn, what was warm water was now cold, you were lucky to get a small piece of pusser's hard left to wash all of your whites and underclothes, and your dirty socks.

Still, there were the fun times, much of the first months on board were spent in learning one's way around the ship, the daily routines, and how to stand up to those senior boys who could make your life miserable given half the chance. There was one in particular, a member of 22 mess quarterdeck port, a nasty piece of work by the name of Blythe, and he had a mate. Both were bully boys and would try to make your life a misery. I learnt which officers would maybe overlook minor faults, as well as those who could be unforgiving and swift to punish.

CHAPTER 25

ASIAN INFLUENZA EPIDEMIC, 1957

The virus that caused the 1957 Asian influenza pandemic had been accidentally released by a laboratory in the US, their scientists sent out to all places over the world in test kits which contained the virus. There were fears the virus could escape the laboratory if opened by the incorrect people, which did eventually happen. The mistake was discovered after the virus escaped from a kit at a high-containment laboratory in Canada. Such an escape could spread worldwide. Towards the end of 1957, the whole of Great Britain was struck down by what was called the Asian Influenza Epidemic, lots of people lost their lives through it, everyone was dropping like flies. By December 1957, there were 3550 people who had died from influenza in England and Wales alone – three times as many flu fatalities as in the corresponding period of 1956.

After the vaccine was made available, deaths fell but a second wave of the virus in November saw fatalities rise once again. There were 100,000 deaths worldwide attributed to Asian Flu, nearly 70,000 in the United States alone. Asian Flu had crept across our gangway around the end of November 1957 and lasted right into the New Year; the *Arethusa* were not clear of it when it finished at around February of 1958, when the last of us were actually clear of it.

It struck very quickly for those on board. First it was just one or two of the boys, who were quickly quarantined in the sick bay, however, the sick bay became full in no time. Then there began a steady flow of ambulances arriving at the foot of the catwalk, and boys who were extremely bad were taken off to the local Medway hospitals, most of whom went to Royal Naval Hospital in Chatham, and hospitals in Rochester and Strood, which all became overwhelmed. Some went even further afield to be placed in intensive care wards.

Remember, there were 240 boys plus the staff on the *Are*. I was one of about 20 boys and staff who did not go down with it at first, it really was really hard work trying to control its spread. The first thing we had to do was to wash down all of the decks, bulkheads, even the deck heads in some places, with some very strong disinfectants.

Then there were those of us who had to make up a quarantine area by rigging up canvas screens, where those who had the flu but not quite as bad as most of the others were placed, these screens gradually moved further up the ship's accommodation deck as more and more boys became ill. Those of us who did not catch it had to look after all those who were being sick, literally, being given our place of duty, some actually helping Sister in the sick bay, some were sent to the galley to help Mo and Stan.

My station to start with was, when one of the boys who had lent over the side of his hammock and let go whatever was in his stomach, then it was out with the buckets of disinfectant and mops and I had to scrub it clean. No sooner had you cleaned that one up, another boy would poke his head over the side of his hammock, here we go again, buckets and scrubbers at the ready.

Our main job was to try to get them to eat or take on fluids; this was also an arduous thing to do, as you had to be on your toes in case it all came back up again and you ended up covered in their vomit. I can remember being helped by quite a few of the Royal Naval hospital staff who came on board to see things were being carried out correctly.

This went on for weeks, then into a couple of months. Those who were released from hospital had to be place in another part of the ship, those of us who were still on our feet were moved ashore into the swimming pool to sleep and eat our meals. As the staff got better, things started to get easier for us. The whole episode went on for about eight to 12 weeks in all. In the end there were about ten or so boys who had not been affected at the time by this Asian flu and were given a clean bill of health. One or two of the ten had contracted the flu bug whilst on an earlier leave period and had become immune when the epidemic hit the ship. Those of us who had worked our butts off all the way through were treated quite well by the ship's staff. As I remember it, we would be granted extra leave periods and privileges. Then a week or two later, about three of us were called before the captain.

I was put on the captain's report, not as a defaulter but as requirements. Along with others of the flu working party, I had to march up to the captain's table, halt by orders, and salute the captain. My divisional officer, Mr Tiny 'The Whiz' Fuller, gave my appraisal; a very good one, I must say. As it was put to the captain, I had, along with 'the few', worked hard during the emergency of the Asian Flu. I got a long lecture from the captain and first officer about how I should behave in the future, that they were entrusting me with this great responsibility. I was to be made up to be acting leading boy of 2 mess, now I was in forecastle port division.

It was on one of these extra leave periods that a number of us were allowed a little relaxation, or a spot of 'local' leave, so we went ashore and had a bit of a muck about around the yacht club, as a number of us before the outbreak were invited onto some of the yachts as crew by some of the club members, thanks to the 'Rev' Simsilliams, who managed to get the invites for us previously. Fed up with that, I was asked by a number of the boys if I could take away a whaler, with permission from the 'Wiz' and went for a sail ourselves. I, as a newly made leading boy, would be placed in charge of taking a boat away, but the 'Wiz' said that as there were a number of us with qualifications to sail a whaler, he was placing the boat and crew in my hands.

Taking a 'banyan' (food pack) with us, we sailed up the river, towards Chatham dockyard, heading out towards Sheerness. We thought we had better not go too far around the river, so full about, sailed back down towards Rochester, stopping off by the trot of warships, mainly destroyers and frigates, which were placed into reserve or mothballs, a few old destroyers and one or two frigates tied up to one of their buoys, to enjoy a bit of scran out of sight of the *Arethusa*. When we had finished our food break, off we sailed again, this time I took the tiller, sailing back down river, tacking, as we went, passing the *Are*, making a small coaster, coming out of Rochester harbour, give way to us as we were under sail, on one of the tacks, took us towards Upnor Castle, or the Royal Engineers depot, where there were a few barges and pontoons. We thought, *This looks like a bit of fun*, so we tied up alongside one of these barges, and being very inquisitive, decided to investigate what was in these barges. It turned out to be ammunition.

I had not been alongside for more than five minutes when there was this loud voice. "Oi, what you lot up too?" It was the security guard or dockyard police. "This is a restricted area, get out of 'ere, don't you know it's dangerous to be around 'ere."

So we quickly got back into the boat, pushed off, quickly got the sails up and off we went, none the wiser. We sailed further down river towards Rochester and, before time was getting a little late, turned around, sailing before the wind, and made good progress back to the *Are*. We tied up to the boat pontoon, stowed the sails correctly back into the sails store, then while cleaning out the boat, there was this voice from behind us, it could not be mistaken for anyone else except the second officer, Ferdie Farrington, slapping his 'Herbert' into the side of his leg, hitting his long black shiny gaiters. "Who was in charge of this boat?"

We all looked at each other, then they all looked into my direction. *Oh my God, what's up now?* I thought. "Me, Sir, Cutts, 207, Sir."

"You do not learn, do you?"

"Learn what, Sir?"

"Don't get clever with me, boy," was his reply.

I am not your boy, I thought.

"You know you are not allowed anywhere near to the Royal Engineers depot, do you not—

"What depot, Sir?" There I was trying to be funny again, trying to put on the 'old green jacket' once again.

"Right, you lot, fall in outside the regulating office and be quick about it."

I, being the last to climb out of the boat, caught a hefty whack from 'Herbert' right across the cheeks of my backside.

There were seven of us, at least three of us were leading boys. I had not long been made up as the leading hand of 2 mess, I think mainly for how I behaved during the flu epidemic. We were all lined up outside the regulating office and were met by the duty chief petty officer boy. He said, "You lot are for the high jump, especially you, Cutts, you were coxswain of the boat."

We had been standing there for about half an hour, my backside still stinging from the swipe of Farrington's electrical flex. By now, a large number of the ship's company had gathered around the regulating office to witness what was going on, all making silly comments. When the footsteps of Farrington's jackboots could be heard approaching, our audience quickly dispersed in all directions. He was accompanied by the first officer. Both stood out in front of us, the first officer proceeded to give us the biggest and loudest rollicking ever heard on the ship, of the dangers of playing around on ammunition barges, then proceeded to praise the work we had carried out during the ships flu epidemic. As a punishment, we were to lose the privilege of 'local' leave. For my pains, I had to bend over and take another two strokes of that bloody black thing, Herbert. Nothing more was said about that incident. As we were not on the barges for long, only a few minutes, looking to see what they were before being interrupted by the security, who made a more serious incident out of it when reporting to the *Arethusa* officer of the day.

It was not long after the ship had been given a clean bill of health and everything was nearly getting back to normal routine that one or two of the lads in the party became very ill and were rushed off to hospital with the dreaded Asian flu. It was not long before it was my turn, being one of the last to drop. Again, off I went to Rochester Hospital and was placed in quarantine. I think I was there for about a week, maybe less, before being transferred to Chatham Royal Naval Hospital until I was fit enough to be sent back to the ship. When I was returned to the sick bay on the *Are*, boy, were we treated like lords. I say 'we' – the three or four of us survivors from the epidemic were given everything we wanted. The lovely sister (cannot for the life of me remember her name, she was a diamond) made sure we were all comfortable, making sure that we were all tucked up nicely every night that she was on duty. It was for all the work and caring we had done for the others over a period of about ten weeks in all, even the captain, first and second officers gave us praise. After it was all over for good, a number of us were invited to stay the weekend with the sister in what was known as Davitt House, her quarters, which was situated on the hill leading to the playing fields. That became another eye-opener. Nudge nudge, wink wink.

CHAPTER 26

27-FOOT COXSWAIN WHALER INCIDENT

Chatham Dockyard Submarine Pens

I had not long been made up as the leading hand of 2 mess when it was deemed that I had been a good boy long enough (taking the flu epidemic into account) to be considered for a position of leading boy. I had by now obtained two good conduct stripes. Whoopee. I had already qualified as a boy coxswain, under the guidance of mainly the 'Whiz' and the padre, Simms-Williams, which allowed me to take any one of the boats away. One of the privileges as a leading boy was also to be allowed with permission to take a boat away, being in sole charge of the boat. We had several types of boats, the smallest was a 14-foot sailing dinghy, which I was able to take out onto the Medway on my own to sail it single-handed. There were a couple of skiffs, a bit bigger than the 14-foot dinghies, which carried a crew of up to four people, sailing or under oars.

The 27-foot whaler was a much larger boat. With a crew of five oarsmen, single-banked and a cox, it could be sailed. It had two masts, nice boats to sail and to have fun in. The 32-foot cutter; this was a bit different, needed a lot of effort and concentration to manoeuvre. It had 12 oarsmen, double-banked, six either side. The 32-foot motor cutter was the same as the other cutter only this one had an engine with Kitchener steering gear. Namely, the engine would only go forward, to go into reverse you had to wind a handle which closed a bucket set up on the rudder, covering the prop. Easy really.

Once having been made up to leading boy, also being one of only a few boy coxswains, I was allowed to book the use of these

167

boats on summer evenings or at weekends. One Sunday afternoon, I indeed had gained permission, even after my little escapade on the Upnor Castle or the Royal Engineers depot, to take a whaler away with a crew of five out for a pull (a row) on the river. You were allowed a certain time, up to two or three hours, I think. Well, off we went with the tide, to make it a little easier. The tide was going to start ebbing soon, so my plan was to take the boat down river towards Rochester. Then I planned to turn around and head back towards the ship about two miles away, on the ebbing tide. On doing so, I made for the Chatham side of the river, by the large building and the dockyard, which gave us a little protection from the headwind and from the little wind that there was. On our return trip, this route brought us past the Royal Naval Submarine pens, still at this time the Royal Navy were building the odd one or two diesel boats (submarines) on the slipway at Chatham dockyard, mainly the 'O' class.

I steered closer towards the wall, which took us out of view of the *Are*'s officer of the day's telescope. I then made fast between, behind the stern of two of the operational submarines. I think they were two of the new 'O' class boats and could have been the older 'T' class, which were there to do their sea trials prior to joining the fleet. I said, "Right, boys, we'll have quick fag break," or a 'lug' as we called it. "We will have a quick smoke and rest then get on our way." I had just got my fags out, taken a couple of drags on it, when this dockyard pinnace came chugging out from behind one of the caisson gates. "Oh no, the bloody dockyard police."

On a loudhailer (not needed, we were only yards away from them), he shouted, "Put those cigarettes out. Who's in charge?"

"I am, Sir," I said.

"Do you know you are in a prohibited area, what are you doing here? You know you should not be here, this is also a no-smoking area."

I tried to play the innocent, on went the old green jacket, by saying one of my crew was not feeling too well and needed a rest, but did not get away with it.

"Throw me your bow rope," was the order.

I tried to say, "Sorry, we'll be alright, we can manage." I hoped he would let us go on our way. Not a chance, the bow rope was securely tied to the rear of the pinnace and he towed us all the way back to the *Are*. Word soon got round that a whaler was being towed back up the river, all of my crew were now getting worried about having cigarettes on us. What should we do, we knew we would be searched, so I passed the word to drop what cigarettes in the water without the dockyard police noticing. On our approach to the ship, all the boys were leaning over the side, shouting, cheering and clapping.

The pinnace let the bow rope go then instructed us to follow him to the *Are*. Doing as told, we pulled the boat alongside the pontoon, we drifted into the boat pontoon, the dockyard police pulled in behind us. We were met by the officer of the day, duty chief petty officer boy, and the duty regulating petty officer boy. The 'copper' told the officer of the watch how he had found us in a prohibited area. Also, that we were smoking, another heinous crime on the *Are*.

Oh dear, I thought, thinking of the little incident on the ammo depot, which only happened a few weeks earlier. I was sure I would be placed in the rattle (on a charge). Into the rattle we all went, six of us standing outside the regulating office, waiting for Ferdie Farrington. He had been ashore in his house enjoying a little rest from his horrible little gits. Well, that's what he called us before charging us. As we knew he had the boat searched before doing the same to us, he found nothing. Did not stop him putting us on the chief officer's report. All six of us were paraded in a line in front of the chief officer's table. He said that he could not deal with us, as it was such a serious charge, so he placed us on the captain's report. We had to wait until Thursday following the usual morning divisions where captain's request men and defaulters were held. The duty regulating petty officer boy called us to attention. Quick march, we were all marched up to the captain's table together, 'off caps'. The captain looked at me shaking his head in the negative, saying that I was in charge of the boat and he would deal with me separately. I then fell out; about turn marched off to the regulating office away from the others.

They got off with extra work detail, loss of pocket money, and loss of shore leave privileges.

I was called back, quick march, halt, off cap. The charge was read out: conduct unbecoming an *Arethusa* boy, bringing the uniform into disrepute. Trespass on Her Majesty's property. Unlawful use of tobacco. Irresponsible conduct, while in charge of juniors. Captain le Mare, he threw the book at me (and it did not miss, hit me straight between the eyes so as to speak). I thought the captain this time was about to explode. His neck had expanded to twice its size, he was turning bright purple, I thought he was going to explode before my eyes. He gave me the biggest lecture I had heard to date, that I had undone his trust in me, bringing the good name of the *Arethusa* into disrepute. The punishment he gave me was loss of my 'hook' (demoted from leading boy), loss of two 'good conduct' badges, loss of leave, loss of pocket money, extra work detail. To top it all off he said he was going to make an example of me by awarding me 'six of the best'.

I nearly passed out at the severity of his punishment. On completion of defaulters, I was marched away under the escort of two petty officer boys to the regulating office. There I was told of when my punishment would take place, then dismissed back to my original messdeck of 21 mess.

Soon after I had to report to my divisional officer's office where he told me what the next thing to happen to me was. Firstly he read the riot act to me, asking what in the devil possessed me to do such a thing. I told my excuse that one of the crew had felt unwell so I pulled over until he was feeling alright, this did not wash with the 'Wiz' either. During my little audience with my divisional officer. Prior to the clearing of the 'lower deck', the 'Wiz' gave me a few words of advice and told me what to expect, what I should do. He ran through the routine with me, after turning to me saying good luck, he said, "Do not let the side down out there."

The same afternoon, the captain 'cleared lower deck', which meant all the ship's company had to muster to whatever part of the ship, normally on the upper deck. This 'clear lower deck' was on the main mess deck, everyone had to fall in front of the main mast, or top of the stairway or companion ladder leading to the gymnasium below. I was marched from the regulating office by an escort of two petty officer boys and a chief petty officer boy in charge giving the orders, to out in front of the whole ship's company, then by two of the chief petty officer boys (I know Guttridge was one, Cre or Mystrik could have been the other, horrible pieces of work, the pair of them). I was dressed in only a pair of flimsy navy-blue sports shorts, nothing else. Mr Farrington and Mr Shackleton took up position directly behind me, two CPO boys either side, nowhere for me to go. Everyone was called to attention, as the captain and First Officer Lt Commander Townsend marched out and addressed the ship's company. Once again they read the riot act to the ship's company, giving everyone notice to behave themselves in future or they too would end up like the silly gentleman before them. The first officer read out the charge once again, then the punishment, which was to be carried out forthwith in the gymnasium.

All the boys were each fallen out in order of part of the ship, and mustered down in the gymnasium. All the officers went down, leaving me until last with my escort, Mr Shackleton, followed by me and the two CPO boys, Mr Farrington, bringing up the rear. He had a handful of canes. The vaulting horse was once again positioned in the middle of the gymnasium, coconut matting around it. There was hardly room to move down there with all 239 boys all in their respective divisions. They were almost on top of me. Mr Shackleton was to administer the punishment. He asked me to choose a cane, which I did with a little apprehension, then at his instruction I was bent over the vaulting horse. I did struggle a little but Mr Farrington held my head down. While the two CPO boys held an arm each, two other petty officer boys held my legs down. I heard Shackleton swish the cane from side to side. The captain gave the order for the punishment to commence. Shackleton was dressed in his smart white vest with the red physical training instructor's badge on the front of his vest, trousers with creases that you could cut your fingers on, brilliant white gym shoes. His hair was slicked back, what he had left anyway. 'Shacks' took a couple of paces backwards, then moved very quickly forwards, as if dancing on his tiptoes, Thwack, the first one landed, my teeth biting the leather of the vaulting horse.

Mr Farrington bent down and whispered in my ear, "Will you not ever learn, boy? Did that hurt, here comes another."

Fighting back the tears, I said something like, "Get lost."

He said, "You can have more than six, you know, if you do not change your attitude."

When it had finished, I was trembling with pain. I felt like killing all of them. I was told to stand to attention, how could I? I was still bent over in two, trying to gain some sort of composure.

"Stand up straight," said one of the CPO boys, who also said, "Say thank you to Mr Shackleton."

I refused, being the stubborn person I was, I again refused. I turned and addressed all who had to witness my punishment. I said, "Sorry to my boat's crew, for their punishment, it was not their fault." A cheer went up from all of the other boys, who were quickly silenced by Ferdie.

Another order from the CPO boy came, to thank the officers, when the 'Wiz' Mr Fuller came forward, got hold of my arm and led me away, saying, "He's had enough punishment." He took me into his office, having given me a lecture on how to behave in future. This is the moment when I thought to myself, I took the treatment that the 'old man' had meted out to me as a child, then I'll take this punishment but from now on I would only look after number one – me. In other words, I might knuckle down a little but I would try and give those in authority a little run around.

After I had recovered sufficiently enough I was allowed to return to my mess, this time back again to 21 mess, 2 mess had a new leading boy. I could not sit down for some time afterwards, the bleeding of the wounds went on for some days after. I had to report to the sick bay to have them treated.

I was treated by some as a hero, but did not feel like one. When the food was issued, the lads in the mess would offer me extra portions from their own plates. When the tuck shop opened, they would offer a 'nutty bar' as I had no pocket money for a few weeks, they even gave me the odd cigarette, now that was hard for some of them. I soon found out who my true friends were on board.

The extra duties I could cope with. The 'sanding canvas' where you had to muster on the upper deck, dressed only in your blue shorts, when one of the duty petty office boys would give you a strip of canvas, while another boy would wash the deck down with sea water, while another would scatter sand over the wet deck, then with, canvas in hand and down on bended knees, you would have to scrub the deck. This was carried out to make the decks look white when it was dry, it was akin to rubbing the paint work on your car down, but at a much larger scale. Boy, did it make your knees and hands very sore.

My main extra duties were to help the captain's steward by cleaning the captain's quarters, cleaning his daughter Petra's shoes, and cleaning their kitchen floor. This turned out to be a very nice punishment. Mrs Adriana le Mare (the captain's wife) soon took pity on you, and would often tell you to sit down. She would say, "Make yourself comfortable," give you a cup of tea in her nice tea service and a piece of her latest cake, saying "Enjoy, I'll tell you if anyone comes." Lovely lady, a true lady in every way.

Other extra duties were in the galley, where I had to help Mo and or Stan, whoever was on early turn to get breakfast ready. Spud bashing, washing and cleaning the galley, looking after the bread locker. So you had to get up much earlier than the rest of the ship's company, you always got an early shake from the night watchman. To do so, he would shake the 'nettles' on your hammock, you had to get out of it straight away, normally without trying to wake those around you. I always made a point of, once being away from my own messmates, on my way up to the washroom and heads, finding something to kick, which would make a nice noise, or knock into a hammock or two, just to wake some of the others up.

On top of doing punishment, I had to do my normal duties or routines throughout the ship so I was kept more than busy, getting very tired. I was told that it was part of life which was called discipline!

After three months' good conduct, I got my good conduct badge reinstated. I never was again made up to be the leading boy (on leaving I was reverted to boy first class). I was about to leave the ship to go to the Royal Navy as an ordinary boy.

CHAPTER 27

CORN BEEF HASH INCIDENT, COOKING TRAYS OVER THE SIDE

My mess for the majority of the time while on the *Arethusa* was 21 mess, which was made up of ten boys, plus a leading boy. Our numbers ranged from 201 to 219. My number was 207. During my time on board the people would change but not the numbers.

During the Christmas term of 1958, 21 mess consisted of the following: 201 'Dick' RICHARDSON (later to become leading boy of 12 mess, then petty officer boy, after I had left chief petty officer boy). 203 Bill BOWES. 205 Peter COSTELLO, a Liverpudlian. He hated every minute of being on the *Are*. 207 myself. 209 David 'Sproggy' MAYNE, from Epsom. 211 David CLEMENTS. 213 Pete PULLEN from Bognor Regis. 215 Jim BINNS (later to become O'Halloran). 217 David WEARE also from around Bognor Regis, I think. 219 Colin 'Wiggy' BENNETT. 77 leading boy was Michael Coyle. Other leading boys of 21 mess that I can remember were 92 Martin HALES, 173 Mick O'BRIEN.187 Tony LUKE. 195 Ollie SIVERTSEN. Four messes to each division, 21 mess were in quarterdeck starboard. Each division had an officer in charge, called your divisional officer. So my divisional officer was 'Tiny' 'The Wiz' FULLER.

Now 'Tiny' Fuller or the 'Wiz' was far from being tiny, he was huge. He was about 5 feet 9 inches tall (about 6 feet across the shoulders) over 20 stones in weight, hence the 'Tiny' nickname, the 'wiz' because his knowledge of all that of seamanship and communications and signals were second to none. He was round-faced, pug-nosed (often glowing bright purple), a genial and very friendly personality, who was a great favourite with all of us boys who were under his care and instruction; he was my divisional officer.

In his naval career, during the war years, he served on the county class cruiser HMS *Sheffield* as their chief yeoman of signals. He taught all means of communications and seamanship, boat-work, and sailing used at sea. He was a very happy jovial type of person, but woe betide anyone who crossed him, he would come down on you like a ton of bricks. It was the duty of each mess to appoint or nominate a person to be cook of the mess for one week, Saturday to Saturday. His duty was to make sure at meal times that the mess was laid up correctly, when a pipe was made – 'cooks to the galley' – he would have to collect the mess 'fannies and trays' – go up to the galley on the upper deck to collect your mess's meals. The cooks' favourite, which we got more than often, was corned beef hash. Other cheap and cheerful meals were either potato cheese, or 'UNOX' – deep fat fried luncheon meat in batter. If you stuck your knife or fork into it, you got a squirt of fat in the eye if you were not on the ball. I am sure the engineers greased their gearings and things they wanted to keep moving, with the leftovers.

On this particular day, I, 'Comic' Cutts, was 'cook of the mess'. The pipe 'cooks to the galley' was made. I was doing my duty and collected the mess trays, etc. from the messdeck but on doing so, said jokingly to my fellow mess mates, "If it's corned beef hash on the menu again, I'll toss it all over the side." Mind you, I was only joking at the time. Well, blow me down. I arrived at the serving hatch of the galley, there was Mo Pavey, cigarette hanging out the corner of his mouth as usual, the ash on the end of this cigarette was about an inch to two long, ready to fall off into, of all things, one of the trays of corned beef hash. *Oh no*, I thought, *what did I say when leaving the mess to come up here?* What was on the menu but corned beef hash.

One wag, a cook of the mess from my adjoining mess, said, "I see we have corned beef hash again, what did you say you would do, Cutts?" I did not answer him straight away, and then I heard the phrase, "You're bloody chicken, Cutts."

Oh dear, fancy saying to me that I was 'chicken'. A rush of blood to the head, I grabbed a couple of trays of the bloody hot corned beef hash.

"Bloody chicken, am I?" was my reply. I tossed them over the side, one landed on the boat pontoon below, the other straight into the River Medway. I got jumped on by both Mo and Stan, plus the duty petty officer boy, whose duty it was to oversee the issue of food, swiftly frog-marched me down to the regulating office.

Coming from the direction of my mess was a chorus. "Oh! It must be corned beef hash then, Cutts is in the rattle again."

I was duly 'put in the rattle' on a charge again. Ferdie Farrington was the officer of the day, why was it always him? He had me put under close arrest, and put on the chief officer's report. Normally I would have been placed on the divisional officer's report, then he would place me on the chief officer's report. However, the charge being a serious one, I was placed directly on Chief Officer (or 'Jimmy the One') Lt Commander Townsend's report.

We had to muster each morning for divisions. We dressed in the rig of the day depending on the time of year. We were still in summer dress or 'summer rig of the day', consisting of a pair of thin blue cotton gymnasium shorts with a canvas money belt around your waist, nothing else. This was a Wednesday morning towards the back end of 1958, around the end of September or first weeks of October. It was a very chilly day with flimsy sunshine, no warmth in its strength; to be honest a grim cold day. On this occasion, I was brought up to the upper deck to join my division quarterdeck starboard at the rear, under escort of two petty officer boys. On this particular morning, following divisions, the chief officer was to hold his request for men and the defaulter's parade. Once again it was my turn to appear as a defaulter. So, having mustered for divisions carrying my cap, the order was given.

"Ship's company – SHUN request men and defaulters to stand fast, rest of the ship's company to your classes and work stations fall out." Immediately following the order to fall out, it looked like organised confusion, with boys frantically running in every direction. All orders must be obeyed at the double, but some had to remain behind to see 'Jimmy the One'. Request men would form up on the starboard side, standing at ease. The defaulters on the port side, standing rigid to attention. We had to remain in this position under the stern eyes of the second officer, Ferdie Farrington, while the chief officer attended to the various requests. Many were requests to be 'made up' or requests for compassionate leave, all kinds of trivial matters. We, the defaulters, were arranged into two ranks and were now wearing our caps. The request men were called forward first, smartly march up to in front of the chief officer, standing behind or rather leaning on his lectern. They would smartly 'chop him one off', salute, his request would be heard, and then he would be dismissed. When the request men had finished it was the turn of the defaulters.

When my turn came, I was ordered to, '"DOUBLE MARCH, HALT," in front of the chief officer (or 'Jimmy the One') Lt Commander Townsend, a PO boy on each side. "STAND STILL, OFF CAP." The morning being very chilly I still had perspiration running from my brow, armpits and down the middle of my back, scared even to move a hair on my rigid form. On the order of an 'off cap' like a coiled spring, my right hand shot to the left side of my head. *Up, two, three,* grasping the left side rim of the cap, *two, three,* holding the rim, bringing my arm smartly down to my right side, *down, two, three.* I remained stiffly to attention. The charge was read out. Conduct unbecoming, in that it did destroy *Arethusa* property, namely two galley trays. The wanton destruction of good food. Two principal witnesses, Mo Pavey and Stan Whitnall, gave their side of the story. Then came the 'how do you plead.'

"Guilty, Sir."

'Jimmy the One' gave his verdict. "I am placing you on the captain's report, in view of the seriousness of the offence, captain's table will be held as soon as possible, in the meantime you are to remain under close arrest."

Being kept under close arrest was certainly no fun at all, I was placed in a compartment, up in the forecastle or fo'c's'le (pronounced folk-saul), where the chain locker was, the door was left open 'ajar' on a small chain. The duty petty officer boy was responsible for looking after me. I was let out to go to the heads and to carry out punishment duty, such as scrubbing the floor of the galley.

I was lucky, the captain's table for defaulters was held the next day. I was collected by two chief petty officer boys who marched up in front of the captain's table. 'Off Cap'. The charge was read out. The captain, Commander le Mare, took his time as he quietly reads the charges, then, taking his eyes from the official log book set on the same lectern as used by the chief officer and the padre to hold his Bible during morning prayers at divisions, he lifted his head again, his piercing glare directly into my eyes. "Anything to say for yourself in defence, boy?"

"NO, SIR," was my reply.

Turning to my divisional officer, Lt 'Tiny' Fuller, the captain asked, "Have you anything to add on his behalf?"

Tiny, true to 'his boys', gave me a glowing appraisal. "Out of character, Sir, very hard worker, easy to teach, always ready to learn."

Captain le Mare returned to the charge sheet, fountain pen in hand and in silence he steadily, and with some conviction, wrote at some length in the book, and then he again lifted his head, stares me straight in the eyes, went an absolute shade of bright red, his neck above his collar was swollen to bursting (I had seen this sight once before). I cannot recall his exact words, unrepeatable. Then he quietly spoke. "I find you guilty as charged."

I was only an ordinary boy with one good conduct stripe. The whole outcome or punishment was to be six cuts of the best (oh, Christ, not again), pay out of my pocket money for the loss of two very good cooking trays (but I did not have enough money in the ship's account), the loss of the one good conduct badge I had gained back after being judged a good boy for six months prior. All shore leave is suspended for one month. Confined to the ship for the same period (so no band practice or swimming), extra punishment duties such as, helping the galley staff with their duties, scrubbing the galley, washing the pots and pans, with a little 'holy stoning' thrown in for good measure.

"DEFAULTER. ON CAP 'BOUT TURN DOUBLE MARCH." Boy, could those chief petty officer boys shout, full of their 'piss and importance'.

CHAPTER 28

SIX OF THE BEST – NOT AGAIN. "THIS BOY DOES NOT LEARN."

The same afternoon, the captain 'cleared lower deck' which meant, as mentioned before in this story, all the ship's company had to muster to a part of the ship, normally on the upper deck. Not this time, 'clear lower deck' was once again held on the main mess deck, everyone had to fall in, in their messes. The captain, chief, and second officer arrived on the main mess deck as before. Then each mess had to form up in their various divisions in front of the main mast, or top of the stairway or companion ladder leading to the gymnasium below.

Having gone through the same process some months earlier, I knew what to expect. Once again, I was marched from my divisional officer's office by two chief petty officer boys, Tiny Fuller bringing up the rear. I was placed out front of the whole ship's company by two of the chief petty officer boys, dressed in only a pair of flimsy navy-blue shorts, nothing else.

Farrington and Shackleton took up position as before directly behind me, two CPO boys either side, divisional officers to their side, nowhere for me to go if I wanted to. Everyone was called to attention, as the captain and First Officer Lt Comdr Townsend marched out and addressed the ship's company. The first officer read out the charge once again, then the punishment. The ship's company then fell out to muster in the gymnasium below. There were a few comments as they did this like 'well done, Cutts' and 'good luck, Comic', 'you've done it now' and 'give us a look of your arse after'.

"KEEP QUIET," was barked out by someone. All the officers went down last, followed by Shackleton. Then came my turn with the two CPO boys. Farrington brought up the rear, with a handful of canes. The vaulting horse was positioned in the middle of the gymnasium, coconut matting around it. I had to march up to the gathering of officers, everyone was there, and I do believe the padre and the sister were there too. I halted in front of them, standing to attention. I had to speak out, slowly, in a clear loud voice, head held high, defiant to the last.

"ORDINARY BOY CUTTS, SIR." Then, Second Officer Farrington was to administer the punishment. I was absolutely crapping myself. I had to say, "Six cuts of the cane, please, Sir." He asked me to choose a cane, then at his instruction I was bent over the vaulting horse, not without a little struggle. Mr Shackleton held my head down at the head of the vaulting horse, while the two CPO boys held an arm each; two other petty officer boys held my legs down. I could not move if I tried to.

One of the things that the 'Wiz' said was, "Try not to grit your teeth too hard together, you might break a tooth or bite your tongue, get a piece of thick rubber or a roll of cloth to bite onto, don't let anyone see you doing it though."

I heard Farrington swish the cane from side to side, measuring his stroke. The captain gave the order for the punishment to commence. Farrington clicked his heels together (just like a Nazi). There was a slight pause as he winds up to full strength for the first stroke; I hold my breath, tense all my muscles, then I hear the vicious swish as the cane descended. Thwack, as it strikes, the first one landed, pain fills my whole body; it is so intense it made me feel sick, how I did not throw up I'll never know, maybe because with my teeth I was biting so hard into the leather of the vaulting horse. Mr Shackleton bent down and said, "Are you all right?"

Fighting back the tears, gritting my teeth, I said, "What do you think?"

He said, "You must say 'yes thank you, Sir'. You can have extras if you wish, say thank you."

"Thank you, Sir."

Once again, my thoughts were that I had never known pain like this before in my life, except for the last time, my whole body shook, it was screaming out with it. This was far different from the beating I got from my old man when using his belt. The pain was very much different, it was awful, this was only the first one, five more to go. The second one fell. Oh my God, this was worse, I did cry out a little. *Don't let the side down.* The leather on the horse took another pounding, and how I did not break my teeth I'll never know.

The same happened after every cut of the cane. I was instructed before the punishment was given, that after the last one was administered, I was to stand up to attention, turn to Mr Farrington and say, "Thank you, Sir." The last one really struck home, all the people who were holding me let go, I just fell to the ground in a heap. I had passed out.

I came around to a voice which said, "Get up and thank the officer for your punishment." I could not, three or four of those around me grabbed hold of me and stood me up, one said, "For Christ's sake, stand to attention like a man and say thank you to Mr Farrington."

The next thing I remember – I must have passed out again – was I woke up in sick bay. Apparently, I had six lovely stripes or angry red welts across my lower regions, all of them were evenly spaced, as if drawn with a ruler, only inches apart. Two of them had drawn blood; hence the sister had placed a dressing on them. The bruises soon appeared, lasting up to six or seven weeks after.

It was not long before I had a visit from my divisional officer, the Whiz, who firstly congratulated me. "Well, you did not really let the side down, he really laid into you this time didn't he, shame you passed out, you must now get back to the mess deck as soon as you can, let the others know you can take it, and not hide in the sick bay."

I could hardly sit down, or even walk, let alone get back to the mess deck. Anyway, I did, after a short rest and to let the intense pain subside a little before I went back to the mess. After I had recovered sufficiently enough, I was allowed to return to my mess, I was a hero, although I felt far from it. The only trouble was I could not sit down properly for days afterwards. Farrington had drawn blood, but after a while it wore off. Believe it or not. I love corned beef anyway, you could serve it to me today. The nightly shower, now that became a very big ordeal, I was put on show for the whole ship's company to come, look, touch and see the damage, with my glowing set of lines running in parallel from side to side across the cheeks of my arse and down the upper part of my thighs. Comments of 'well done, Ken' and 'that'll teach you, cuts for Cutts'.

The extra duties would turn out to be the worst punishment. Like 'sanding canvas' which was the upper deck had to be scrubbed once again. House maid's knee, you must be joking, it was worse than that! Another punishment was I was placed on galley duties once again, my first job was in the bread store, where I had to prepare the 'slickies' (slices of bread, in trays for all, plus those for the PO boys and chief PO boys) then there was also the margarine machine. The margarine was supplied to the ship in very large square tins, one would last a normal family a year, I would think. I had to open the tin, and then put it in this large mincing machine, at the turn of the handle, it would give one small flower-shaped portion of margarine, enough for one slice. The cooks of the mess would come up at breakfast time, collect whatever there was for breakfast, and then they would have to pass the 'bread locker' where I would be situated. I had to ask how many there were in that particular messdeck, then turn the handle that number of times, one for each person. For my own divisional messes, I would turn the handle a little way backwards, then slowly, forwards which made the size of the portion margarine a bit larger than the others, and I would slip them an extra slice or two.

After six months' good conduct, one could apply as a request man to have your good conduct badge reinstated. This I did, I had to apply first through my divisional chief petty officer boy, who in turn took my request to my divisional officer 'Tiny'. Then I had to be brought up before the captain, when he held his next 'table' where 'Tiny' Fuller had to read out a report on my progress with regards to my conduct over the last six months. He always gave a glowing report on every boy. Guess what my favourite meal is today, yes corned beef hash. I love it.

After this incident, the two cooks, Mo Pavey, Stan Whitnall, and I became very good pals; I often got jobs in the galley. 'Spud bashing' (peeling the potatoes), that was a good one, all I had to do was to fill the spud peeler situated in the galley, just let it run until all the skin was taken off of them, then load them into a large vat for cooking.

ADMIRAL OF THE FLEET, LORD LOUIS MOUNTBATTEN OF BURMA VISIT

Once a year we would have a visit from a notable person to come and inspect the ship and to award various prizes to the ship's company. It was my privilege to be a side party on the day that Lord Louis came to the ship, and I with others piped him aboard. As on this day I was part of the gangway staff as bosun's mate, I do believe that Bernard Pitcher 166 was the quartermaster. Another that came during my stay was The king of Belgium.

I did whenever possible have a go at any and all the sports on board, but fell foul of Shacks a couple of times during my stay on the *Are*, having been punished with six of the very best a couple of times. He took a very dim view of that. Cricket was my main game, having found out how to play it properly while at boarding school before coming to the *Are*. I think it was Mr Willy Wightman who took the cricket team. I did make the ship's team, only playing one or two games against outside opposition, playing up on the sports ground. Climbing up the steep hill to the sports ground was perfect training for anyone who wished to be part of a mountaineering team to climb Everest. I am sure the air was much thinner up there on the playing fields, or was it that I was so out of breath through having to run up to the top of that goat track we had to climb?

Football I was not that good at all, nearly always being placed in goal, not good at that either, but I did and enjoyed it when I did. Cross country running I used to hate, what was the idea of such a sport, to run halfway to Strood on top of the hill and then back again? No sense in it at all. Swimming, that again I partook when asked or even told to by Mr Hartree, who tried his best to get me into his water polo team, but my pony kept drowning or rather I did. Then there was boxing. I got caught by the PTI 'Shacks' having an argument with a mate, a pushing and shoving disagreement, so, it was both of us down to his gymnasium, out with the boxing gloves, everyone had to witness a grudge fight. We had to knock seven bells out of each other. Well, according to Shackleton, I showed promise. I had to join his boxing team. Yes, I did enjoy it, doing quite well, winning several fights and competitions, getting back into his good book.

CHAPTER 29

TRAINING SHIP
ARETHUSA BAND

I first joined the ship's band soon after arriving on the *Are*, being told that it was a doddle. The first instrument I played was the base euphonium, but I did want to play the trumpet. However, after a while I was to play the snare drum for a while, then went onto the tenor drum, had a go at the base drum as well, and before I left I had a very short spell as drum major, did a few practices and one march to church on a Sunday.

Even when I was on the *Are*, Bob Morton must have been getting on, but he was always smart and, on the ball, an ex-Royal Marine bandsman. He wrote most of our music himself, his favourite was 'The Chieftain', we would always be playing it.

My first experience within the band was to play the base euphonium, it was nearly as big as I was. I first tried to get to play the trumpet, but due to my buck teeth I could not get a proper note out of it as the mouthpiece was too small. Bob Morton always got a tune out of us, despite the fact that the majority of us could not read a note properly. On our sheet music, we used to have to write in the finger movement, above the note so the right valve was depressed at the right time. In rehearsals, there were many times I received the treatment of being walloped by whatever Bob Morton had to hand, for playing a wrong or bum note.

One of the band's tasks was to lead the Sunday march to Upnor Church for morning service. After having divisions on board, on completion, all would fall in on the foreshore (or the hard). One of the only times you were allowed to wear footwear. The band paraded all nicely turned out in our white gaiters and belts. Bob Morton at the rear, Drum Major John Jolly for most of the time I was on the ship, out front. He would call out. "Band ready."

Bob Morton would order, "'The Chieftain' please, gentlemen."

Ferdie Farrington, all done up in his black shiny gaiters, would give the order to 'parade shun, into line 'eft turn. Quick march'.

The chief petty officer boys of each division would call out the time. One would say, "Eft, Oit, Eft, Oit, Eft, Oit'."

Another would put an 'H' in front. "Heft, Hoit, Heft, Hoit."

The division bringing up the rear, quarterdeck, their chief petty officer boy trying to outdo the other two, would be shouting louder, calling, "Keep in step, left, right, left, right." Each would have their own style of calling time.

We would often be called upon to parade at local town's carnivals, such as Tonbridge or village fetes; Paddock Wood being a favourite one. A lot of young girls would follow us everywhere we went. We often attended large parades up in London, like the cenotaph. I remember on one of them, there we were marching through London, crowds of people cheering us, on our way to the Royal Albert Hall for the evening remembrance parade. I was still pumping out the tunes on the base euphonium at this time, chest stuck out like a peacock, I sighted out of the corner of my eye this elderly gentleman, smartly marching alongside us. I took a sideways glance to my left-hand side as this person was marching alongside me, swinging his arms with a walking stick in one hand. I had to take another quick look, blow me down, I could not believe my eyes, it was my dear old grandad. I could not believe it, it put me off my playing, I missed a number of notes before I got it back together, I felt so very proud with my grandad marching alongside me, making me put on a bit more of a swagger. He had come up from Dorking on the Green Line bus. So I must have written home to say what we were going to be doing.

As bandsmen we were allowed to go ashore to the band hut for band practice. The hut was situated next to the swimming pool, on the hard, and it also gave us an opportunity for a quick smoke in the bushes behind the hut. Being in the band got us out of other cleaning duties. After playing the base euphonium, I got a little tired of it, carrying the heavy thing around, which had to be cleaned spotless. I asked if I could be put on the trumpet, dear old Bob Morton took one look at my teeth, saying I do not think so. Anyway, he gave me a try, true to his word I could not hit any of the high notes, so I asked to go into the drum section, at first on the snare drums. So his first words were, "Can you do 'mummer, dadder' (using the drum sticks properly) on the side drum?" I could, but as I was one of the bigger boys in this section, I joined Petty Officer Boy Ken Cooke (quarterdeck port) on the tenor drum. I soon mastered the stick swinging, loving every minute of it.

The band used to also give concerts on board or what was called a 'sod's opera'. Always on Sunday divisions followed by marching up to the church for church parade. There were many invitations for the band to partake of local hospitality around the Medway towns, on Saturday or Sunday afternoons. At least once a year, normally during the summer, the ship held an 'open day' where the atmosphere on board was one of great anticipation, with lots of young girls. Tea and cupcakes were always available on the mess deck for everyone. 'Shacks' had his boys doing a gymnastics display on the main deck, and swimming displays given by Fred Hartree in the swimming baths. Seamanship displays by the 'Whiz'. The people came in their thousands while the band after their display on the foreshore, played sweet music under the baton of bandmaster 'Bob' Morton, and at the end of the day, the band put on a marching display. Once everyone had left the ship, the cleaning up had to be done.

As different boys left the *Are*, it made vacancies within the band. I eventually did get to play the bass drum for a short time before playing the side drums or snare drum before getting a short period as drum major due to my extended stay on the *Are*. Why did I join the band? Well, I thought it would be a bit of a skive, a bit of a laugh, how wrong I was. I got into the routine, plenty of band practice in the small band hut on the foreshore, you could make as much noise as you wanted, followed by a smoke behind the hut. Band practice was at least two evenings a week, as well as Saturdays and Sunday afternoons. I stayed playing the base euphonium for about a year because I always wished to play the drums.

Jolly was our drum major for most of the time I was in the band and he was a great friend, Cooke was the other tenor drummer, and bass drum I think was Baker, side drums were Hepplewaite, and trombone was Culverson. Just some of the names I can remember.

I think it was at the beginning of 1958, when I was just 14. The Bandmaster came up to me and asked me to join a few others to have a chat about the Royal Marine band. He was telling us all about what sort of training they gave young boys like us. Then came the question. "How would we like to join the Royal Marine band?" I think at the time three of us put our hands up, saying yes, we would like to. As it turned out, the three of us, I cannot think of the other two, were then sent off to the Royal Marine School of Music in Deal, Kent. When we arrived in *Arethusa* uniforms, we were laughed at by the boys who were going through the music school, each learning how to play three musical instruments at a high standard before being transferred to the Royal Marine band.

I and the other two had only gone down there for an appraisal, to see if we were up to playing or learning music, consisting of a two week stay, taking a few little examinations. I wanted to be a bugler/drummer, but even into the second week I could not get the right notes out of the bugle, the big teeth in the front got in the way so I could not get the right notes out, I could only do it on the side of the mouth, but that was not good enough. So, it was back to the *Are*, having had a little view of life elsewhere.

Shortly after you join the *Arethusa*, one is put into the boxing ring with someone about the same size as yourself, you have to knock seven bells out of each other, so that the officers can see what you are made of, and until Shacks think you had enough. The day came when I had to go up against one of the lads who joined me. Having come from Sunnydown, where we had done just a little boxing, I had a little idea of how to move about to get out of the way of a windmill. This lad came at me, all guns blazing, thrashing at clear air, I side stepped him a couple of times, caught one or two around my ear hole. Neither of us really wanted to hurt each other. However, we made quite a fight of it. Mr Shackleton, the PTI, said he wanted a word with us both. It turned out he was quite impressed with the two of us and told us both we were in his boxing team, whether we liked it or not. This was another section to be in, already in the band, the boxing team was another way to get out of cleaning routines. So, I now had to get involved in boxing training as a member of 'Shack's' team of special boys, just like his gymnastic display team. The boxing team took part in fighting other local boxing clubs, often during the evening, so it meant getting away from the ship in the evenings.

There was also the annual boxing tournament on the *Are*, most of the sports on board were against another division, so I boxed for quarterdeck starboard for the 'Whiz'. The first boxing competition was during 1957. I had three fights with other members of the other divisions losing in the semi-finals to the eventual winner. The next year I won the competition and as a bonus I was awarded the best style cup in 1958.

Then one day there was a clash of events, the band and boxing team had an outing on the same day, I had to make a choice, so I went with the band. This meant upsetting 'Shacks', so I was not one of his blue-eyed boys anymore, which happened soon after the corned beef incident anyway – I was already in his bad book from that little incident.

CHAPTER 30

CAPTAIN'S SATURDAY ROUNDS

Weekend and other routines

I was placed into a mess deck, mine was 21 mess as I've already mentioned, this mess deck was about 15 feet wide by possibly 20 feet long. There was a wooden table in the middle, placed hard up against the bulkhead (wall) at the bottom. There was a long wooden bench on either side of the table, at the head of the table was where the leading hand or leading boy of the mess sat. At the bottom of the wooden table were the mess shelves, which held all of your aluminium plates, utensils, all your mess 'fannies' (pots and pans to you landlubbers), a cupboard for mugs and knives, forks and spoons. Each person sat in his place on the table according to seniority, as explained earlier.

Every Saturday routine was one of the main events of the week, which were captain's rounds. Your mess deck had to be cleaned, spotless. First the table top had to be void of any stains, so it had to be scrubbed until it was white, so it was scrubbed every day to keep it up to standard for the Saturday rounds. Woe betide anyone who made a mess on it, the benches had to be the same, glowing white wood, cleaned by using lime juice if you could get hold of it, used to bleach them white. Do not get caught doing it. Then there was the mess 'fannies' of various shapes and sizes, these were always heavy types of aluminium but they had to shine so you could see your face in them. The plates were also made of aluminium not so heavy, but these had to shine or even glow better than the fannies. We used to clean these utensils with Brillo pads, finest wire wool pads, impregnated with a soap, but to keep your Brillo pad fresh, because you were only allowed so many to each mess, we used to keep them in a large glass jar, with all the leftover little pieces of soap. We added water and let it settle into a thick jelly with our Brillo pads soaking in this liquid. We used to give this mixture a name, however, it escapes me at the moment.

To get the plates to really shine, we would first clean and shine them with duraglit chrome polish to start the shine, rub them off or polish with newspaper, then you had to scrub them with the Brillo pads soaked in this jelly soap mixture, working up and getting a heavy froth, then smartly dip each plate into clear boiling hot water, holding them between two fingers on the rim (like you might with a DVD disc) so as not to smug them in anyway or you had to do it again. Each mess had their own secret mixture and ways of getting the best shine, which proved hard to keep to yourself without giving away your secrets to the next mess, as there were always spies walking around to see how you did it.

When all was cleaned, you had to set up a presentation of your mess area, most messes tried very hard to outdo the next. There were 24 messes. Each division had four messes, ours were 17, 19, 21 and 23 messes, the best division would be given fried eggs for Sunday breakfast. The best actual mess was rewarded with a cake for Sunday tea. Quarterdeck starboard division won many of the best divisions, my mess also won best mess more times than I can remember. The mess cleaning routine was to get me into a lot of trouble on joining my first ship in the Royal Navy, HMS *Bulwark*, but more about that later.

There was a yacht which had been bequeathed to the *Arethusa* for training purposes, including a sum of money to help with her upkeep. The *Glen Strathallen* was a steam yacht, first built as a trawler and later converted and fitted with a larger engine. Unfortunately, it was not possible to operate the ship under cruising conditions as to run her economically she would have to have been in constant use and able to pay her way. So, she laid alongside the *Are*, just as something to look at over the side and wish that she could be used to train those of us on board in seamanship, and watchkeeping. She did get a little use as occasional classes were taken on board and the padre used her for communion classes. Sometimes some of us boys were taken over to her and instructed on her construction and engines and general details, some worked on her, chipping, scraping, painting, and helping in her general upkeep. Staff also used it on special occasions, and also lived on board. The bequest stated that if she could not be of any further use, she was to be sunk as somewhere for divers to be trained on, this was carried out sometime in the early '70s.

As a young boy, from the very start from walking my first steps on Box Hill, being brought up in wooded areas, I was surrounded by trees. So I mastered the art of climbing up even the most difficult of trees at a very early age. So, from that early age right up to the present I have always been a climber, of anything, from trees, gas lamp posts to many other challenging structures. Such as masts. Why, because they were there. During my time at sea, I have climbed up many high structures, mainly masts, carrying items such as paint tins and brushes. I mastered the art of tying off a boatswain's (bosun's) chair. A single small piece of wood (for one) like a seat on a child's swing with four holes, through which is passed a looped strop. The four ends or loops are at about chest high, where a single long rope is attached, which is fixed at the highest point of where you are working. The bosun's chair enables you to move up and down while working or painting a mast or maybe the ship's side. I learnt this art from the bosun on the *Are*. I seem to get muddled up trying to remember the staff names, and I cannot for the life of me remember the bosun's name. A lovely man who taught me a lot. Smelt of strong tobacco, he smoked or rolled his own, they were like tar, his cigarettes I mean. He may have been 'Pegleg' Mr Taylor.

During April of 1959, the ship's company was on Easter leave. I had remained back on board as a retired party, until when the ship's company returned. Those who had volunteered for retired party took their turn on going on leave. However, on my scheduled return after Easter leave, I was to join my intake for the Royal Navy at HMS *Ganges*. However, once again fate was on my side. Whilst I was on leave, I felt a bit unwell, with stomach pain, living at my grandparents' place in Holmside Cottages, Mid Holmwood, but at the time staying at Cathy's place. I was in a little pain, I kept on saying, "It's OK, I'll be alright, nothing to worry about." People became a little concerned. Ricky, Cathy's mum, said I ought to see a doctor.

All naval personnel had to see a particular doctor in your area, as I was now waiting to join the Navy. I had to visit Dr Brice, in South Street (not my own GP) . I went to Dorking to see this so-called Royal Navy-approved doctor, obviously he got paid more to see those in the Forces. Cathy came with me to hold my hand to see this very old-fashioned doctor. He examined me, rubbed his chin, saying, "You are in a bad way, old chum, you need to report to the hospital as soon as possible, I'll arrange a bed for you, you have grumbling appendicitis." He left it at that. He said for me to make my own way up to the hospital and that they would be expecting me. So off I went with Cathy, both walked back home to her place, about two and a half miles, where I put a few things into a small attaché case and proceeded with Cathy holding my hand to walk back into Dorking, up the hill at St Paul's Road to the Cottage Hospital.

On my arrival at the hospital, I was very close to passing out, the pain was so intense, Cathy was so concerned she was in tears. The matron took hold of me saying, "We have been expecting you for over two hours or more now, where have you been?"

When we had given our story of being told to make our own way here, and collect some sleeping clothes first, the matron of the hospital went absolutely spare. I was in bed ready for an immediate operation within minutes. My appendix had ruptured between the time I had seen Dr Brice and the time I arrived at the hospital. I was told I was very lucky indeed not to have lost my life through it, caught just at the right time, just minutes after it had burst. It could have been far worse if it had gone on any longer.

I was placed in a ward of eight beds, mine was placed in the corner of the ward farthest from the door, the other patients were very old men, most of them died while I was there. The nursing staff were very good to me being the very youngest, especially one, a night nurse from Malta, Maria Mifsud, I remember her name, used to sit on my bed watching the television and telling me stories of her motherland.

In those days when you went into hospital for an operation, they kept you in for at least two weeks, in my case it was up to three weeks and I was only supposed to be on leave for two weeks over Easter. So the inevitable happened, I missed my intake into HMS *Ganges*. So, upon my discharge from hospital, I received a visit from a welfare lady, sent by the *Arethusa* to explain to me that I had now missed my entry into HMS *Ganges*, and would have to wait until the next intake in September. In the meantime, I was instructed to take another fortnight's leave to help with the recovery, then to return to the *Arethusa*.

After a short convalesce at home – I was now five weeks into my leave, two of which were now sick leave – I returned to *Arethusa* as ordered. What was I going to do when I got back? I did not have classes to go to as I had already passed out from the *Are*. I had kept my number 207, so my place on my mess was still intact. I had nowhere to go, I did not wish or want to go back home to Goodwyns. I could not go forward to HMS *Ganges*, having missed my intake. I did not exist as far as the *Are* was concerned. My social workers made a case for me not to return to my parents, due to the behaviour of the 'old git', so it was decided that the social services would sponsor another term.

So the *Are* accepted me back and placed me 'out of routine'. I first had to report to the sick bay for another two weeks convalescing on board. Oh boy! What a life I had, to be looked after by our lovely sister, she was a smasher, and in looks as well in her temperament, nothing fazed her. I got to get to know her quite well, but do you know I now cannot for the life of me remember her first name or surname, one day it will come back to me.

It was soon after this that I had been requested to visit the 'sin bosun' or padre in his small office next to the sick bay. On entering his cabin, I was told to sit down, "You are not to worry, you are not in any trouble this time." His next words shocked me somewhat. The padre said, "What surname name do you wish to use when you enter the Royal Navy?"

"Pardon?" was my reply. "What do you mean?"

The padre went on to explain, "We, the *Arethusa,* had to write to your next of kin, your mother, to confirm what name was to be used, as there is not any record of there being a Kenneth Brian CUTTS to be found. We now have her reply with your new birth certificate and the name on it is CHANDLER (my mother's maiden name), not Cutts."

Apparently, I was not registered at all until 1st June 1959 so I did not exist until then. How freaky is that? This has proved to be a bit of a nightmare proving what Mother has told me then and since, another long and unbelievable story. To be told later when the facts are available if any can be found.

Blimey, I thought, *why has this happened?* Then Padre Simms-Williams passed me the letter for me to read, but overcome somewhat, I asked for him to read it for me. In essence, what Mother told me in the letter was that my father was a Canadian Soldier, over here in England during World War II, who had gone to France during the D-Day landing and had not returned. He was placed as missing in action. You could have knocked me over with a feather. Padre then repeated his question. "So, what name are you going to use to join the Navy with?"

My reply was, "What do you think? Chandler, of course."

After a few more moments of explanation from the padre, I left his cabin, dancing all the way to my mess, shouting, "I am not Cutts anymore, I am a CHANDLER now!"

CHAPTER 31

OUT OF ROUTINE. PAINTING THE SHIP, BOSUN'S PARTY

Oh, what to do with me. So I was placed in the bosun's party with Ray Alfold 204 and a few other lads. If you remember, the summer of 1959 was a very hot one. On the bosun's party you did not join in with the ship's routine of going to school, doing parades, etc. Instead you had a little fun. You were classed as 'out of routine'.

Unfortunately, I was a bit of an awkward sod, to say the least, throughout my time on the *Are* I tried very hard to buck the system, sometimes a bit of a skate. The exception was when I was made up for a very short while acting leading boy of 2 mess, which did not last, and did not get past the 'acting'. So, I left the ship as an ordinary boy. So I returned to helping with all the routines within the sick bay. I even considered joining the Navy as a sick berth attendant (nurse) but that was only a passing fancy.

When it was time to return to normal daily routine, I was sent for by my divisional officer, 'Tiny' Fuller (who had the hots for our sister). "Sit down, young Ken." He then poured me a cup of tea, then he started to explain that I had missed my intake into HMS *Ganges*, which of course I already knew. "The next intake is not until September 1959, another four months ahead. What are we going to do with you? We cannot send you home (*oh goody*, I thought) so what the captain and chief officer have decided is to put you to work with the bosun. You will learn a lot from him if you put your mind to it, which will hold you in good stead for the Royal Navy. When you passed out before Easter your record had improved." I was voted the most improved boy for the Easter term, I must have lost my old 'green jacket' for a while. "We are going to also give you back your once-earned leading boy status, you can have your hook back (an anchor worn on your left sleeve, same rank as corporal) as an extra privilege staying in my division under my care, on 21 mess. Now what a turn up for the books."

This meant that I was to be summoned to the captain's table. On the following Thursday I was standing in the requestment line and not the defaulters. Felt rather odd being on this side of the main deck. It came my turn to march forward, halt, and salute Captain le Mare who was standing in front of me with a big smile on his face. "What an improvement in your behaviour during the last few months, it is nice to see you here before me in a pleasant manner rather than to be punished, Cutts." The 'Whiz' soon put him right, with an apology from Captain le Mare. "Sorry I mean Chandler. I do believe it is going to be hard for us to now get used to calling you Chandler rather than Cutts, a new start all around."

When the requests had all been carried out, it was great, I was back as a 'killick' without the normal duties, I did not have a mess to take charge of, but still sat on 21 mess under Leading Boy Mick O'Brien 187 and the petty officer boy was Ollie Sivertsen 195, who went on to be head chief petty officer boy. The only duties I carried out as a leading boy was that of being duty watch, or quartermaster on the gangway, with the odd regulating office duties.

I was placed on what was called 'out of routine' for the remainder of my time on the *Arethusa*, which meant there was no school work, no divisions, no parades, or guards to take part in. Many duties could be found for you to do, such as being sent to the laundry, which was housed in an old Nissan hut which ran alongside the swimming pool on the foreshore, or you could be sent to the pantry, or the galley (not a bad duty, you got extra food) or perhaps one went to assist the engineer, electrician (a Mr Thomas as I recall), or maybe the carpenter, or to give him his true title, Shipwright Mr Bill Dowling, who's workshop was also on the foreshore, where the Venture Centre is now. You could help the gardener, or, if like me, one was very lucky, they were sent to work with the bosun. All the jobs had their various 'perks'.

Now back on the mess deck, where I started, now doing a job I liked and got on with, working for the bosun's party, and there was not anything he did not know about seamanship. His workshop was way down in the bottom of the ship, down on the keel, next to the tailor's shop, and adjacent to the after locker flat. When you walked into his workshop, it was a true bosun's store, the smell of the various ropes, twines and canvases hit you, sent a shiver down your spine. All around the bulkheads (walls) were all the tools of the trade, all in their particular place, nothing was ever out of place. If I had used a tool and placed it back in the wrong position, he would in no uncertain terms tell you where it should be.

I reported to the bosun on my first morning, along with Roger Alfold 204 from quarterdeck port, he was also a leading boy and, like myself, not able to take up whatever service he was going into. I think he eventually went into the Royal Navy, as a 'Jack Dusty'. However, all the time I was on board, the foremast would always beckon, a personal challenge. I knew that one day I would climb to the very top, before I left the ship. I had many tries during the two and half years on board. I had attempted the feat several times, without actual success. First few occasions, I got to the upper or second platform. This is where the Jacob's ladder starts. Then a little further onto the 'crosstrees' where the third or upper yard is fixed. I often got to this part, often going out onto the third yard to sit at the end where the stays met which was holding it up, at least you had something to hold onto. From here, the third yard, it is about another 30 feet to the top of the mast via the Jacob's ladder. Now if anyone tells you it is easy to climb a Jacob's, yes, maybe, if you do it properly, or if the Jacob's ladder is rigged so that one could climb it properly, with your body sideways on, the ladder between your arms and legs, so that you are climbing with one arm and one legs on opposite sides of the Jacob's ladder. Easy doing it the correct way. Not on the *Arethusa's* Jacob's ladder, for a start. It was rigged so tightly against its mast you could not get your legs behind it. It was fixed too tight to the mast; there was no room to pull it away from the mast. You had to climb this Jacob's as if ascending a normal ladder, it could only be accessed from face-on, the front. The first few feet to the third yard were not too bad.

Using your feet as if climbing a normal ladder, but your hands or fingers will get trapped if you hold onto the rounds, you have to hold the side wires of the Jacob's. So you are on your way to the top. Every time you put your foot on a round (rung or ratline) there is less room, until you only have room for your toes, causing difficulty in getting purchase and not allowing you to put your full weight onto it. Not only do you have this problem, but there is another, the Jacob's is getting narrower the higher you go. Halfway up the Jacob's, you pass the 'goose neck' where the fourth yard would have been situated. On upwards. The final rounds are only wide enough to get your hand onto them to grip, but this is very difficult as these rounds are very tight to the mast and pinch your fingers. The next serious obstacle is once at the top of the Jacob's ladder, you have nothing to hold onto, only the mast itself, in a 'bear hug' type of hold. You are still not at the top, there is a good nine or ten feet further to go before reaching the button. (or truck which is the rounded top of the mast)

Once on the third yard, the other lad with me decided he would try first, he got halfway up the Jacob's, could not go any further. My attempt, as I have already explained, was extremely difficult. I reached the top of the Jacob's the first time I had been this far. I dared not look down. The motion of the ship was not helping, it was swaying slightly from side to side, and up there it was magnified much worse. I then shimmied up to the truck without stopping, in one quick motion threw my arm across, quickly followed by the second arm, and pulled myself up, trying my hardest to pull myself up onto my stomach but it was impossible to gain the truck. Trying my hardest but could not balance as there was not that much room, or anything to grab or to hold onto. Looking down, the other boys were cheering. That was enough for me, I had actually only touched the truck, I did not sit or stand. Now comes the hardest part of all. I started to retreat back down by sliding down by means of a bear hug to Jacob's ladder. I soon got the incentive. Out of the corner of my eye, I saw Ferdie Farrington coming out of his house at a rate of knots. I got off the top of the Jacob's ladder in no time. I thought to myself, *I have got to get down very quickly, or else.*

Just below my feet was the forestay which went down to the bow spit. I quickly, not thinking of the consequences if I fell, slid down the forestay using hand over hand, but sometimes just sliding. The friction made my hands and legs, which were wrapped around the two- to three-inch wire, very hot, in fact I did get a blister or two. I managed to get down onto the bow spit before Ferdie had crossed the catwalk and entered the ship. Being clever, or so I thought, I made for the forward heads (toilets), dived in one of the traps feet up so I could not be seen from the outside. Oh no, it did not work, Ferdie was on the ball. He shouted, "Come out, Cutts, I know you are in there."

By this time, the others had come down below to see what was going on. I came out from my hiding place, Ferdie grabbed my ear, and frog-marched me out onto the mess deck where I got the biggest rollicking, followed by three whacks of his 'Herbert' across the back of the thighs.

Now I have heard boys telling the story of how they used to regularly climb to the top of the mast and sit on the button, and some have even said that they have stood on the button. I have only seen one other boy sit on the button. Who he was, I cannot say, memory loss again? I have heard the absurd stories of boy's holding onto lightning conductors, for balance, poppycock. There were no such things on top of any of the masts of the *Arethusa*. Each mast had its lightning conductor, but this was only a thin wire or aerial sticking up, leading to a copper strip; it would certainly not hold a person's weight for balance. They must have been thinking of the HMS *Ganges'* mast.

I came to love all four masts; they consisted of the FORE MAST, which was 175 feet high, the only mast on board which the boys were allowed to climb. The MAIN MAST, also 175 feet high. The MIZZEN MAST, which was 180 feet high and JIGGER MAST, which was 145 feet high. How do I know this? Because I painted and cleaned each mast in turn. During my period of being 'out of routine' with Pegleg Taylor, the boatswain's party, I had the privilege to climb every mast. The first job we had to do was replace the caulking on the poop deck. Great fun, wearing old overalls, covered in tar and tallow, forcing this cocktail in between each plank of decking. Painting the masts was hard work, but enjoyable, rigging up bosun's chairs, pot of paint attached to the underside of the chair by means of a 'sky hook', long tom paintbrush tied to your wrist, smaller paint brushes attached to your belt. Up to the top, first job, scraper in hand, with a bucket of soapy water under your chair, cleaning off all that seagull guano from the tops of the trucks, but this time one had a lifeline attached very tightly. Once the truck was cleaned off, the seagull scraped off and left to fall on those below; to paint the top you could only use the long tom paint brush to reach the parts you could not with the small brush. I still could never see how one could sit or stand on any of them – the most difficult thing to do, impossible.

I do know of one person who did fall from the mast, which happened just before I joined the ship. He was number 89 and I met him at one of the Old Boys' Association reunions. He said that he was skylarking around on the upper yard, and where the topmast joins the main part of the mast, he said he slipped and he fell off. It must have been over 100 feet. He went on to say, "By some miracle I managed to land in the net, my knee went through the mesh and hit the heads (toilets) roof which boomed like a drum, must have hit my head early in the fall as I remember none of it. I was very lucky (you can say that again), I had not broken anything. I had torn a couple of muscles and had only bad rope burns. The doctor said I had survived the fall because I was 'well-padded'." That evening, the ship's company had tomatoes and bacon. With true humour, someone declared it to be 'Nelson's guts'.

Alfold and myself, with the help of a couple of other lads, painted, renewed a lot of the stays, ratlines, rounds on the ladders, shrouds, even the Jacob's ladders,. Most of the rope work was all renewed by us over a three-to-four-month period, in that joyfully hot summer of '59. We looked as though we had spent years in the tropics.

'Rob Roy' was the final examination you had to take when leaving Arethusa. These were taken up by the last weeks of your last term on board; they consisted of every subject you had undertaken during your time on board, from all the those in the classroom, reading, writing, mathematics, science, physics, to swimming marching, shooting, rowing, sailing and kit musters and personal hygiene. You had to attain a certain pass mark to gain your 'Rob Roy', which in turn meant you were about to leave the ship for good. Having taken the 'Rob Roy' and passed you were now able to nominate which service you wished to join.

The first choice I gave was to be a passenger steward on the Cunard liners; I made my wishes known to my divisional officer, who went through all the necessary information with me, telling me I would have to go to the King Edward VII Nautical College in Greenwich, a Merchant Seaman college, to be trained but the captain would have to write to my guardian for their permission to send me there. No such luck, my mother had written back saying, *no he cannot join the Merchant Navy*. I was to go into the Royal Navy as my grandfather had done before me, it was their wish that I had to comply with. OK then. The next step for me was to sit the examinations to enter the Royal Navy. I remember it was leading up to Easter of 1959, just 15 years, three months old. Around 20 of my term went off to number 2 Dock Road, Chatham; the Royal Navy's recruiting office.

I tried everything to fail the entrance exam; but kept being told, "Don't be silly, we know you can write, read, and do mathematics." The medical was again passed with flying colours, the aptitude tests – to show you were not a complete divvy – were also passed with flying colours. Then came the eyesight tests, to see if you were colour blind or not. I tried to fabricate my answer by saying I was seeing the wrong numbers, that did not work either, just got the biggest rollocking (for mucking about with the recruiting chief and his staff as they had made a complaint about me and a couple of other who were trying but not succeeding in swinging the lead) from my divisional officer 'Old Tiny' Fuller when I returned to the ship.

CHAPTER 32

HOW CATHY CAME INTO MY LIFE, BEGINNING 26TH AUGUST 1958: 62 YEARS

My first meeting with Cath was on one sunny summer's day in 1958, on one of my leaves from the *Arethusa*. At the time I lived with my grandparents, just across the Common at Mid Holmwood where she attended church meetings with her family at a small building used as a Pentecostal Church, and during the week held a youth club. My first cousins, Valerie and Iris, would also attend with them along with the Sunday school. I'd wander over the common, accompanied by cousin Peter, Val's older brother, to have a chat and catch up with what was going on around the area while I was away. Also to get up to a little mischief.

A lot of my time during this period was spent with Peter and two other cousins, Melvin and his brother Tony fishing down on Bondies Pond, which had been stocked up by the local lads and my Uncle 'Bun', father of Melvin and Tony. The girls would often come down to the pond while we were doing a little serious fishing, and would start mucking about, being chased off by us boys for making us miss our bites, so not many fish got caught while they were about.

Now when on leave from Arethusa, I never stayed with Mother, I would always go straight to Grandmother's.. When my leave had finished, and it was time to return to the ship, I would always travel back to Rochester, Kent, on my own, aged 13 years, back to the *Arethusa*, dressed in my best number one uniform, all nicely cleaned and pressed by my grandmother. I looked like the 'bee's knees'. I wonder whether the youth of today could travel such distances on their own.

Returning from one of my leaves, on a Saturday at about 11am, I left Grandmother's catching the 414 London county bus, which ran from Horsham to Croydon, via Dorking North Train Station. However, on this occasion the bus was running late, making my journey a little uneasy. Would I miss my train, thus, missing my connection back to Kent?

As the bus approached the station, I noticed that the porter on the platform was making ready the train's departure and to set the train off towards Waterloo, whistle in his mouth. As I entered the station, I shouted, "Please hold the train!" I arrived on the platform just as the porter and guard were about to send the train on its way. On seeing me struggling with my kit bag and rather out of breath, the porter grabbed my kit bag and, throwing open the carriage door, placing my kit into the compartment, said, "Here you are, Jack, nearly missed it."

I jumped into the first carriage but as the train was about to depart, I was grabbed by another firm set of hands from a person on the train, who picked up my kit bag and threw it up onto the luggage rack above my head, saying, "Sit down, young Ken, make yourself comfortable." So I made for the corner of the compartment, slumping into its seat, hands covering my face, very short of breath. Having gained my composure, feeling a little embarrassment, I turned to thank the person who had assisted me. Unbeknown to me, I had entered a single compartment carriage which was nearly full. In those days, the train's carriage was set up as individual compartments; some of the carriages had a corridor towards the outside so that one could walk from one compartment to another. What I had done was to climb aboard a single compartment, with no corridor, the train now moving out of Dorking North Station, so if I wanted to change the compartment, I could not, so I was feeling a little embarrassed.

Looking up, to my surprise, was a sight for sore eyes; the person who had assisted me onto the train was no other than Cathy's Dad and was accompanied by her family. Well, we all got talking about my uniform, the *Arethusa*, just talking in general. The Russells were on their way to see the sights of London. The questions then started as to where I was off too.

I must make it abundantly clear that, although I knew of the Russell family at this stage, I also knew where they lived, in one of the new council houses just built on Goodwyns Estate, in Glory Mead. I had not at the time ever been introduced to Cathy, who was a little younger than myself. I was 13-and-a-half at the time. We all got chatting. I then informed them of my story, that my journey was taking me back to the training ship *Arethusa*, which was a nautical boarding school anchored in the River Medway at the village of Upnor near Rochester, Kent. Various questions were asked about the uniform I was wearing, which I explained to them, and what the *Arethusa* was for, why I was sent to the ship, how long I had been on it (which was about three months). Then they asked how long would it be until my next leave, which would be after the summer term, around August. Just talking in general, passing the time of day.

The train was approaching Waterloo where I was to disembark to change trains. Before I got off the train, Cath's dad wanted to take a look at my cap so I handed it to him. He gave it a good inspection, tried it on, as you do. It was rather too big for his head then he passed it back to me. He had taken a good look, made some remark about it being a daft hat and not a beret or peaked cap like the army wore. I put it back on my head, to be properly dressed. I said goodbye to everyone because I had to change trains and made my way to catch the Charing Cross train, which stopped at Waterloo East station for a train back to Strood in Kent. It was quite a distance to walk across the bridge to the right platform. As we were about to part, Cathy asked if she could write to me. I was a little embarrassed at being asked, and blushing somewhat, I gave her my address. We then went our own separate ways.

I got settled in the carriage of the train to Strood, and I was running my fingers through the lining of my cap when I came across a ten-shilling note. How did that get there? There was only one explanation, it must have been what Cath's dad had been up too. This was a lot of money in those days. What it meant to me was half a term's pocket money in the bank. I had already been given a ten-shilling note from 'Old Joe' who lived across the common from my grandparents' house and who seemed to take a shine to me. I used to drop in on him as he was disabled, more later in this story to follow with regards to Joe.

On my arrival back on board, I had to declare all the money I had with me, for the first time ever I had a whole pound to my name, which had to be banked. This amount would last me all through the summer term – roll on pay day each fortnight.

Cathy had written to me, I believe that I may have written back on several occasions (if she could read my writing) during that summer term. From all of this, to everyone involved around us, it looked as if we were going out together. Mind you, we did not really have a clue about each other, only in letters, I hardly knew Cathy or anyone else at home for that matter at this time of my life. Those who were involved with the both of us knew nothing of our get together on the train, except Cathy's immediate family.

So it was while I was on leave during the summer of 1958 that I again was staying with Gran and Grandad, as I could not stay with the person who I had to call my dad, Cutts, as he was still so horrible towards me still. So while on summer leave, I remained at Holmside Cottage. My two cousins, Valerie and Iris, Avril and Ruth, Cathy and a small gang of friends from Goodwyns, would also congregate there during the late spring and summer evenings to use the hall of the youth club and sometimes to attend Sunday school.

It was during this time that my mother (God bless her cotton socks) had strong words with me one day, saying to me, "You now have a career going to sea, which would be spoilt by your fraternisation (as she put it) with that Russell girl, she gets up to no good and is a bad influence on you." So I would make sure that when Mother was around I would be seen to be out with the girls just talking, but especially if Cathy was around. I certainly went out of my way to make sure that we did meet from time to time during the next year.

On returning home on one of my leaves, way back before getting to know Cathy, there was a case the 'old Man' supposed to remain a certain distance from me, brought in by the social services, so, this is why when on holiday from boarding school or on leave from the Arethusa I would live with my grandmother but during my first leave back in the summer of '57 when on my first leave from the *Arethusa* it was decided by the authorities that were in charge at the time that as I was now older, the restriction could be lifted, everything would be all right now that as I was in uniform, that the old man would be all right towards me. WRONG! There was an incident, I did something to upset the 'old git'. I think I had picked up and read the *News of the World* Sunday newspaper before him and creased it somehow. He flew at me, threatening me with the fire grate poker, screaming that he would knock my block off, and to go to my bedroom. Mother, by the way, was out somewhere, so I ran into my bedroom, slamming the door behind me. Little did I know the door had been fitted with a deadlock, click went the lock, the 'old git' had locked me in, but what he had also done was to screw all of the windows shut because I had previously been sent to my room and I escaped through the open window. This, as far as I was concerned, was the last straw.

Now locked in my bedroom, I laid down on my bed to hatch a plan to get revenge, about what to do next to upset this monster, and how I was going to get out of this predicament that I was now in. It was starting to get very dark by now, thinking of possibly breaking one of the window panes, looking up at the windows, I noticed that the small window called the top light or vent window at the top was slightly open. I jumped up from my bed, taking a long examination of it. I was much fitter having been on the *Arethusa* for a few months, being taught to get out of tight situations. I gave it a try; got my head and shoulders out through the small window. I returned into the room, got all my meagre belongings together, threw them out of the small window out onto the grass verge, then squeezed out through that small opened window, being very careful not to make too much noise or even break any of the glass in the windows. After several near misses I eventually succeeded.

Collecting all of my belongings together and into my small brown attaché case, I lowered myself carefully, firstly onto the outside windowsill, lowered myself slowly onto the grass without a sound, collected up all of my required kit into my small kitbag and equally small attache case and ran around to my Aunt Hilda's (Mother's older sister, and Pete and Val's mother) who kindly put me up for the night on the floor of Peter's bedroom.

The next morning, when I should have been getting up for breakfast, Mother tried to get an answer from me, alas she tried the door, found it locked, had a row with the 'stupid old git', opened the 'prison' to find that I was not there. She put two and two together, got the wrong answer, flew – or she would have done if she had wings – around Hilda's. She had a barney with her, but I had already left and was in the process of walking one-and-a-half miles to my grandparents' house to get away from the horrible person masquerading as my I-will-not-say father, not knowing any difference until about a year or two later.

I was on leave again, now one summer on, in 1958. I believe it was leading up to this period and to my coming home on summer leave. I had just completed two weeks of volunteering to stay onboard the *Arethusa* as a retired party, while the main body of the ship's company members started their leave proper, which was to leave just a few boys onboard as a skeleton crew to keep the ship running. By volunteering, I had an extra week added to the normal leave pattern. I was again staying with my grandma and grandad.

Again, Mother would remind me of what she had said some year or so before. "That Russell girl won't do you any good, she's a bad influence on you." Mother tried everything to stop me from seeing Cathy (still going strong some 62 years later). What did the old girl know anyway? She was calling the kettle black – look how she behaved in her youth, to have two children out of wedlock before she was 18. I am the second product of her little misdemeanours. Mother took the full detailed secrets to her grave. Yes, I do feel it's extremely bad of her not to tell the truth of how I came into this world.

On arriving home, during the second half of the school holidays in August, I was invited to go on an outing with the pastor Kenny McCarthy's Sunday school which met in the youth hut across the common. The coach was to leave from Goodwyns

at 8:30am on Saturday the 26th August 1958 from St. John's
School on Goodwyns. I said that I would be honoured to join the
outing, along with my cousins. Valerie and Iris Head. I boarded
the coach as instructed, all were ushering me towards the rear of
the coach. There on the back seat, was Cathy, Colette and Peter
Russell, who had got there first. Never mind, there was enough
room for a couple more to sit. I could see there were only one or
two seats vacant. Valerie Head and friends, with Cathy, had
grabbed the whole back seat. When I had arrived, I noticed that
all this was a possible set-up when they all started talking loudly.
"There's room for one more back here," was the chant from the
girls. All settled in, off we went to Bognor Regis or it could have
been Littlehampton, not too sure. We had a great day out, lots of
fun was had by all.

That was the start of a great romance between Cathy and
myself. On the way back from Bognor, I do believe we had our
first kiss, well snog anyway, as that was the way they put it in
those days – having a snog. It was all set up by Valerie, I am sure.
The story here is history; we have been together ever since. This
was, I believe, when we first got together, although we had been
around before that, we just did not really hit it off until the trip.
So now we were going steady at this time, I didn't have long to go
on the *Arethusa*.

My next leave was to be the Christmas leave. I spent nearly all
of it with the Russells at Glory Mead, only going back to my
grandparents well after midnight. I did spend a few hours and
some days at Gran's, often down the Norfolk Arms with Grandad
and Uncle Bun and friends from the village. We had many a party
to go to, but during the winter it got rather cold, so walking home
back to Gran's late at night was quite an ordeal, especially walking
up Spook Hill. This was before the bypass was put in, it could get
rather scary, no wonder it was called Spook Hill. I started to spend
a lot of time with the Russell family, staying at 12 Glory Mead,
Goodwyns almost every day while at home on leave, not to leave
until the early hours of the morning, having to walk home all the
way to Mid Holmwood to my grandparents'. Sometimes I even
stayed the night on a 'put-you-up' at Cathy's.

Cathy and I kept in touch during the spring term, between January and April. This is when I undertook all my final examinations before leaving the *Arethusa*. They were called 'Rob Roy' examinations (why they called after a Scotsman I do not know). Well, I passed them, just, by the skin of my teeth. I then had to take the entrance examinations to join the Royal Navy, which were carried out at 2 Dock Road, Chatham. Again, just passing for entry during the month of May that year. I still had another six months to do on the *Arethusa* before joining HMS *Ganges* after the next Easter leave. Unfortunately, things were about to change at the end of my Easter leave of 1959.

I started to experience an acute pain in my stomach, it got so bad that after a few days I said to Cath I think I need to go to see a doctor. I could not go to my family doctor, Howard Goode in Bentsbrook Surgery North Holmwood, the only doctor I was allowed to see was one who was registered with the Ministry of Defence, a Forces doctor for the area I lived in. This was a Dr Brice whose surgery was situated in South Street, Dorking. At the time I was, as usual, staying at my grandparents' address.

Off I set off with Cathy from Gran's house, who came along with me to hold my hand. I was in such pain. Cathy and I caught the 414 bus from outside the Norfolk Arms public house on the A24 Horsham to Dorking Road, into the bus station in Dorking, walking hand in hand down the road a short way to the doctor in South Street, Dorking. We entered the doctor's surgery, I saw the doctor who was looking rather old and tired, sitting behind a large antique desk and he started to examine me. Doctor Brice then turned to me and said, "I think you are suffering from appendicitis, can you go up to the general hospital, I'll book you a bed now." He then telephoned the Dorking General Hospital who did not have any beds available, but on telephoning the Cottage Hospital, found that they had at least one bed. I then enquired whether an ambulance would take me. His reply was, "Certainly not, go home and pack a small bag with pyjamas and personal belongings that you might need in hospital, then you should make your way to the Dorking Cottage Hospital in South Terrace, they will be expecting you."

Cathy and I went to go home to my Gran's in Holmwood to pack a small case with pyjamas and washing gear. We walked to Glory Mead, Goodwyns Estate, to tell Cathy's mother what we were doing. Then from there we both walked to my grandparents' in Mid Holmwood, explained everything to dear old Grandmother, who flipped and hit the roof to find that I had walked all the way out of Dorking to her house, suffering from appendicitis.

There were no phones so Gran could not ring anyone to take me to the hospital, but gave us the money for the bus fare for our return to Dorking, catching the 414 or 439, alighting at the Dorking Bus Station situated on Horsham Road, now known as Townsville Square housing development, opposite St. Paul's Road. So, off the both of us went, we walked up the long hill of St. Paul's Road, then at the top, into South Terrace, to the Dorking District Cottage Hospital.

Eventually we arrived some two-and-a-half-to-three hours after setting out to see the doctor. As we both walked through the front doors into the hospital, the first person to greet us both was a very stern matron, who immediately saw my condition and was furious at the state that I was in. She gave both Cathy and I a stern telling off because the staff had been expecting us to arrive much earlier and in an ambulance, and they had been looking for us for about an hour or so. Straight away, the matron got a nurse to go and get a wheelchair to take me to the ward. The matron was beside herself, asking who was responsible for making us walk here in that condition. I told her it was Dr Brice. In the meantime, a nurse was summoned to look after Cathy who was taken to one side. I am not sure what the nurse asked Cathy, who was sent on her way back home.

A nurse, in the meantime, appeared with the wheelchair from the ward, which I had to get into. There seemed to be a little panic in their demeanour. I was then whisked off to my bed, helped into my pyjamas by the nurse and put to bed. She informed me that the doctor had been summoned and was on his way to see me. The nurses were buzzing around me, quickly getting me prepared for the operation to remove the cause of all this pain.

The doctor came to examine me some moments later; he was appalled to hear the story of my going to the doctor in South Street, who made me make my own way to the hospital. It turned out that I had ruptured my appendix and was in rather a bad way. The doctor arranged for me to be operated on immediately to save any further complications such as blood poisoning. Within minutes of arriving in the hospital, I entered the operating theatre. I was told I made a bit of a noise, saying that I should not be there as I had to return to the *Arethusa* because I was about to join the Royal Navy. Nobody, it seems, was interested in what I was saying when I was under. I managed to come through the operation all right, being young and very fit, according to the doc. When I came around from the anaesthetics, both the surgeon and matron were at my bedside. They explained to me how lucky I was, as the appendix had perforated (burst), which was far more serious as it could in those days have caused death. So I was to be kept in hospital under observation as it may have entered into my bloodstream which would lead to blood poisoning.

The ward that I was placed on had six beds in it, all the other beds were taken by elderly gentlemen, suffering many ailments, always coughing, snoring and calling out for the nurses throughout the night and making various other noises constantly, and dying. Soon the empty bed was changed, cleaned and filled with yet another old gentleman, the beds were not vacant for very long. I often had to press the attention call button to get the night nurse to see whomever was in trouble. I must say, all the nursing staff were very good towards me making such a fuss of me and only at the age of 15 years old.

My stay was to turn out to be for 14 days before they would let me out, which was way over my leave entitlement, but the *Arethusa* had been informed of my predicament and of course I had missed my intake or entry into the Royal Navy at HMS *Ganges*. During my stay in hospital, during the night on three occasions, I had to summon the night nurse to the ward as a fella in one of the other beds close to mine had made funny noises and just died. Three times that happened. While I was in hospital, I was the blue-eyed boy of the nursing staff, anything I needed,

I only had to ask. One young little Maltese nurse was more than accommodating, she used to bring me in extra food and sweets and chocolate, used to make a big thing of tucking me in at night, making sure that I could sleep with the aid of one or two extra tablets, to shut out all the noise.

I had lots of visits from Cathy and her family, some of my relatives came to see me but I only saw my mother once during my whole stay. Now on the mend, Cathy and I were now closer and going steady, as they say. I still had Mother on my back, telling me that Cathy was no good for me. Having undergone my extended period of leave and then recovery, I had soon to return to the *Arethusa*. On my discharge from hospital, I started to spend a lot of time with the Russell family, almost every day while at home on leave, not leaving 12 Glory Mead until the small hours of the morning, or staying the night, downstairs on a put-you-up.

During this time, I received a visit from a welfare lady, sent by the *Arethusa* to explain to me that, due to the problems of where I stayed while at home, my grandparents were getting on a bit and were feeling the strain of having me about, I could not be asked to return to Goodwyns while the old man was still around to be treated as he felt. Taking into consideration the past court order for him to cease his behaviour, which had not done, I was informed that social service would sponsor me another term on the *Are*. I was to return to the *Arethusa* (that is another part of this story already covered in Chapter Six).

I had to return to Arethusa. From September 1959, I was away for most of the next year training at HMS *Ganges*. I did come home on leave for Christmas 1959. Most of the time was spent with Cathy and her family, although at the time my mother was still living at 18 Stubs Hill on Goodwyns. This is where I slept for a few days before getting so fed up with the old man's treatment of me, which did not change much even with me being now in the Forces. Once again, I approached my grandparents and spent the rest of the time between 12 Glory Mead and Holmside Cottages. Then it was back to *Ganges* in the new year. Cathy and I did not write that much, not every day because I could now phone her, no mobile telephones, or computers in those days. To get in contact with each other we had to arrange a time that I could call the public telephone box opposite the Goodwyns shop in Oak Ridge. There we could talk for as long as the money lasted. The only person who had a telephone in their house on the street was the Cannons at No.3 Glory Mead. Cathy often babysat for them, so this was another way in which we communicated, always at a predetermined time.

Easter and summer leave were much the same. Mother had moved into No. 7 Oak Ridge by now, which was to be my base once again until the old git got too much for me to take, then it would be back to Grandmother's. Cathy and I managed to see each other as and when I was allowed, going out to the pictures and the occasional theatre to see some 'rock and roll pop groups' of the day, with one or two trips to the coast or to visit her relatives in Kent, in the Thames van owned by her father Jack, with the family plus me sat in the bac, on seats and cushions added for our comfort.

During the autumn of 1960, I finally passed out from *Ganges*, sent on leave before joining HMS *Cambridge*, a gunnery school down in the West Country. We were still enjoying each other's company when we could, keeping up the telephone calls.

On completion of my gunnery training at HMS *Cambridge* in 1961, after a short stay in the Royal Naval Barracks Devonport of H.S *Drake*, the Navy then had to decide where they were going to send me. From here I should have gone to sea on my first ship as a junior seaman but they had other ideas. They drafted (posted) me to Royal Naval Barracks Portsmouth, HMS *Victory* to eventually be trained for the Royal Tournament at Earls Court in West London. I was to join up with the Royal Naval Display Team for that year, our display was to be the Cutlass and Hornpipe. This turned out to be a three-month training programme to learn all the moves that we had to know and work up to the tournament. It would be three weeks doing the actual displays with another few weeks touring the country, showing off the Royal Navy.

This meant during this period of time, both Cathy and I had nearly every weekend to get together. At the end of the display team, and before being sent on three weeks' summer leave during the end of July, I was informed that I was being drafted back to HMS *Victory* (Royal Naval Barracks Portsmouth) as ship's company. I was to wait for a flight to join my first ship, which was to be HMS *Bulwark*, a converted aircraft carrier, now a commando carrier, for an 18-month commission in the Far East, based in Singapore.

Things did not happen as quickly as the Royal Navy wanted, with the charter airline, British Eagle Airways Unions, having pay disputes, going on a work-to-rule which delayed my departure somewhat. As it turned out I was as an under-aged seaman, I was kindly 'volunteered' to go Porton Down (that's another chapter to this account of my life) for experiments into the 'common cold', as it was put, but in the long term has had rather serious complications to my health.

Finally, I arrived in Singapore at the beginning of November 1961. From 1961-1963, I was away on the commando carrier HMS *Bulwark*.

In 1963, Cathy and I saw the New Year come in at a party at an ex-school friend's house, who lived on Box Hill at the top of Pebble Hill Road, in a large white house. As it turned out, it was a very good party. Unfortunately it was very cold and snowy, and turned out to be one of the coldest ever winter months, which made it difficult to get there but we did. Then, after having the problem of getting home, I remember trying to walk down Pebble Hill in the ice and snow as it was getting rather bad as the night went on arriving down where it was nearly flat road, we were met by Cathy's dad in his little old green Ford Thames van. About half a dozen of us poured into it. After skidding all over the place and finally getting a grip on the road surface, we were off.

I know it is rather daft, but I cannot actually remember how I proposed to Cathy. I remember going on a shopping trip to Guildford, a matelot with money to burn in his pocket, when I looked into a jeweller's shop halfway up the high street. In the window were obviously a lot of rings. Cathy did take a shine to one, a nice opal, so we went in, tried on a lot of rings, finally choosing the first opal ring that took her eye from the start. I do believe that when we had finished our shopping expedition, we took a train from Guildford to Wandbrough, visited 'Mummy Martin' at Red Leys, where I introduced Cathy to her. I think it was there that I actually got down on one knee and asked Cathy to marry me. Then it was back home. Cathy, being so excited, ran in showing off her new ring to her mother Ricky – such a nice person – who congratulated us both. Then her two sisters and brother wanted to see it. Her dad, Jack Russell, was out somewhere on a fiddle or something. When he did come home, he made some negative remarks, which was his way. Asking when we intended to get married, I said, "Not for at least a year,"

"I should hope so," was his reply.

PICTURES

One Kenneth Brian aged months

Grandparents

One Kenneth Brian aged 4 years

Freddie 6 – 9 months

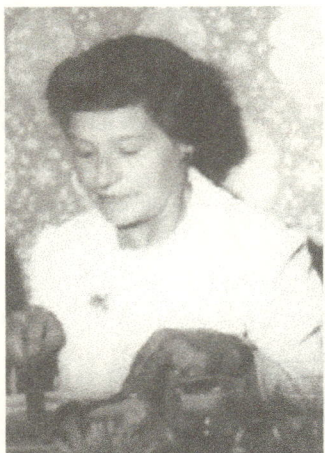

"Mummy Martin"–
Red leys

"Parkie (left) – Birdie (right) – (Circa 1972)

The white house sanatorium hospital for children

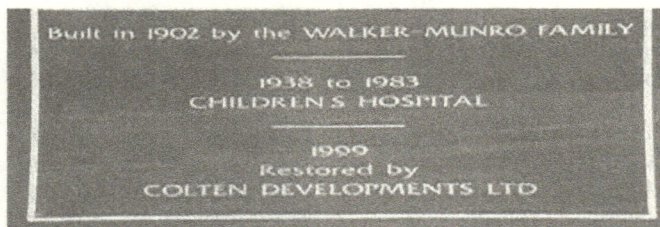

Name plate on the wall at the entrence to the white house today

Sunnydown boarding school

Winners of each age group fancy dress dorking general hospital fete

Training Ship ARETHUSA

Moored in the River Medway at UPNOR

Scrubbing the decks by holystoning punishment

Slinging the hammock for sleeping

Arethusa Band

Some of us up the mast in 1958, shows you just how large the mast was, this photo was taken of us on the first yard arm, I am second from the left, no I have not got my hand on my hip I am holding tight to the for stay. 'Lugger' Pope is the one showing two thumbs, first left, third left at the rear is 'Sproggy' Mayne 209, not sure who the others are.

The captain's daughter Petra le Mare and friend

*(Tea for six aboard the ARETHUSA but the invitation
does not extend to the boys at drill)*

What a Handsome Fella. Outside No.12 Glory Mead, Goodwyns.

The lovely girls from left to right: Cathy, Valerie, Avril and Iris

*I have my hand on my hip showing off my new badges as being
Drum Major of the Arethusa Band. This was taken during
the summer of 1959 just before I left the Arethusa to
join HMS Ganges (I had a great tan then)*

www.ingramcontent.com/pod-product-compliance
Lightning Source LLC
Chambersburg PA
CBHW030824090426
42737CB00009B/860